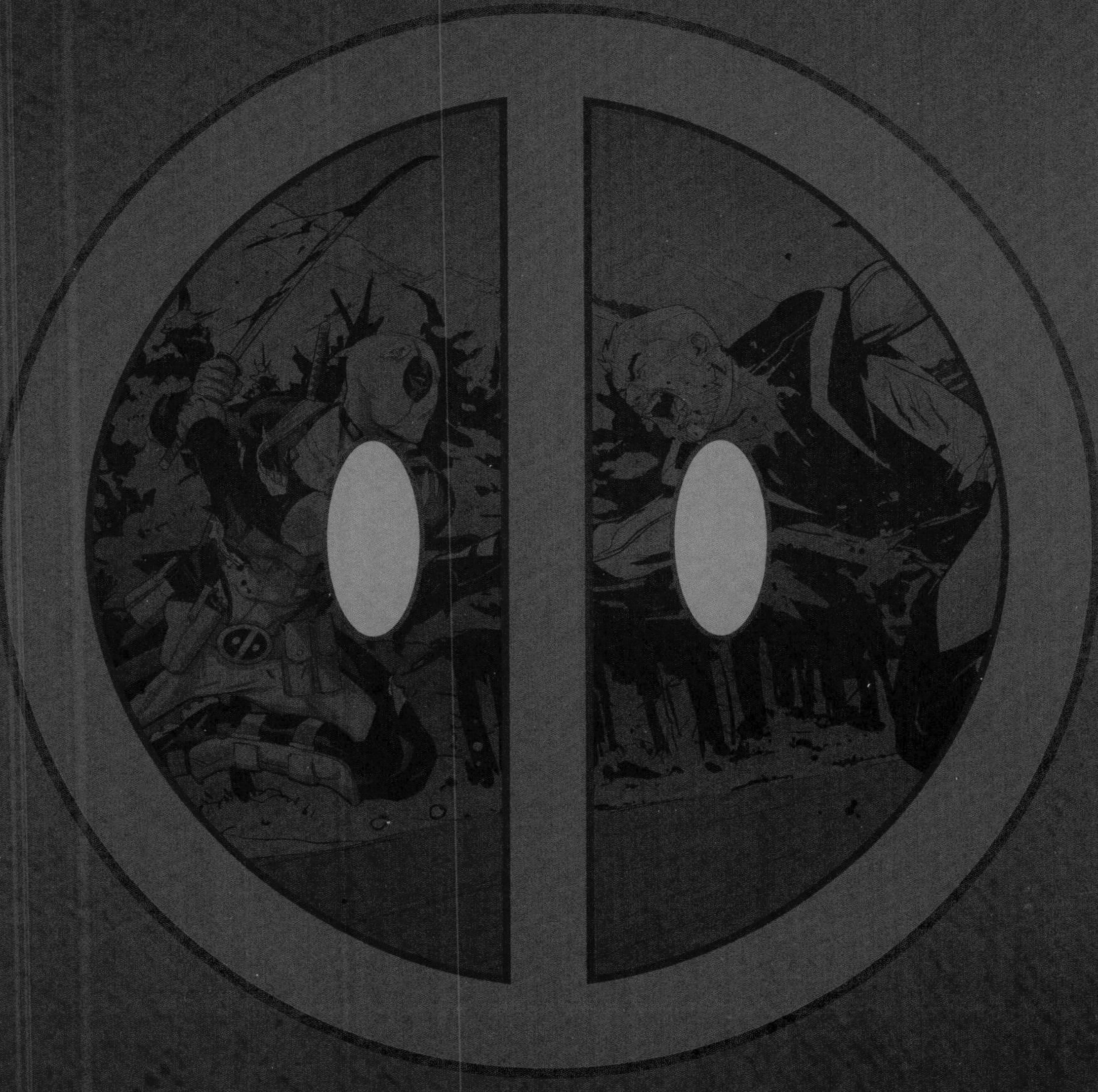

THE WORLD'S GREATEST COMIC MAGAZINE!

DEADPOOL

"DEADPOOL vs. SABRETOOTH"

GERRY DUGGAN
writer

ISSUES #8-11

MATTEO LOLLI
WITH IBAN COELLO [#10]
artists

RUTH REDMOND
color artist

MIKE ALLRED & LAURA ALLRED
cover art

ISSUE #12

SCOTT KOBLISH
artist

NICK FILARDI
color artist

SCOTT KOBLISH & NICK FILARDI
cover art

VC's JOE SABINO
letterer

HEATHER ANTOS
assistant editor

JORDAN D. WHITE
editor

DEADPOOL created by ROB LIEFELD & FABIAN NICIEZA

collection editor JENNIFER GRÜNWALD
associate editor SARAH BRUNSTAD
editor, special projects MARK D. BEAZLEY
vp, production & special projects JEFF YOUNGQUIST
svp print, sales & marketing DAVID GABRIEL
book designer ADAM DEL RE

editor in chief AXEL ALONSO
chief creative officer JOE QUESADA
publisher DAN BUCKLEY
executive producer ALAN FINE

DEADPOOL: WORLD'S GREATEST VOL. 3 — DEADPOOL VS. SABRETOOTH. Contains material originally published in magazine form as DEADPOOL #8-12. First printing 2016. ISBN# 978-0-7851-9619-8. Published by MARVEL WORLDWIDE, INC., a subsidiary of MARVEL ENTERTAINMENT, LLC. OFFICE OF PUBLICATION: 135 West 50th Street, New York, NY 10020. **Printed in Canada.** ALAN FINE, President, Marvel Entertainment; DAN BUCKLEY, President, TV, Publishing & Brand Management; JOE QUESADA, Chief Creative Officer; TOM BREVOORT, SVP of Publishing; DAVID BOGART, SVP of Business Affairs & Operations, Publishing & Partnership; C.B. CEBULSKI, VP of Brand Management & Development, Asia; DAVID GABRIEL, SVP of Sales & Marketing, Publishing; JEFF YOUNGQUIST, VP of Production & Special Projects; DAN CARR, Executive Director of Publishing Technology; ALEX MORALES, Director of Publishing Operations; SUSAN CRESPI, Production Manager; STAN LEE, Chairman Emeritus. For information regarding advertising in Marvel Comics or on Marvel.com, please contact Vit DeBellis, Integrated Sales Manager, at vdebellis@marvel.com. For Marvel subscription inquiries, please call 888-511-5480. **Manufactured between 7/1/2016 and 8/8/2016 by SOLISCO PRINTERS, SCOTT, QC, CANADA.**

10 9 8 7 6 5 4 3 2 1

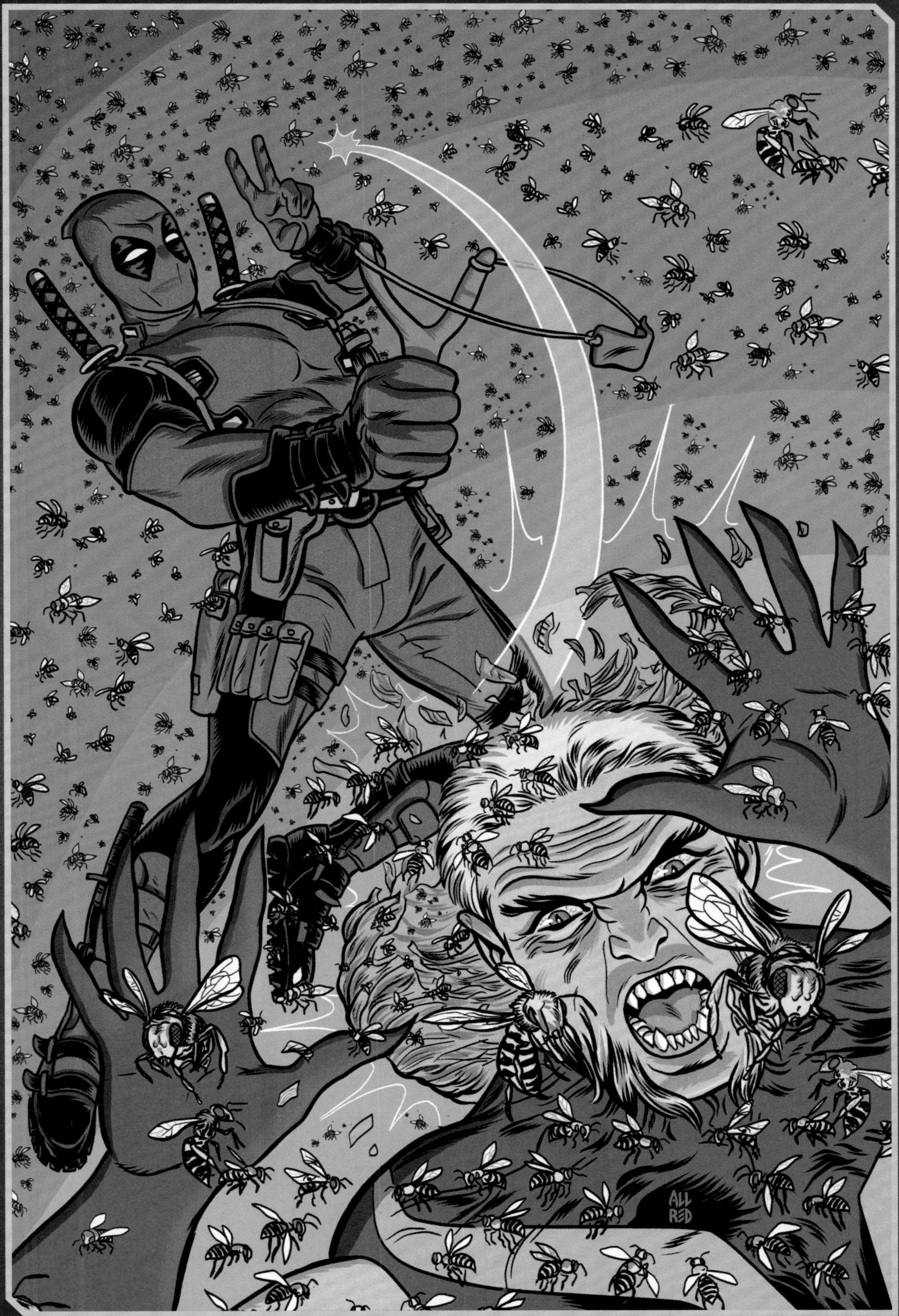
ALL
RED

NIGHTMARE ON MEMORY LANE

Avenger...Assassin...Superstar...Smelly person...Possibly the world's most skilled mercenary, definitely the world's most annoying, Wade Wilson was chosen for a top-secret government program that gave him a healing factor allowing him to heal from any wound. Somehow, despite making his money as a gun for hire, Wade has become one of the most beloved "heroes" in the world. Call him the Merc with the Mouth...call him the Regeneratin' Degenerate...call him...

DEADPOOL

OH, HEY THERE--DEADPOOL HERE! YOU KNOW--THE MERC WITH THE MOVIE.
MAN--LAST ISSUE WAS A BIG ONE.
NOT BECAUSE IT WAS MY 25TH ANNIVERSARY.
NOT BECAUSE YOU ALL GOT TO KNOW MY EMPLOYEES, ***THE MERCS FOR MONEY--SLAPSTICK, SOLO, MASACRE, FOOLKILLER, TERROR*** AND ***STINGRAY***--A LITTLE BETTER.
AND NOT BECAUSE WE SPOILED *HARRY POTTER AND THE HALF-BLOOD PRINCE.*
NO, IT WAS A BIG ISSUE BECAUSE I FOUND OUT ***SABRETOOTH*** WAS INVOLVED IN THE DEATH OF MY FAMILY.
THE ONLY PROBLEM? I'M UNDER THE IMPRESSION THAT MEANS HE ***KILLED*** THEM...WHEN REALLY HE WAS JUST WATCHING WHILE I KILLED MY PARENTS.
THAT MIGHT CAUSE SOME TROUBLE, MAYBE.
THE ADVENTURES OF
KittyPooL
DEADPOOL
25TH ANNIVERSARY!

LI'L DEADPOOL ART BY
IRENE Y. LEE

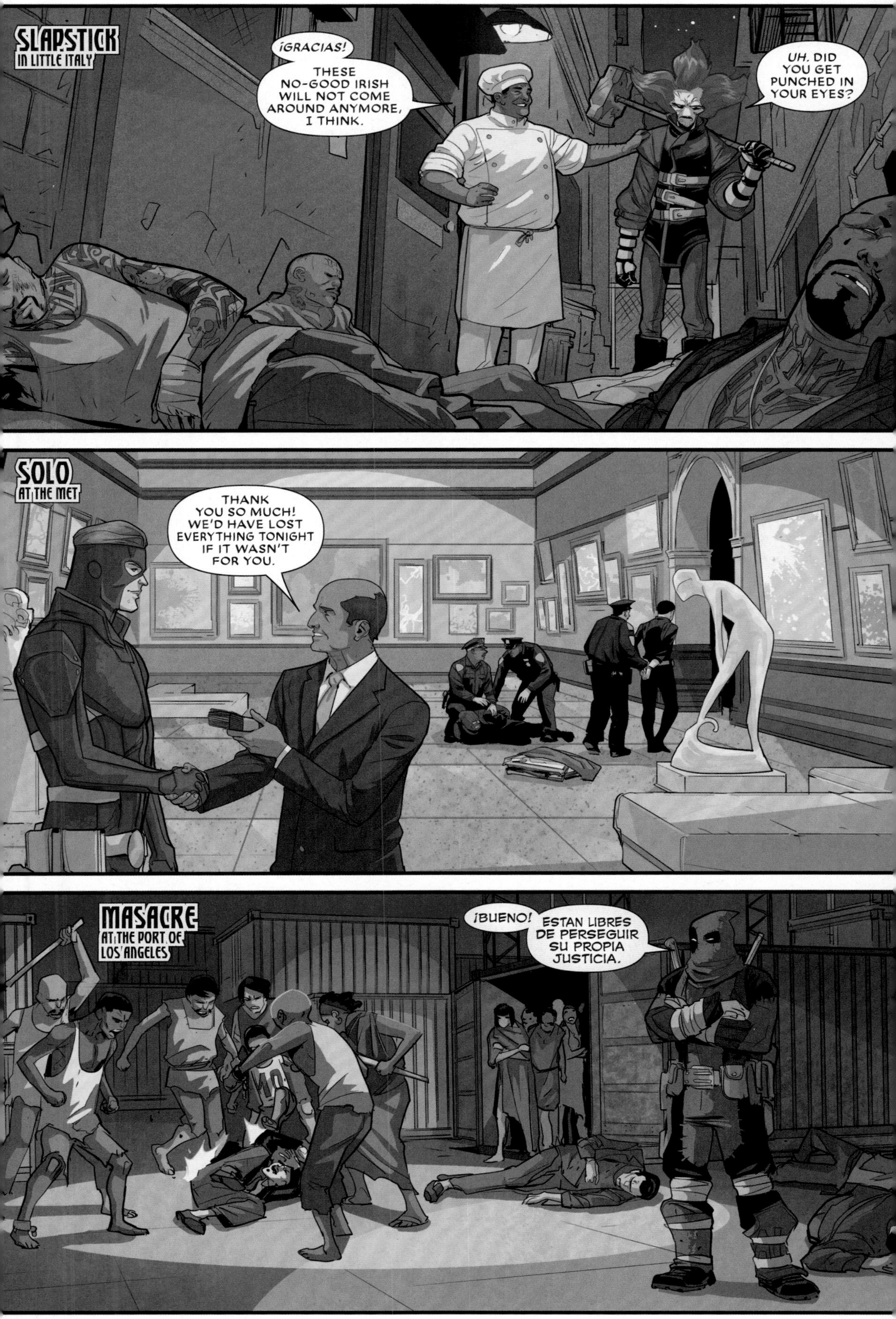
SLAPSTICK IN LITTLE ITALY
¡GRACIAS!
THESE NO-GOOD IRISH WILL NOT COME AROUND ANYMORE, I THINK.
UH. DID YOU GET PUNCHED IN YOUR EYES?
SOLO AT THE MET
THANK YOU SO MUCH! WE'D HAVE LOST EVERYTHING TONIGHT IF IT WASN'T FOR YOU.
MASACRE AT THE PORT OF LOS ANGELES
¡BUENO!
ESTAN LIBRES DE PERSEGUIR SU PROPIA JUSTICIA.

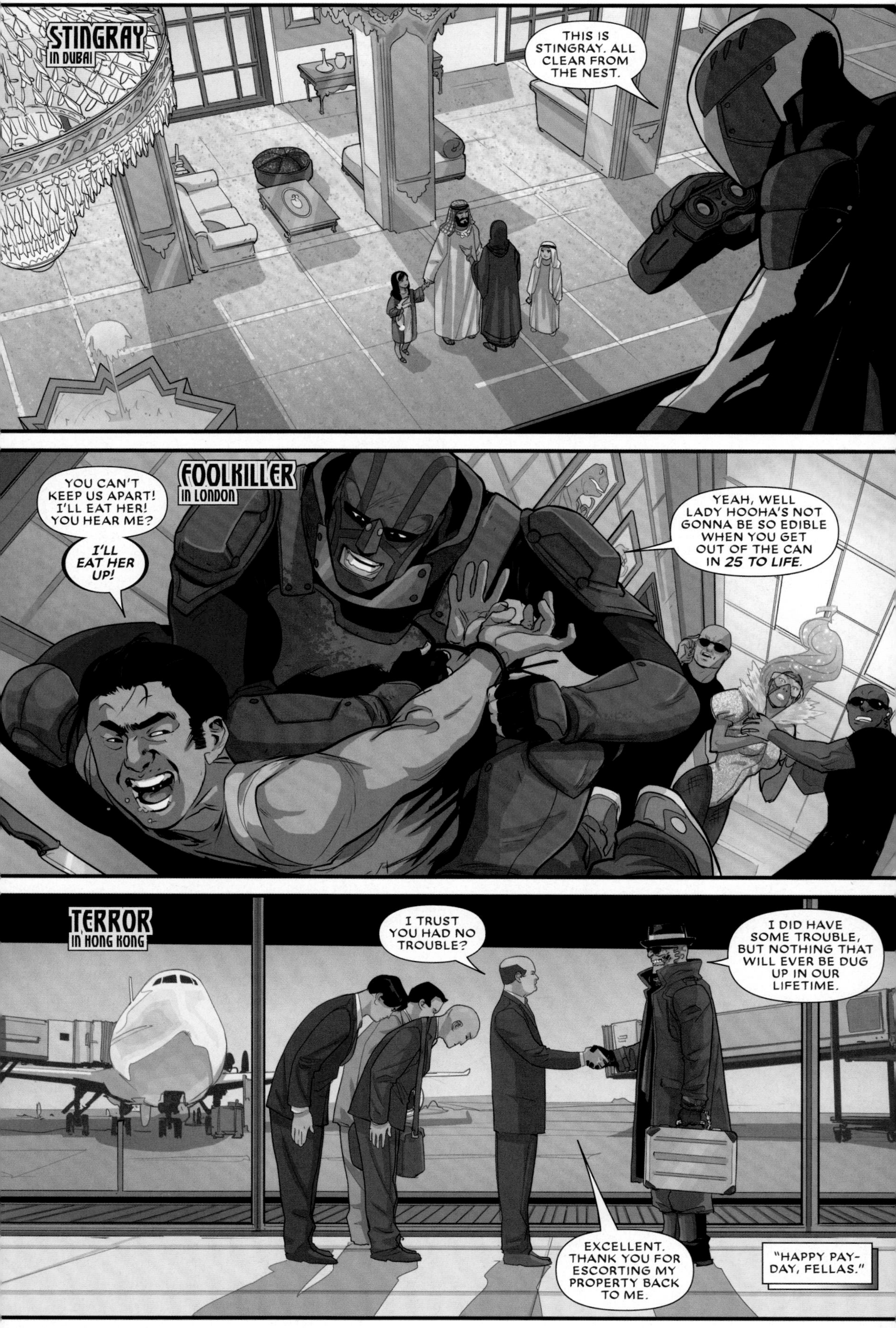
STINGRAY
IN DUBAI
THIS IS STINGRAY. ALL CLEAR FROM THE NEST.
FOOLKILLER
IN LONDON
YOU CAN'T KEEP US APART! I'LL EAT HER! YOU HEAR ME?
I'LL EAT HER UP!
YEAH, WELL LADY HOOHA'S NOT GONNA BE SO EDIBLE WHEN YOU GET OUT OF THE CAN IN 25 TO LIFE.
TERROR
IN HONG KONG
I TRUST YOU HAD NO TROUBLE?
I DID HAVE SOME TROUBLE, BUT NOTHING THAT WILL EVER BE DUG UP IN OUR LIFETIME.
EXCELLENT. THANK YOU FOR ESCORTING MY PROPERTY BACK TO ME.
"HAPPY PAY-DAY, FELLAS."

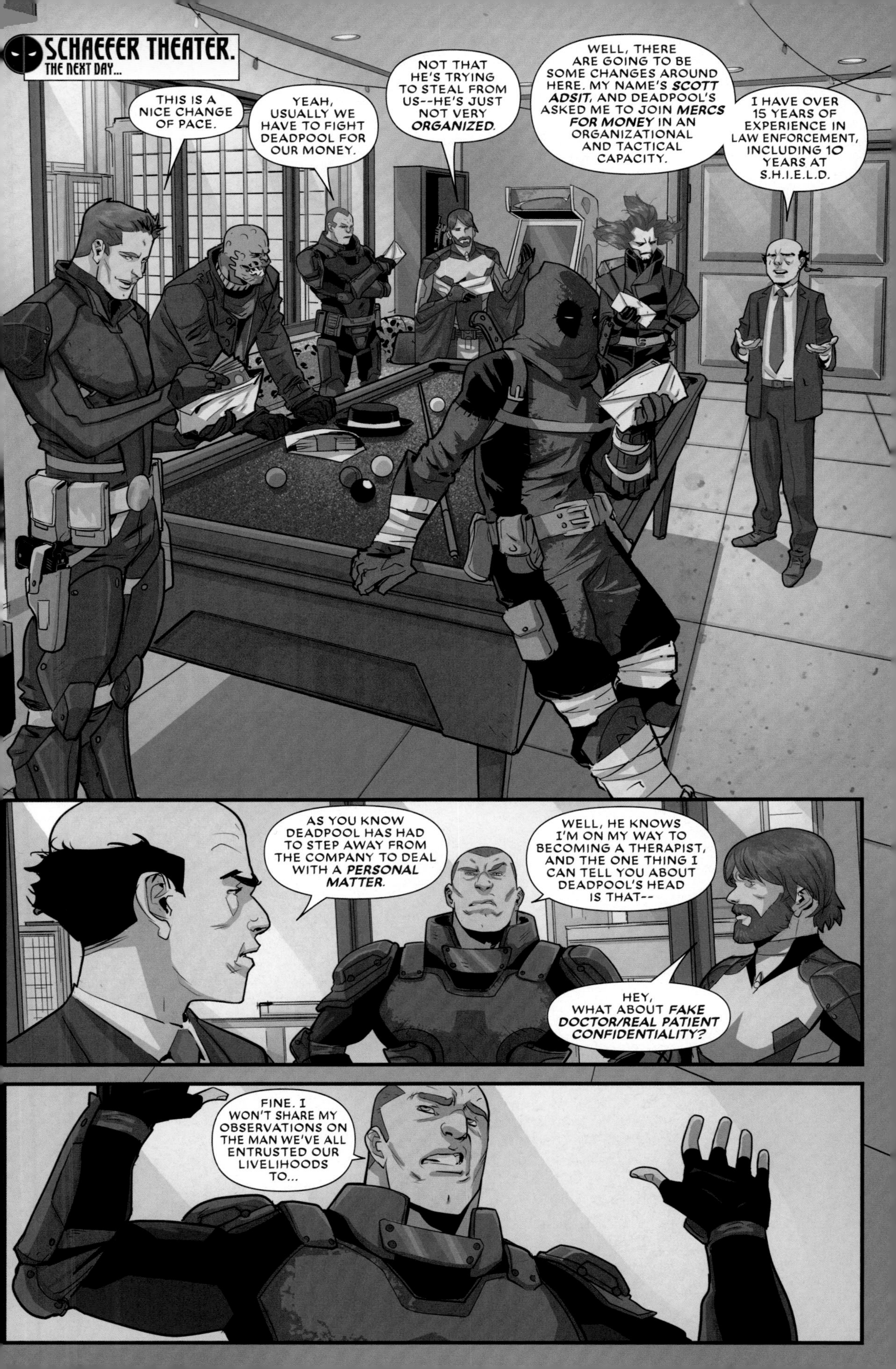
SCHAEFER THEATER.
THE NEXT DAY...
THIS IS A NICE CHANGE OF PACE.
YEAH, USUALLY WE HAVE TO FIGHT DEADPOOL FOR OUR MONEY.
NOT THAT HE'S TRYING TO STEAL FROM US--HE'S JUST NOT VERY ORGANIZED.
WELL, THERE ARE GOING TO BE SOME CHANGES AROUND HERE. MY NAME'S SCOTT ADSIT, AND DEADPOOL'S ASKED ME TO JOIN MERCS FOR MONEY IN AN ORGANIZATIONAL AND TACTICAL CAPACITY.
I HAVE OVER 15 YEARS OF EXPERIENCE IN LAW ENFORCEMENT, INCLUDING 10 YEARS AT S.H.I.E.L.D.
AS YOU KNOW DEADPOOL HAS HAD TO STEP AWAY FROM THE COMPANY TO DEAL WITH A PERSONAL MATTER.
WELL, HE KNOWS I'M ON MY WAY TO BECOMING A THERAPIST, AND THE ONE THING I CAN TELL YOU ABOUT DEADPOOL'S HEAD IS THAT--
HEY, WHAT ABOUT FAKE DOCTOR/REAL PATIENT CONFIDENTIALITY?
FINE. I WON'T SHARE MY OBSERVATIONS ON THE MAN WE'VE ALL ENTRUSTED OUR LIVELIHOODS TO...

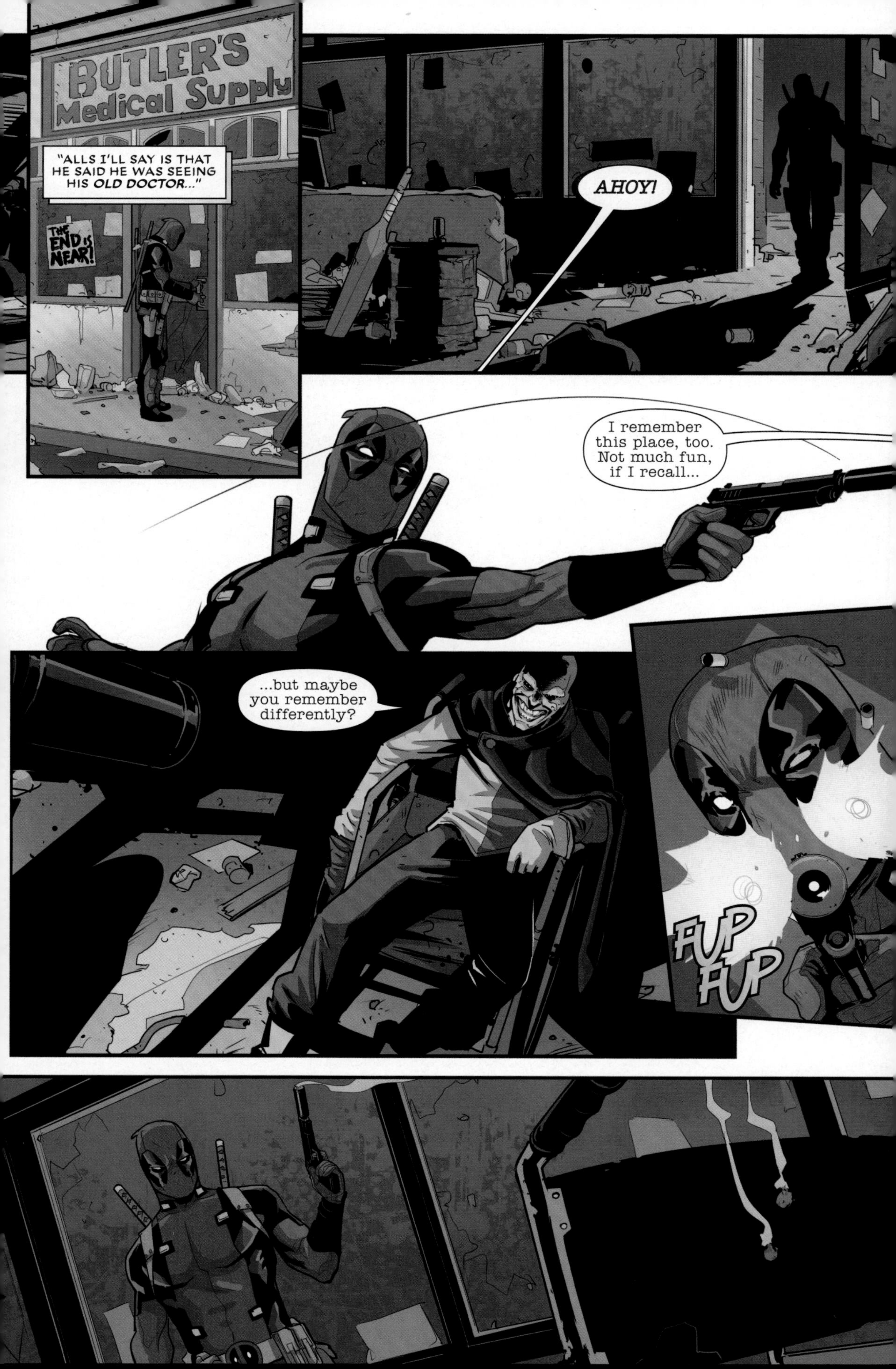
BUTLER'S
Medical Supply
"ALLS I'LL SAY IS THAT HE SAID HE WAS SEEING HIS OLD DOCTOR..."
THE END IS NEAR!
AHOY!
I remember this place, too. Not much fun, if I recall...
...but maybe you remember differently?
FUP
FUP

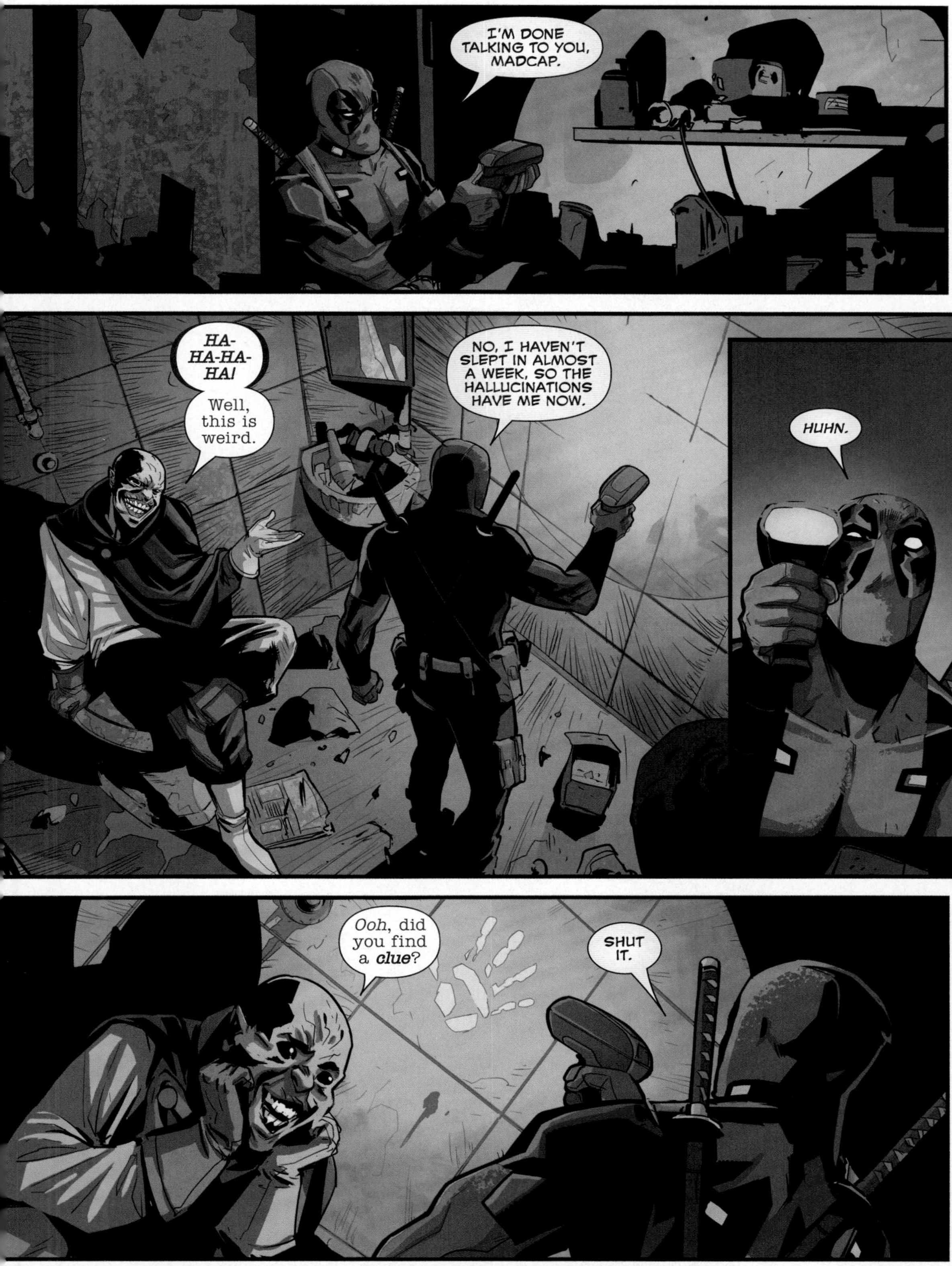
I'M DONE TALKING TO YOU, MADCAP.
HA-HA-HA-HA!
Well, this is weird.
NO, I HAVEN'T SLEPT IN ALMOST A WEEK, SO THE HALLUCINATIONS HAVE ME NOW.
HUHN.
Ooh, did you find a clue?
SHUT IT.

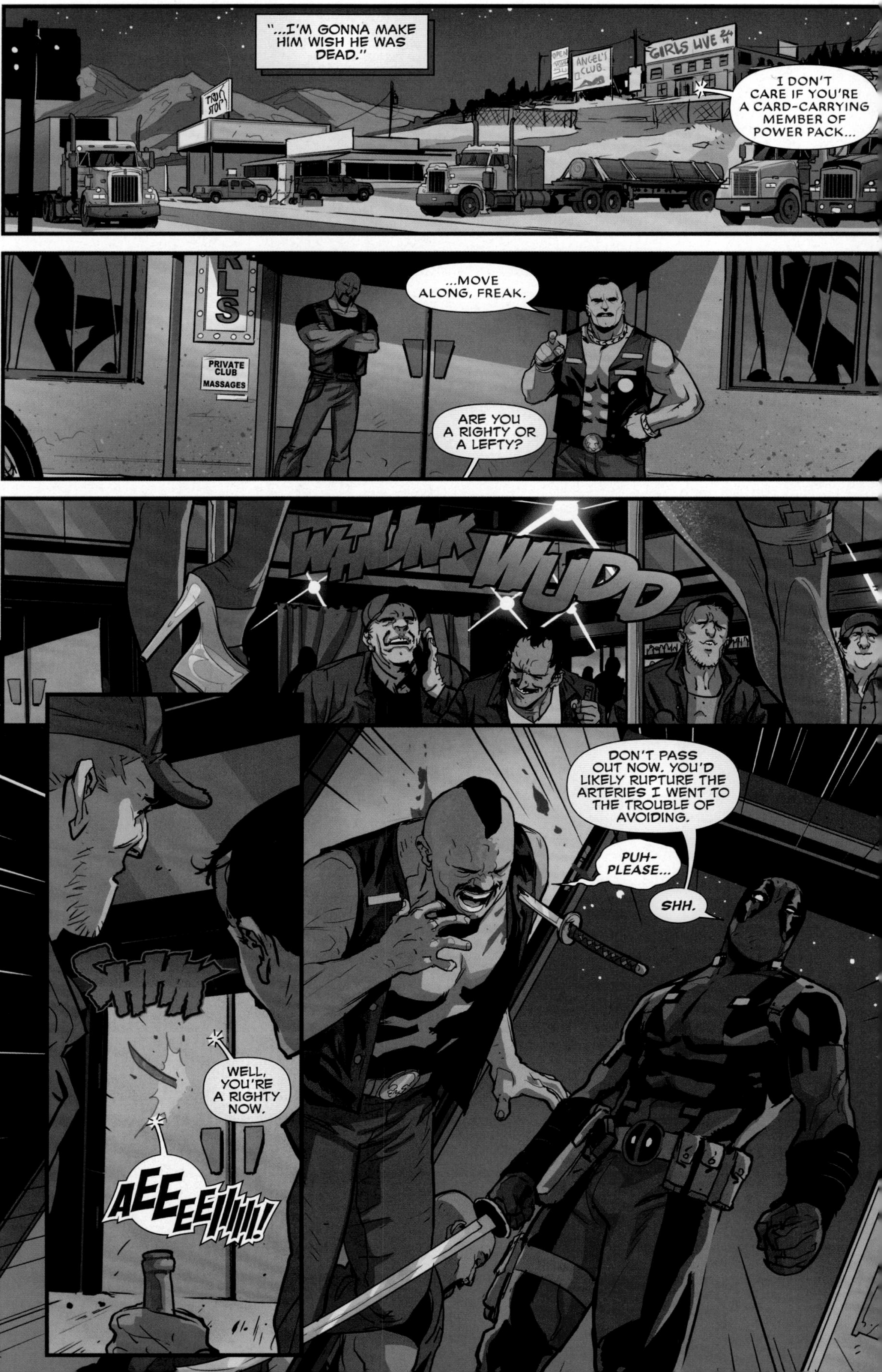
"...I'M GONNA MAKE HIM WISH HE WAS DEAD."
OPEN
ANGEL'S CLUB
GIRLS LIVE
I DON'T CARE IF YOU'RE A CARD-CARRYING MEMBER OF POWER PACK...
...MOVE ALONG, FREAK.
PRIVATE CLUB
MASSAGES
ARE YOU A RIGHTY OR A LEFTY?
WHUNK
WUDD
SHHK
WELL, YOU'RE A RIGHTY NOW.
AEEEEIIIIII!
DON'T PASS OUT NOW. YOU'D LIKELY RUPTURE THE ARTERIES I WENT TO THE TROUBLE OF AVOIDING.
PUH-PLEASE...
SHH.

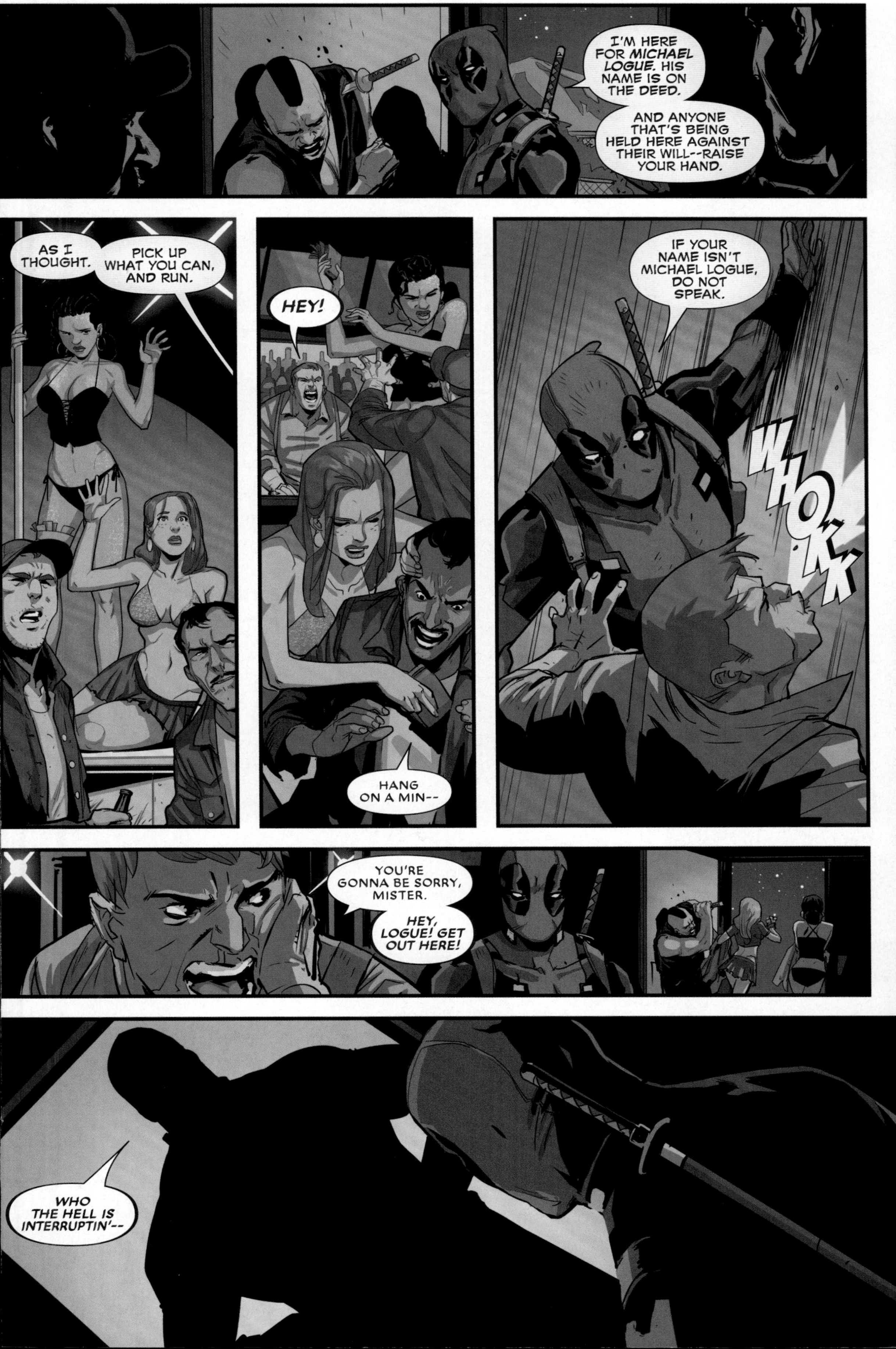

I'M HERE FOR MICHAEL LOGUE. HIS NAME IS ON THE DEED.
AND ANYONE THAT'S BEING HELD HERE AGAINST THEIR WILL--RAISE YOUR HAND.
AS I THOUGHT.
PICK UP WHAT YOU CAN, AND RUN.
HEY!
HANG ON A MIN--
IF YOUR NAME ISN'T MICHAEL LOGUE, DO NOT SPEAK.
WHOKK
YOU'RE GONNA BE SORRY, MISTER.
HEY, LOGUE! GET OUT HERE!
WHO THE HELL IS INTERRUPTIN'--

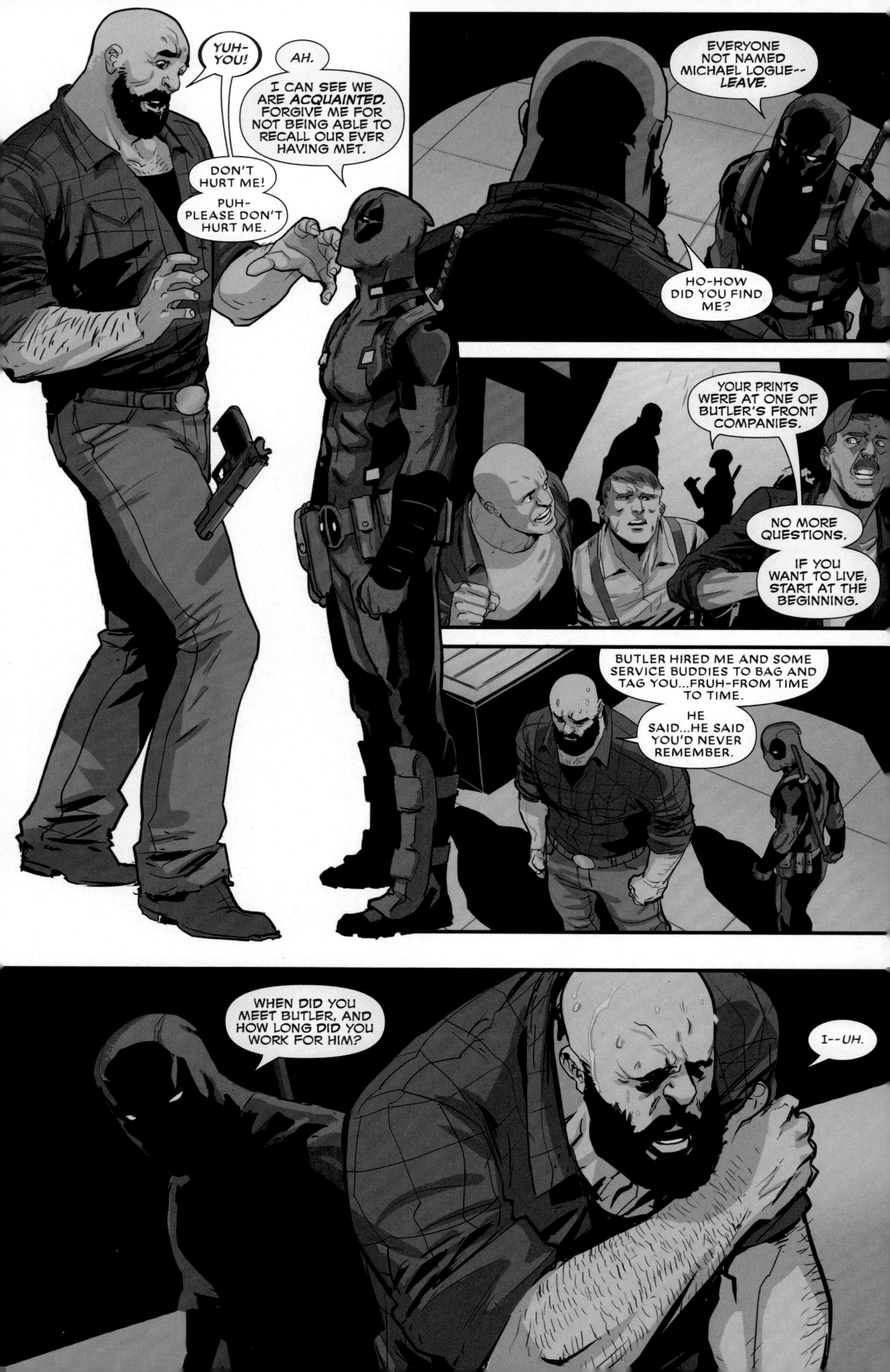
YUH-YOU!
AH.
I CAN SEE WE ARE ACQUAINTED. FORGIVE ME FOR NOT BEING ABLE TO RECALL OUR EVER HAVING MET.
DON'T HURT ME!
PUH-PLEASE DON'T HURT ME.
EVERYONE NOT NAMED MICHAEL LOGUE-- LEAVE.
HO-HOW DID YOU FIND ME?
YOUR PRINTS WERE AT ONE OF BUTLER'S FRONT COMPANIES.
NO MORE QUESTIONS.
IF YOU WANT TO LIVE, START AT THE BEGINNING.
BUTLER HIRED ME AND SOME SERVICE BUDDIES TO BAG AND TAG YOU...FRUH-FROM TIME TO TIME.
HE SAID...HE SAID YOU'D NEVER REMEMBER.
WHEN DID YOU MEET BUTLER, AND HOW LONG DID YOU WORK FOR HIM?
I--UH.

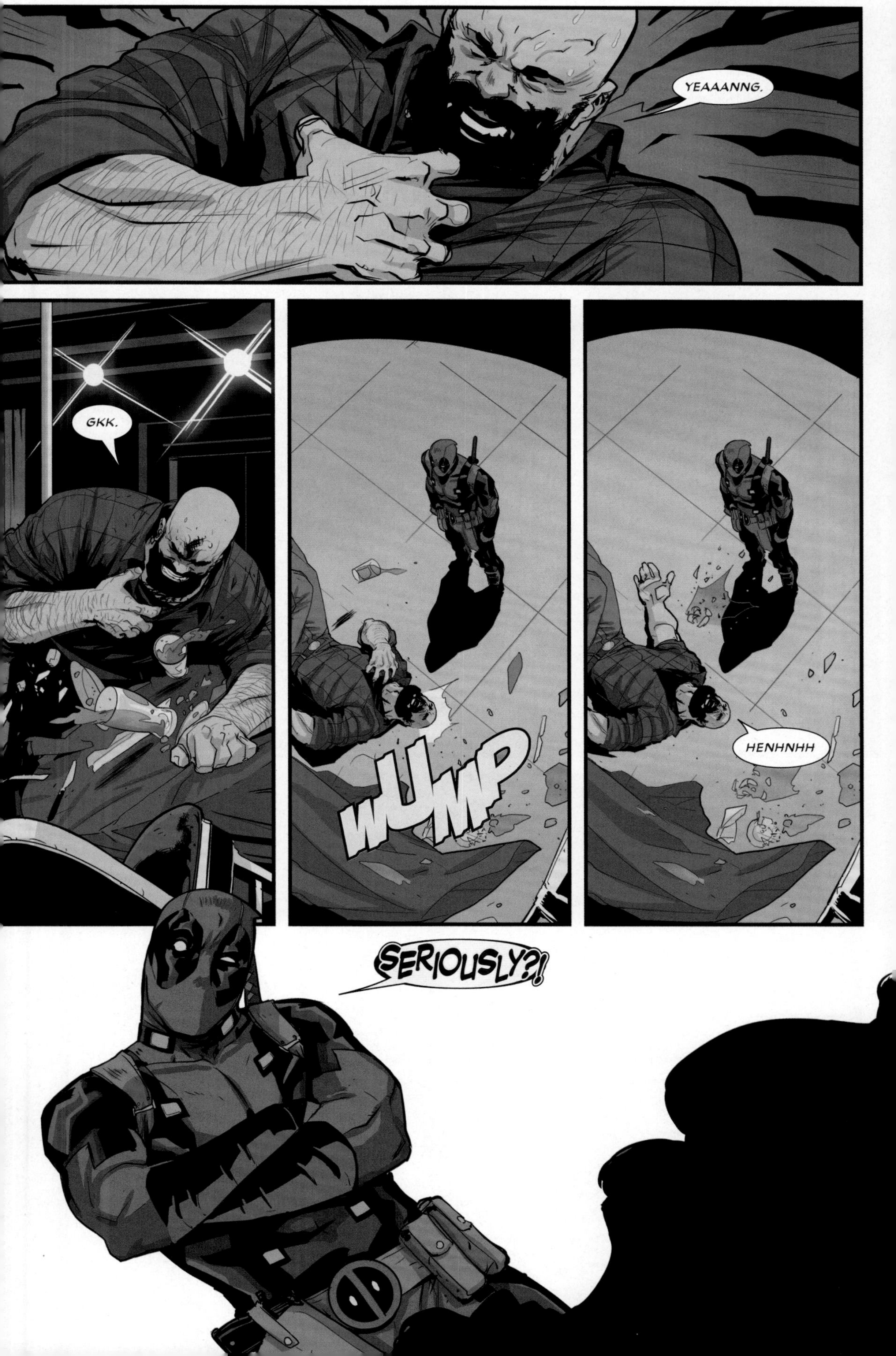
YEAAANNG.
GKK.
WUMP
HENHNHH
SERIOUSLY?!

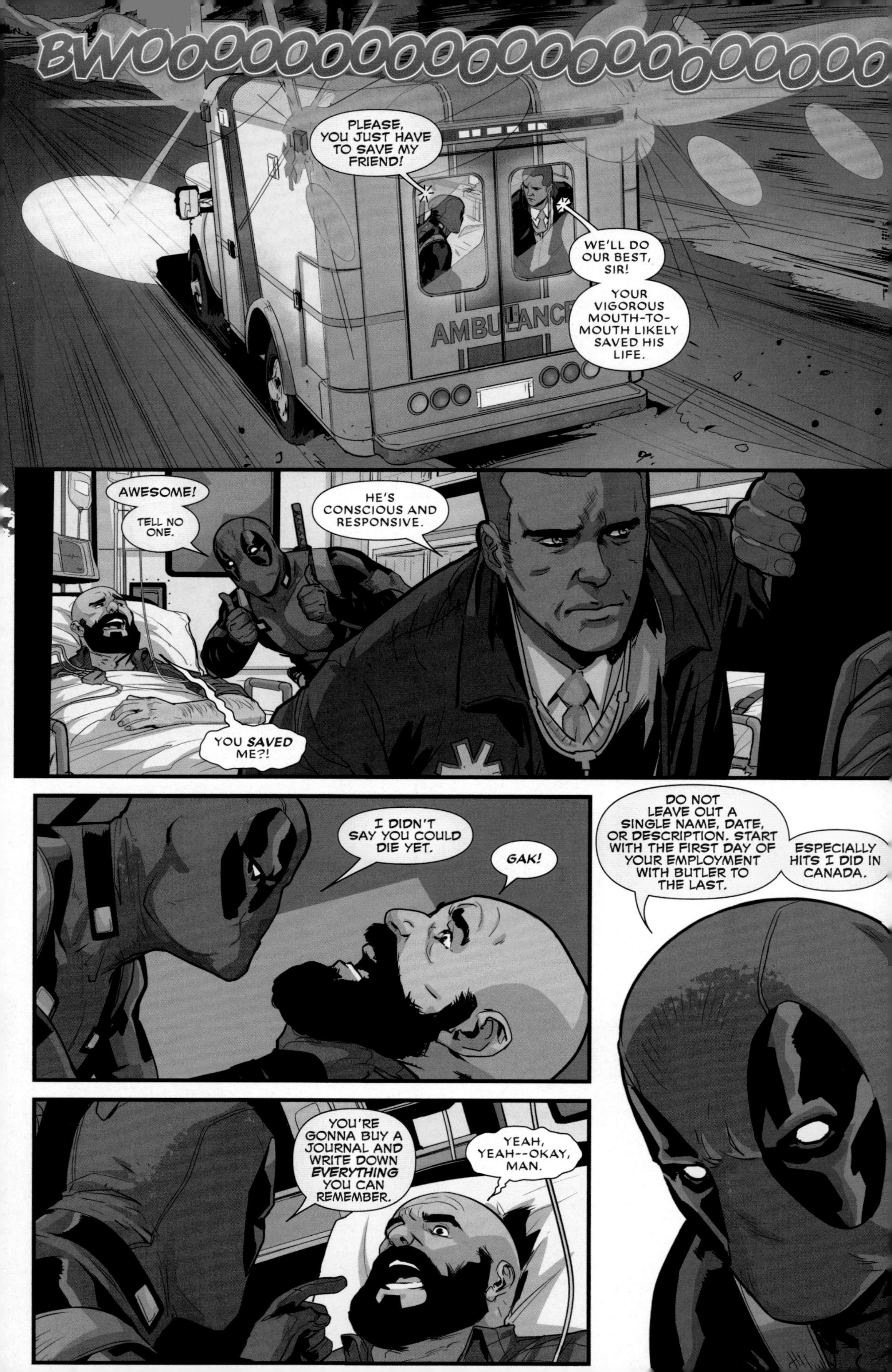
BWOOOOOOOOOOOOOOOOOOOOOO
PLEASE, YOU JUST HAVE TO SAVE MY FRIEND!
WE'LL DO OUR BEST, SIR!
YOUR VIGOROUS MOUTH-TO-MOUTH LIKELY SAVED HIS LIFE.
AMBULANCE
AWESOME!
TELL NO ONE.
HE'S CONSCIOUS AND RESPONSIVE.
YOU *SAVED* ME?!
I DIDN'T SAY YOU COULD DIE YET.
GAK!
YOU'RE GONNA BUY A JOURNAL AND WRITE DOWN *EVERYTHING* YOU CAN REMEMBER.
YEAH, YEAH--OKAY, MAN.
DO NOT LEAVE OUT A SINGLE NAME, DATE, OR DESCRIPTION. START WITH THE FIRST DAY OF YOUR EMPLOYMENT WITH BUTLER TO THE LAST.
ESPECIALLY HITS I DID IN CANADA.

I REMEMBER THERE WERE *TWO* OF YOU THAT TIME.

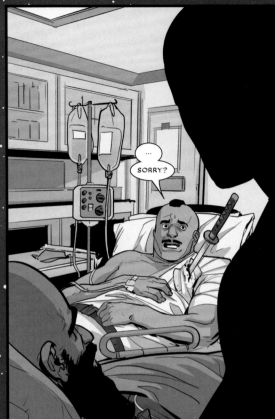

... SORRY?

I WAS WITH SOMEONE ELSE? WHO WAS THE OTHER GUY? WAS IT SABRETOOTH?

HEY, MAN-- HE'S HAVING A CARDIAC EMERGENCY-- LEAVE HIM ALONE!

SORRY!

WRITE EVERYTHING DOWN. I'LL BE BACK FOR THE BOOK WHEN I RETURN FROM CANADA.

YEAAOOOW!!

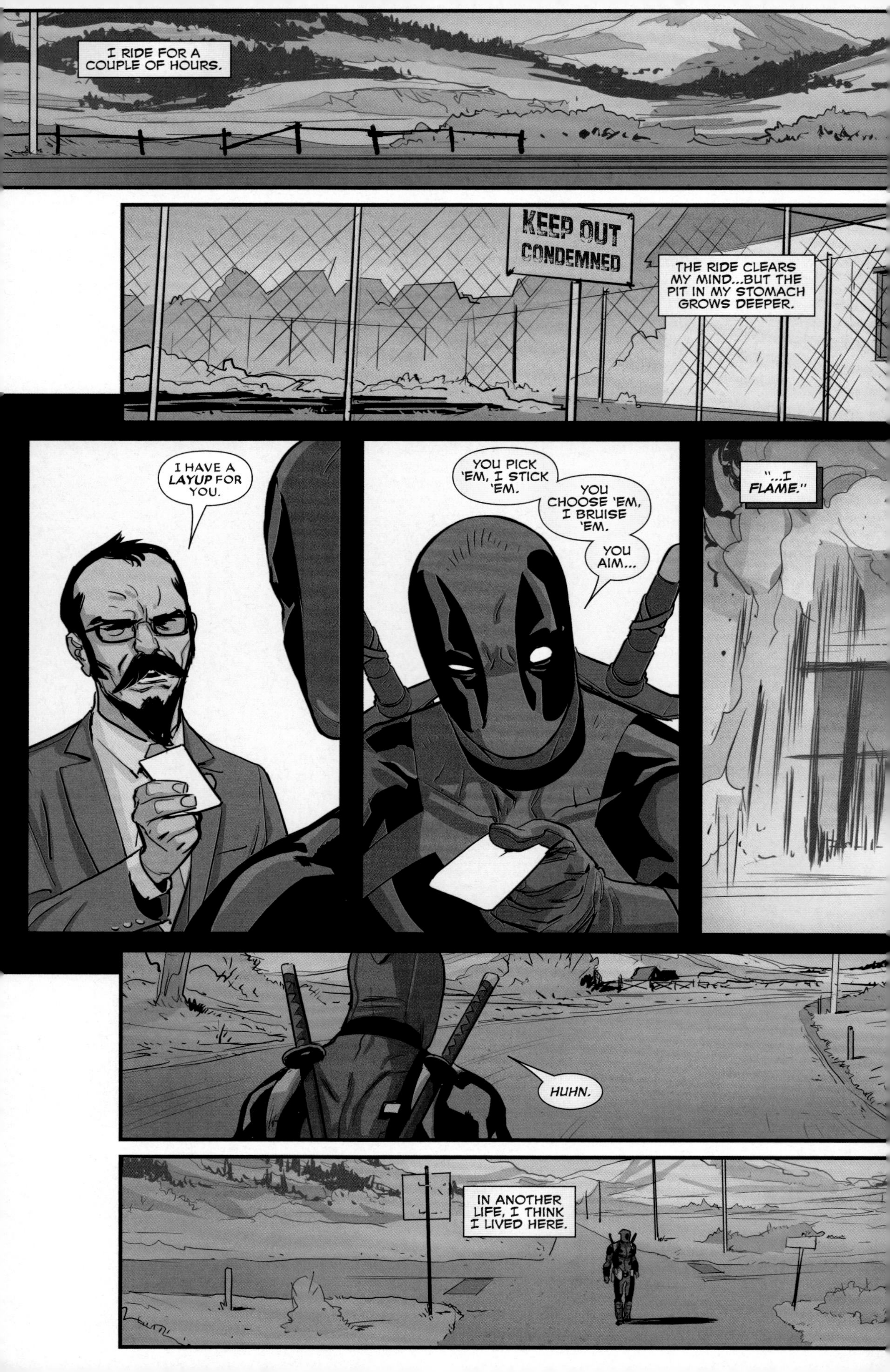

I RIDE FOR A COUPLE OF HOURS.
KEEP OUT
CONDEMNED
THE RIDE CLEARS MY MIND...BUT THE PIT IN MY STOMACH GROWS DEEPER.
I HAVE A *LAYUP* FOR YOU.
YOU PICK 'EM, I STICK 'EM.
YOU CHOOSE 'EM, I BRUISE 'EM.
YOU AIM...
"...I *FLAME.*"
HUHN.
IN ANOTHER LIFE, I THINK I LIVED HERE.

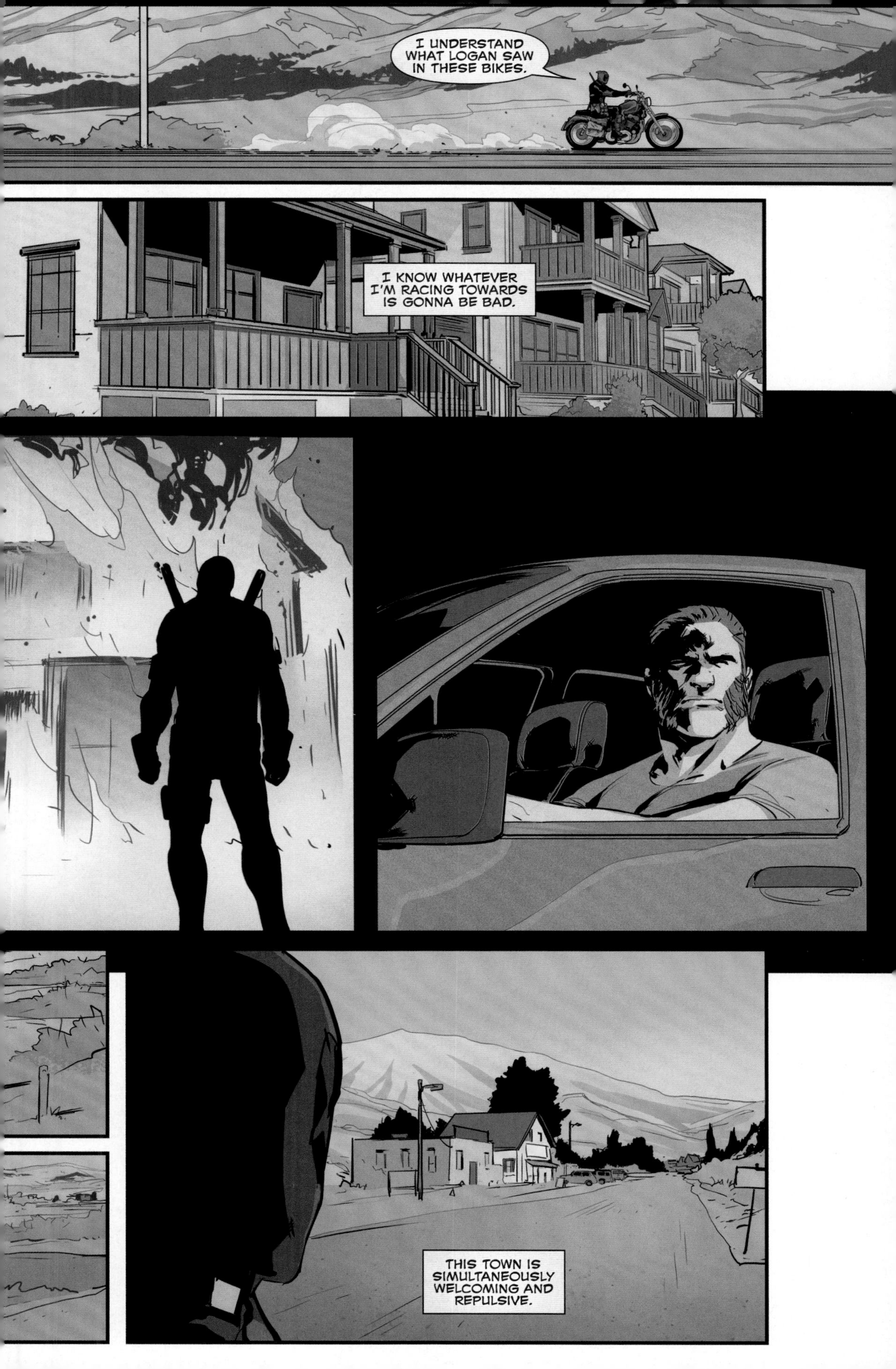
I UNDERSTAND WHAT LOGAN SAW IN THESE BIKES.
I KNOW WHATEVER I'M RACING TOWARDS IS GONNA BE BAD.
THIS TOWN IS SIMULTANEOUSLY WELCOMING AND REPULSIVE.

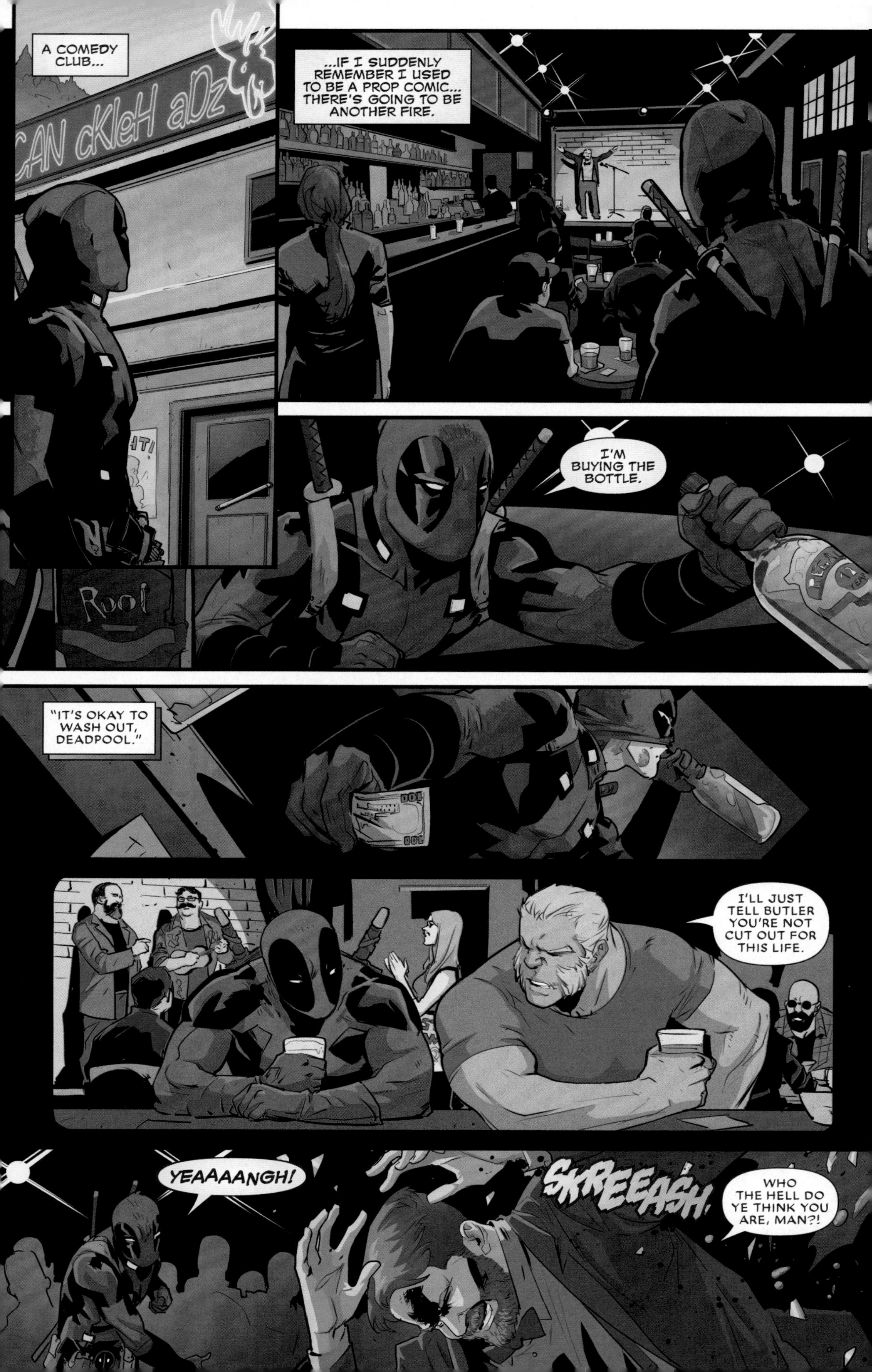
A COMEDY CLUB...
CAN cKleH aDz
...IF I SUDDENLY REMEMBER I USED TO BE A PROP COMIC... THERE'S GOING TO BE ANOTHER FIRE.
I'M BUYING THE BOTTLE.
"IT'S OKAY TO WASH OUT, DEADPOOL."
I'LL JUST TELL BUTLER YOU'RE NOT CUT OUT FOR THIS LIFE.
YEAAAANGH!
SKREEASH
WHO THE HELL DO YE THINK YOU ARE, MAN?!

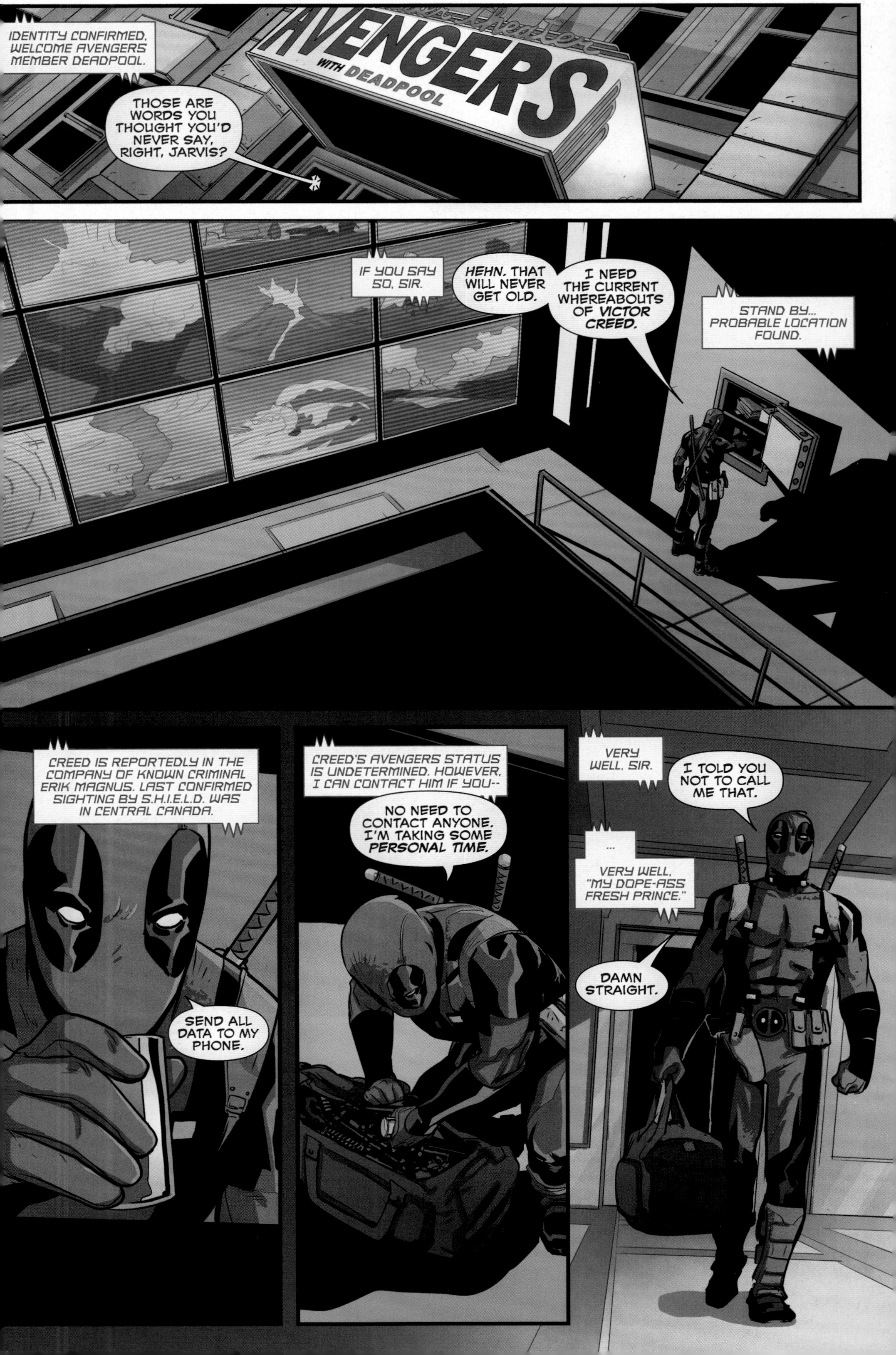

AVENGERS
WITH DEADPOOL
IDENTITY CONFIRMED. WELCOME AVENGERS MEMBER DEADPOOL.
THOSE ARE WORDS YOU THOUGHT YOU'D NEVER SAY, RIGHT, JARVIS?
IF YOU SAY SO, SIR.
HEHN. THAT WILL NEVER GET OLD.
I NEED THE CURRENT WHEREABOUTS OF VICTOR CREED.
STAND BY... PROBABLE LOCATION FOUND.
CREED IS REPORTEDLY IN THE COMPANY OF KNOWN CRIMINAL ERIK MAGNUS. LAST CONFIRMED SIGHTING BY S.H.I.E.L.D. WAS IN CENTRAL CANADA.
SEND ALL DATA TO MY PHONE.
CREED'S AVENGERS STATUS IS UNDETERMINED. HOWEVER, I CAN CONTACT HIM IF YOU--
NO NEED TO CONTACT ANYONE. I'M TAKING SOME PERSONAL TIME.
VERY WELL, SIR.
I TOLD YOU NOT TO CALL ME THAT.
...
VERY WELL, "MY DOPE-ASS FRESH PRINCE."
DAMN STRAIGHT.

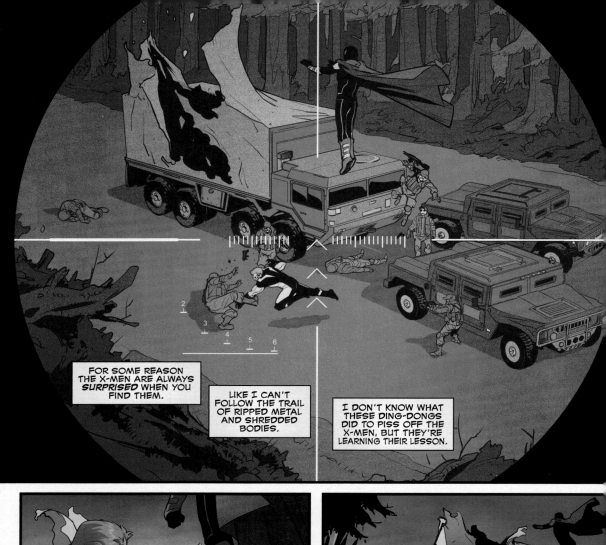

FOR SOME REASON THE X-MEN ARE ALWAYS *SURPRISED* WHEN YOU FIND THEM.

LIKE I CAN'T FOLLOW THE TRAIL OF RIPPED METAL AND SHREDDED BODIES.

I DON'T KNOW WHAT THESE DING-DONGS DID TO PISS OFF THE X-MEN, BUT THEY'RE LEARNING THEIR LESSON.

THERE'S CREED.

I THINK I CAN CORRECT FOR WIND FROM THIS DISTANCE...

...BUT I'M AFRAID MAGNETO WOULD CATCH THE BULLET, SO I WAIT FOR *PLAN B.*

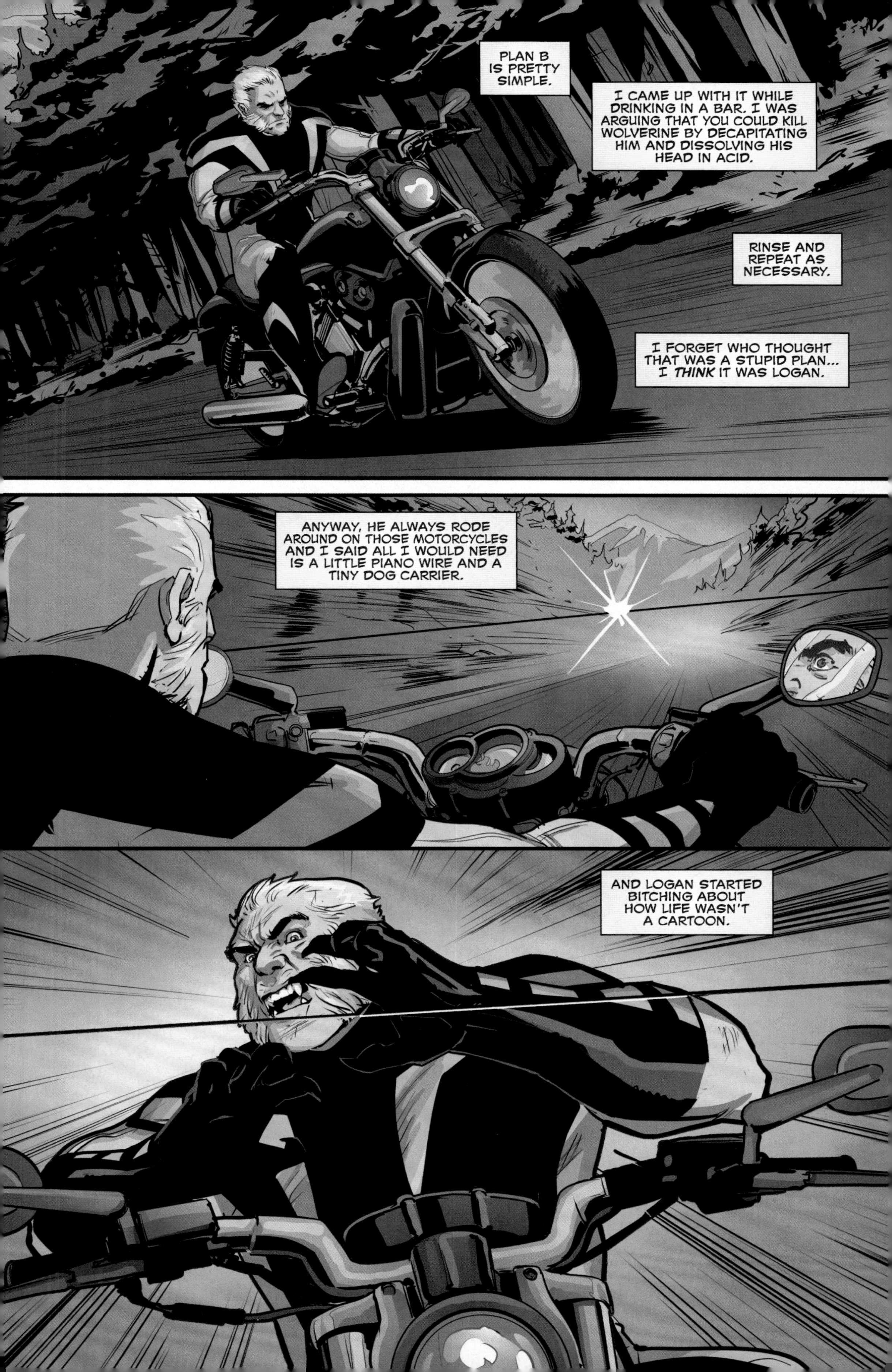
PLAN B IS PRETTY SIMPLE.
I CAME UP WITH IT WHILE DRINKING IN A BAR. I WAS ARGUING THAT YOU COULD KILL WOLVERINE BY DECAPITATING HIM AND DISSOLVING HIS HEAD IN ACID.
RINSE AND REPEAT AS NECESSARY.
I FORGET WHO THOUGHT THAT WAS A STUPID PLAN... I *THINK* IT WAS LOGAN.
ANYWAY, HE ALWAYS RODE AROUND ON THOSE MOTORCYCLES AND I SAID ALL I WOULD NEED IS A LITTLE PIANO WIRE AND A TINY DOG CARRIER.
AND LOGAN STARTED BITCHING ABOUT HOW LIFE WASN'T A CARTOON.

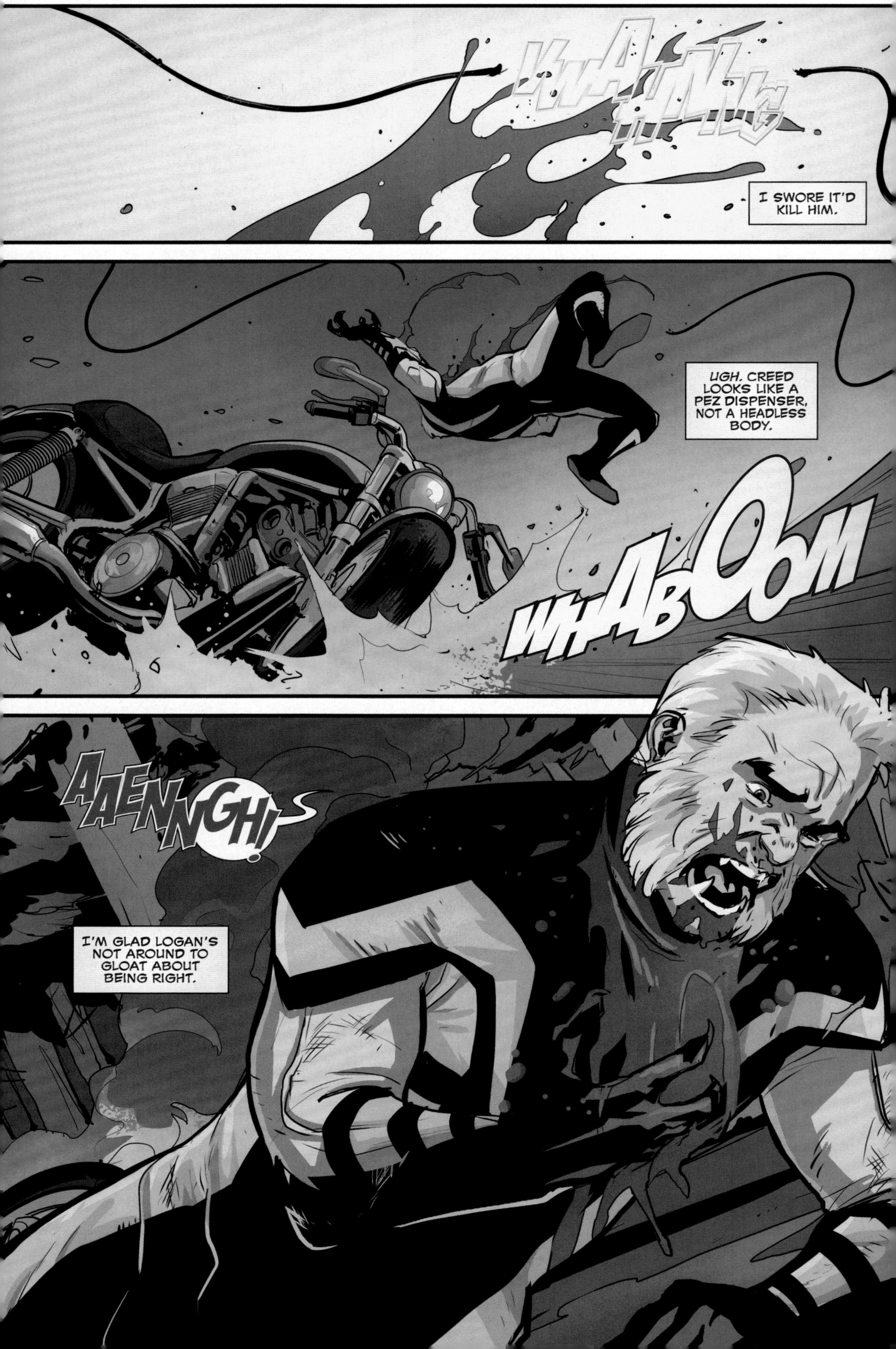
KWAANNG
I SWORE IT'D KILL HIM.
UGH. CREED LOOKS LIKE A PEZ DISPENSER, NOT A HEADLESS BODY.
WHABOOOM
AAENNGH!
I'M GLAD LOGAN'S NOT AROUND TO GLOAT ABOUT BEING RIGHT.

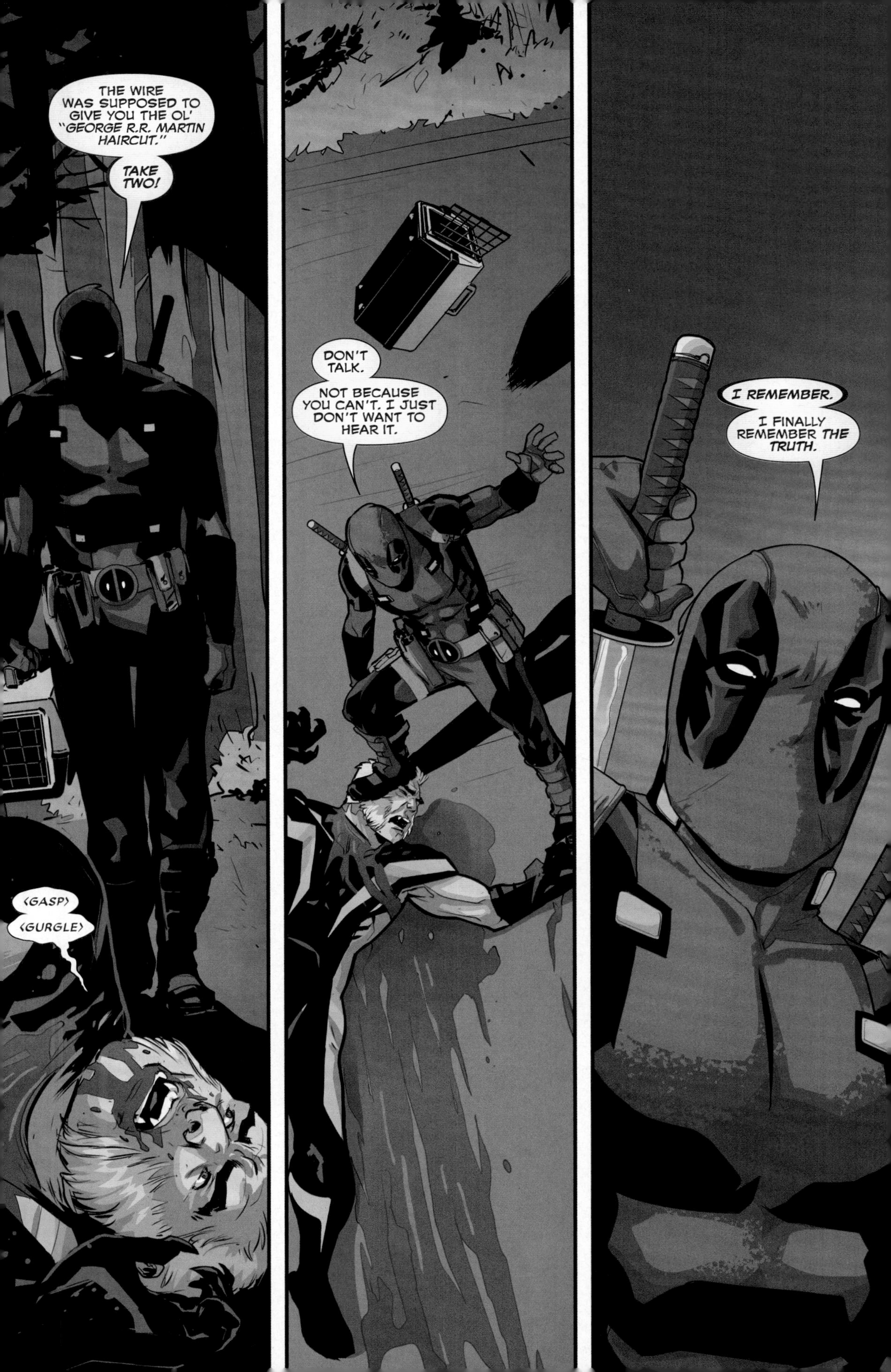
THE WIRE WAS SUPPOSED TO GIVE YOU THE OL' "GEORGE R.R. MARTIN HAIRCUT."
TAKE TWO!
<GASP>
<GURGLE>
DON'T TALK.
NOT BECAUSE YOU CAN'T. I JUST DON'T WANT TO HEAR IT.
I REMEMBER.
I FINALLY REMEMBER THE TRUTH.

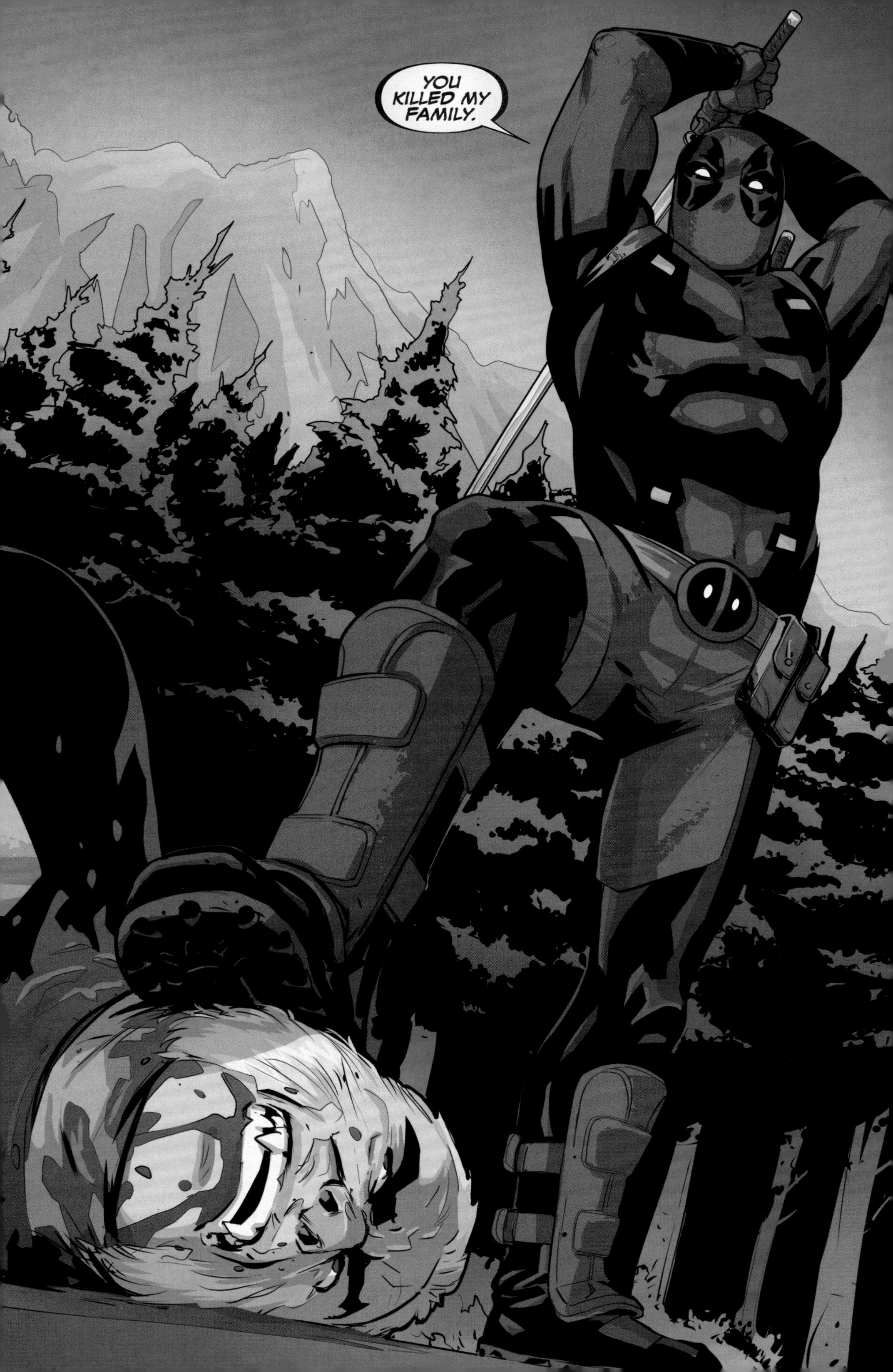
YOU KILLED MY FAMILY.

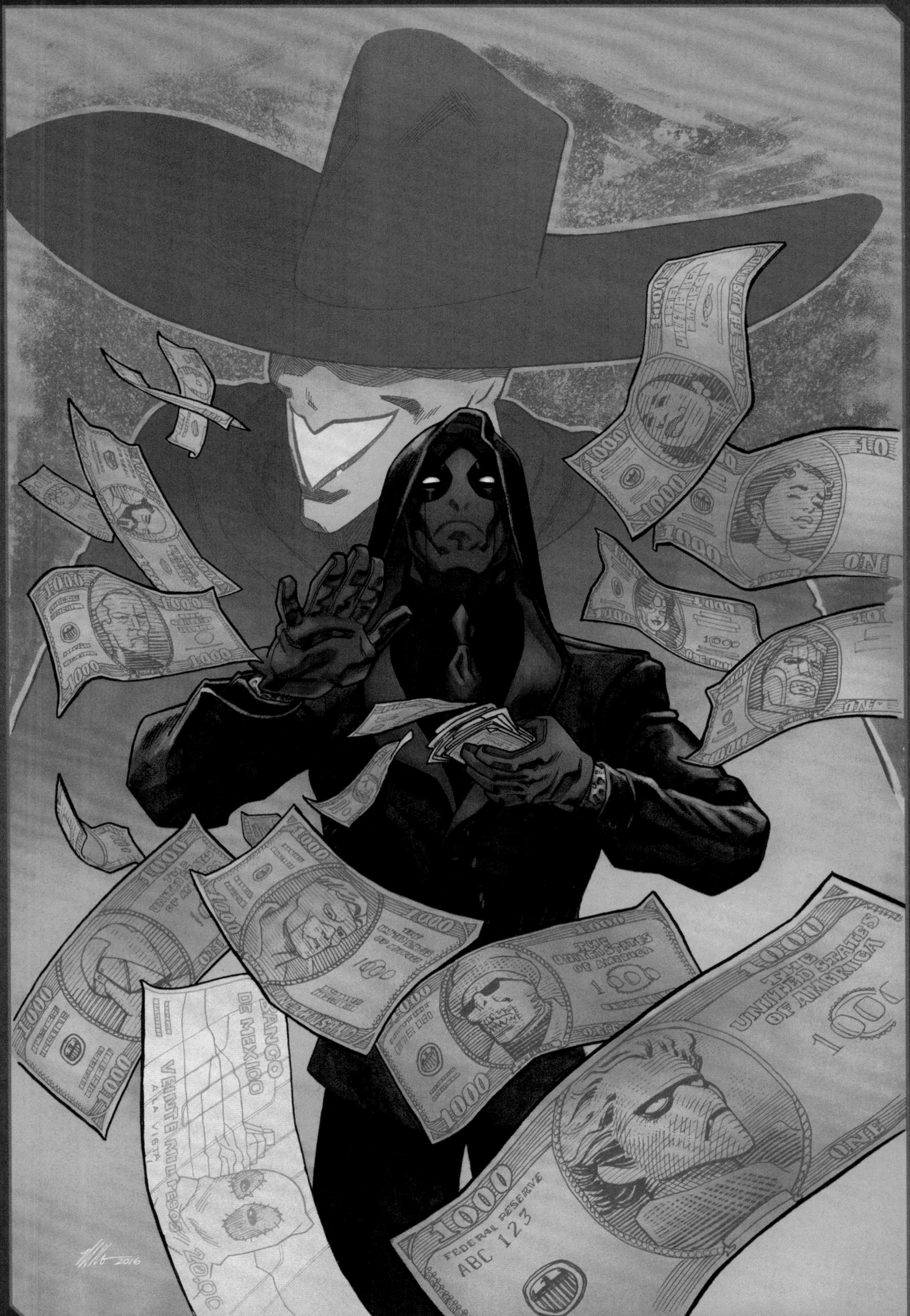
THE UNITED STATES OF AMERICA
1000
ONE
BANCO DE MEXICO
VEINTE MIL PESOS
A LA VISTA
FEDERAL RESERVE
ABC 123
2016

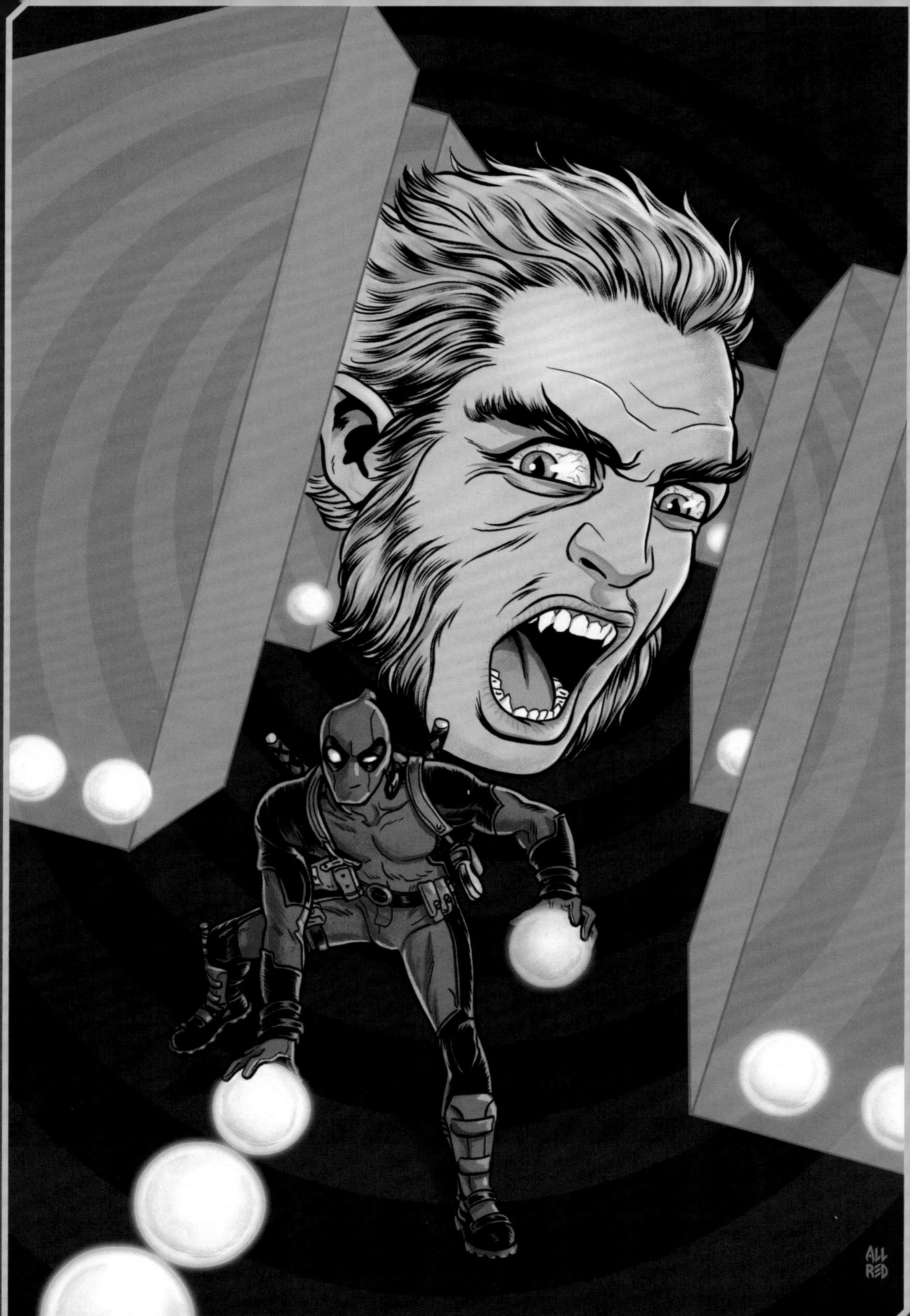
ALL
RED

9 TO ME, MY EX-MAN

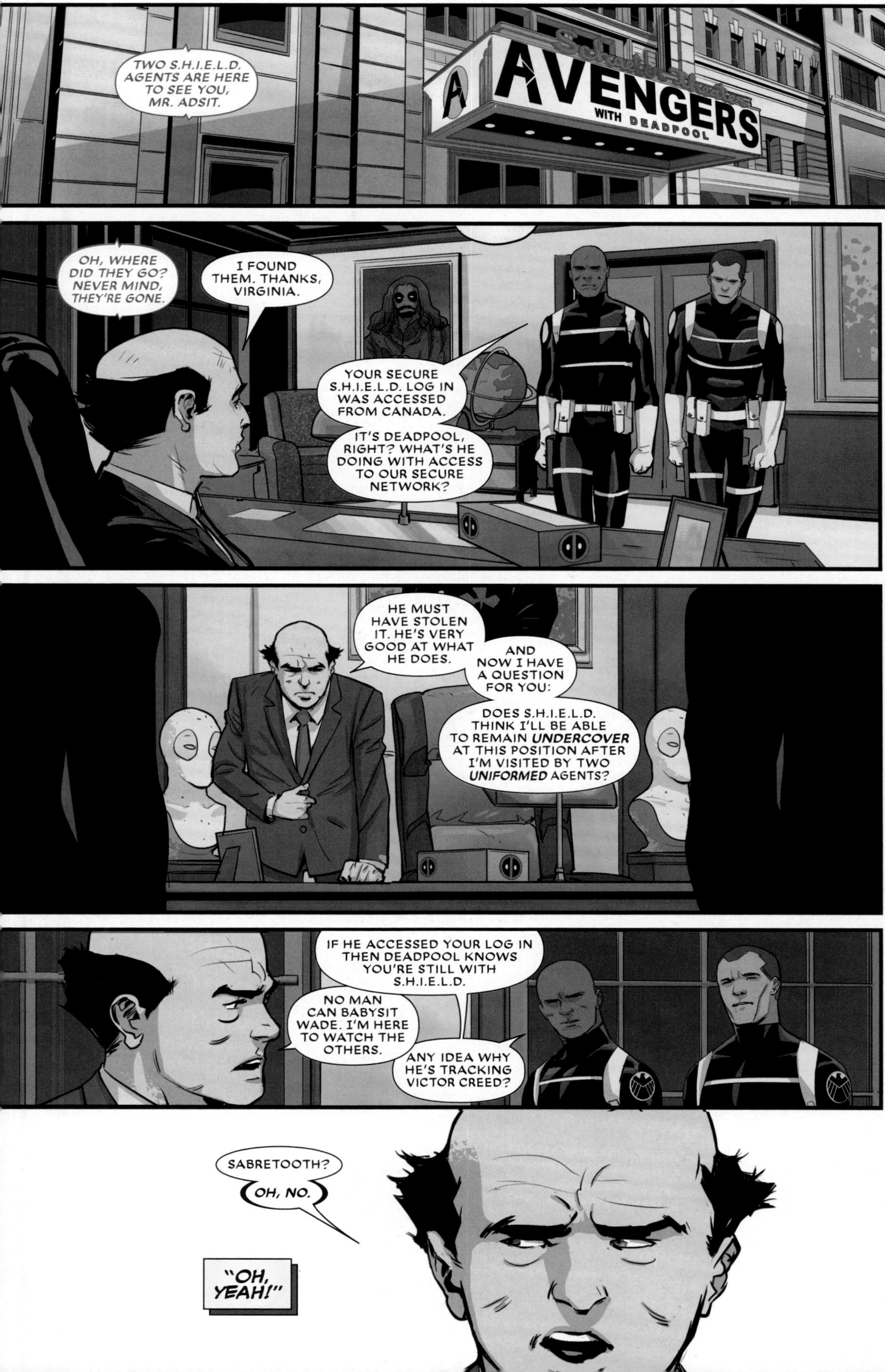

AVENGERS
WITH DEADPOOL
TWO S.H.I.E.L.D. AGENTS ARE HERE TO SEE YOU, MR. ADSIT.
OH, WHERE DID THEY GO? NEVER MIND, THEY'RE GONE.
I FOUND THEM. THANKS, VIRGINIA.
YOUR SECURE S.H.I.E.L.D. LOG IN WAS ACCESSED FROM CANADA.
IT'S DEADPOOL, RIGHT? WHAT'S HE DOING WITH ACCESS TO OUR SECURE NETWORK?
HE MUST HAVE STOLEN IT. HE'S VERY GOOD AT WHAT HE DOES.
AND NOW I HAVE A QUESTION FOR YOU:
DOES S.H.I.E.L.D. THINK I'LL BE ABLE TO REMAIN *UNDERCOVER* AT THIS POSITION AFTER I'M VISITED BY TWO *UNIFORMED* AGENTS?
IF HE ACCESSED YOUR LOG IN THEN DEADPOOL KNOWS YOU'RE STILL WITH S.H.I.E.L.D.
NO MAN CAN BABYSIT WADE. I'M HERE TO WATCH THE OTHERS.
ANY IDEA WHY HE'S TRACKING VICTOR CREED?
SABRETOOTH?
OH, NO.
"OH, YEAH!"

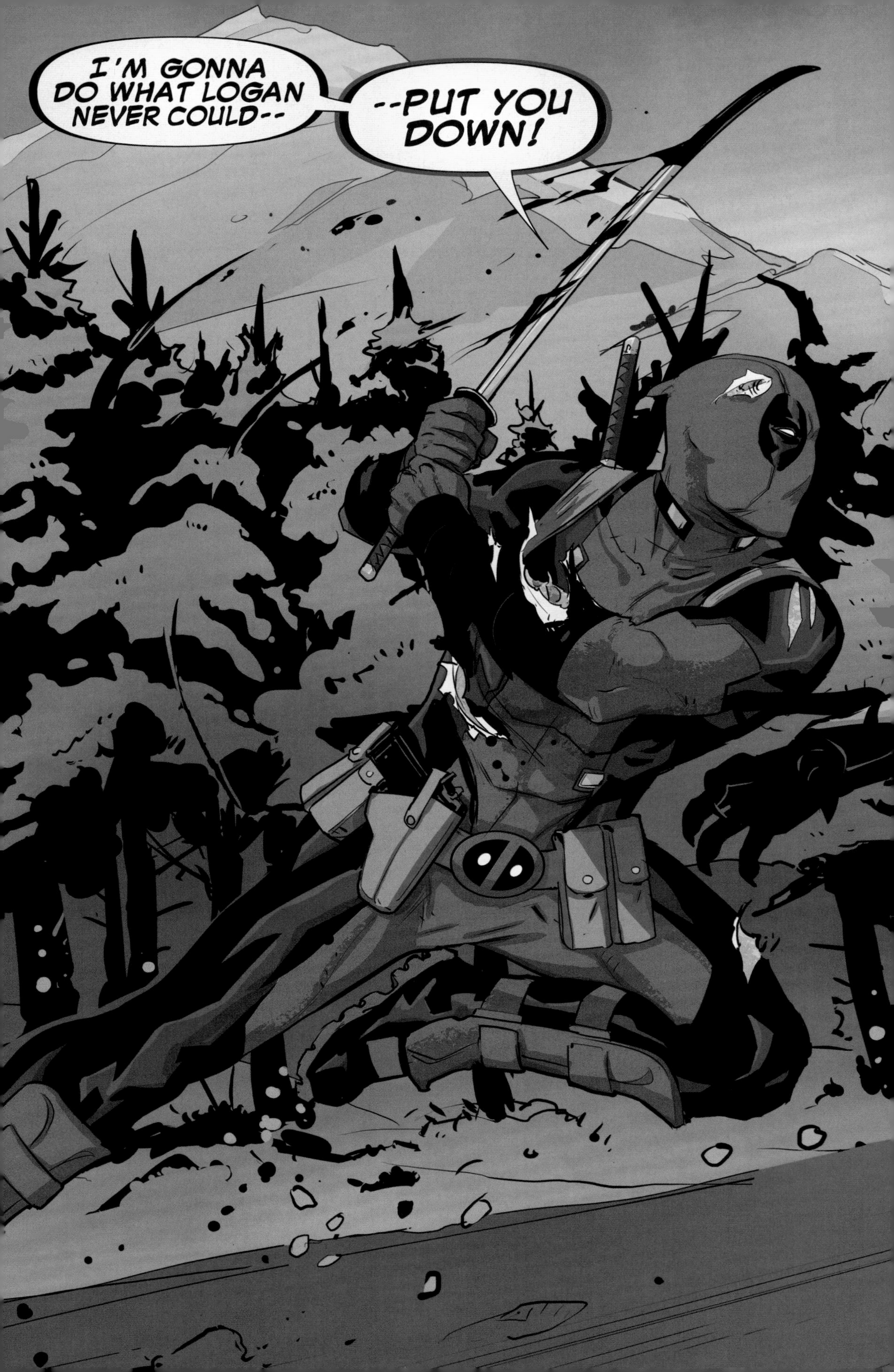
I'M GONNA DO WHAT LOGAN NEVER COULD--
--PUT YOU DOWN!

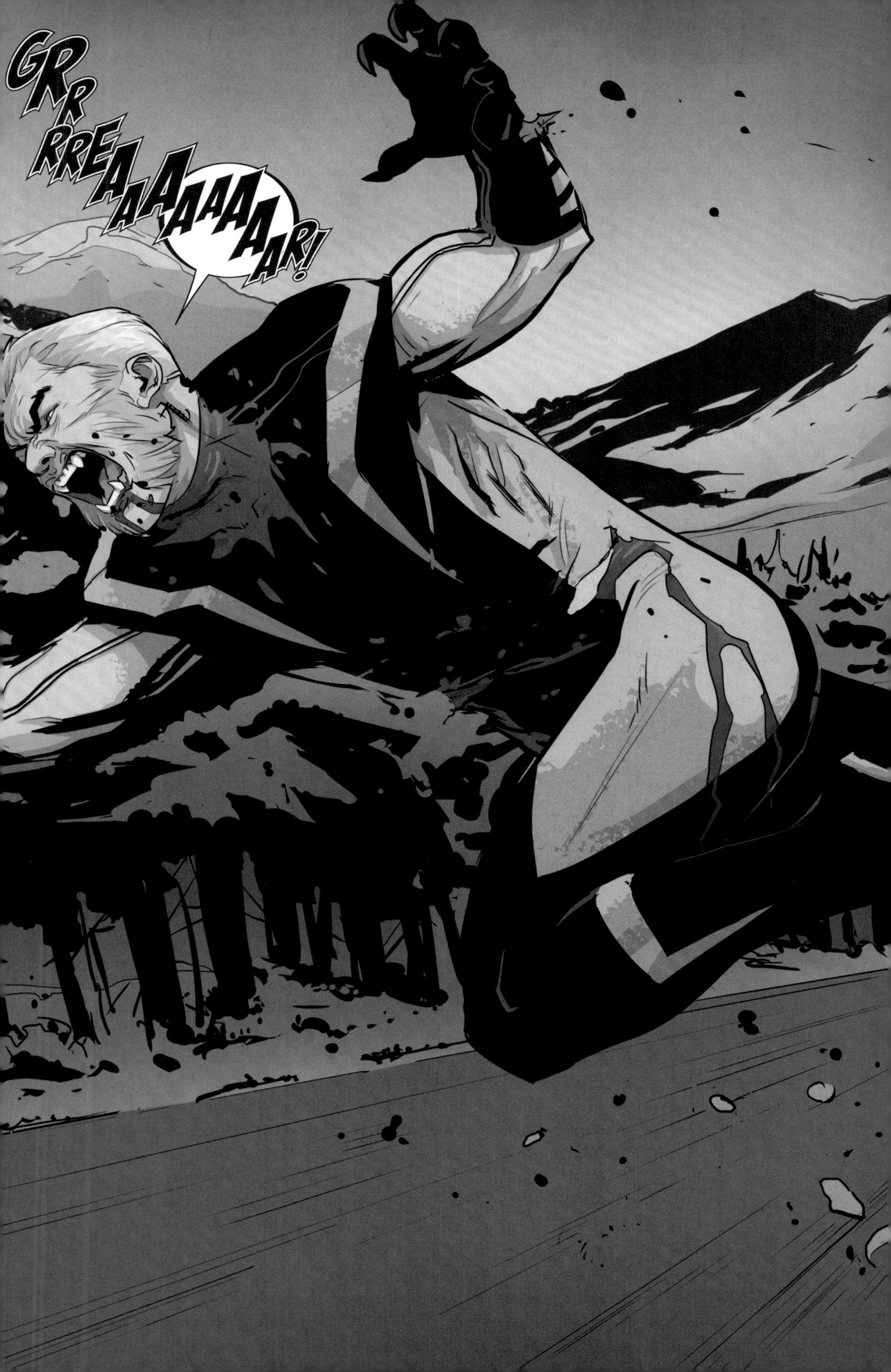
GRRRREAAAAAAAAR!

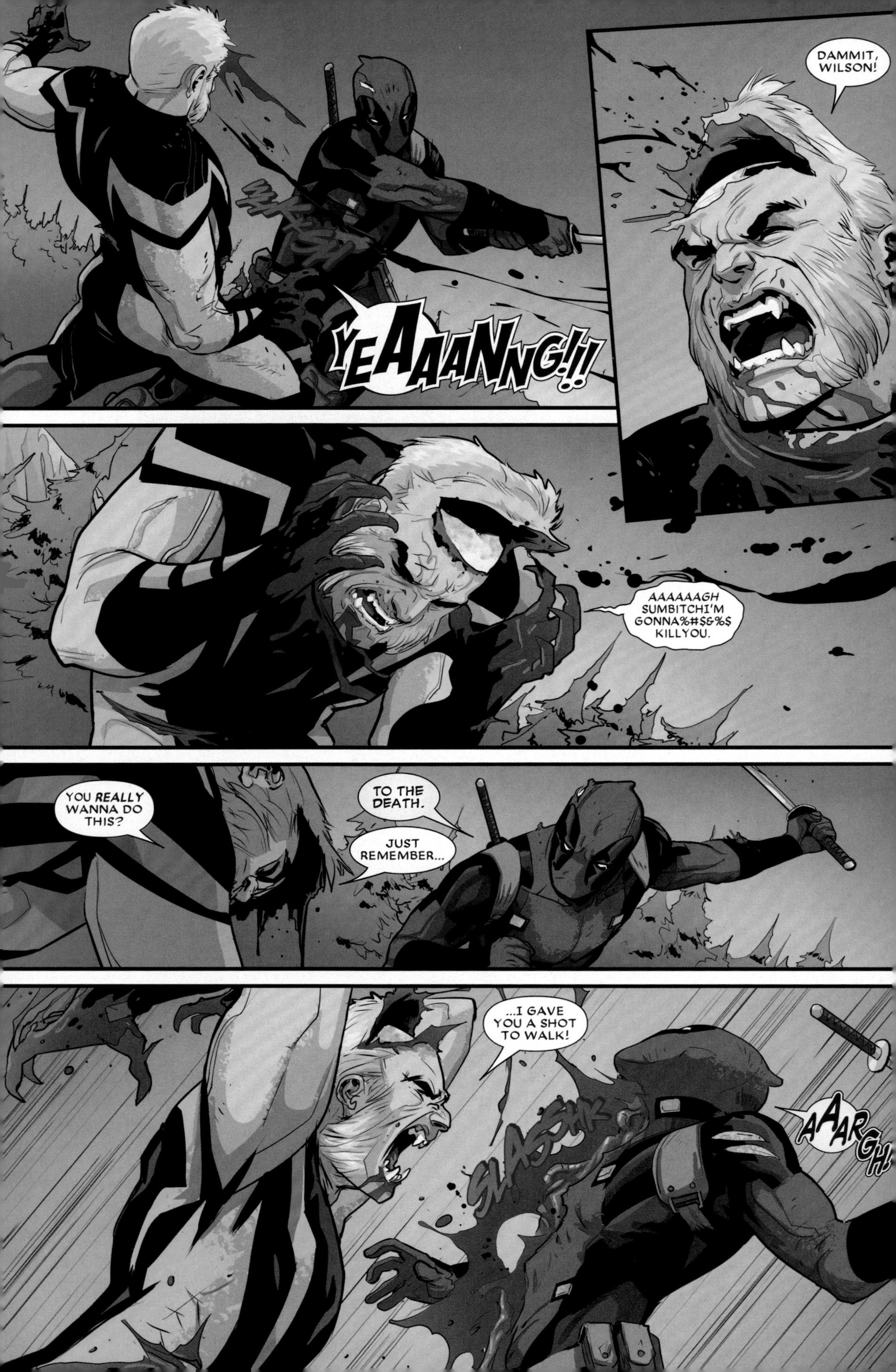
YEAAANNG!!!
DAMMIT, WILSON!
AAAAAAGH SUMBITCHI'M GONNA%#$&%$ KILLYOU.
YOU REALLY WANNA DO THIS?
TO THE DEATH.
JUST REMEMBER...
...I GAVE YOU A SHOT TO WALK!
SLASSHK
AAARGH

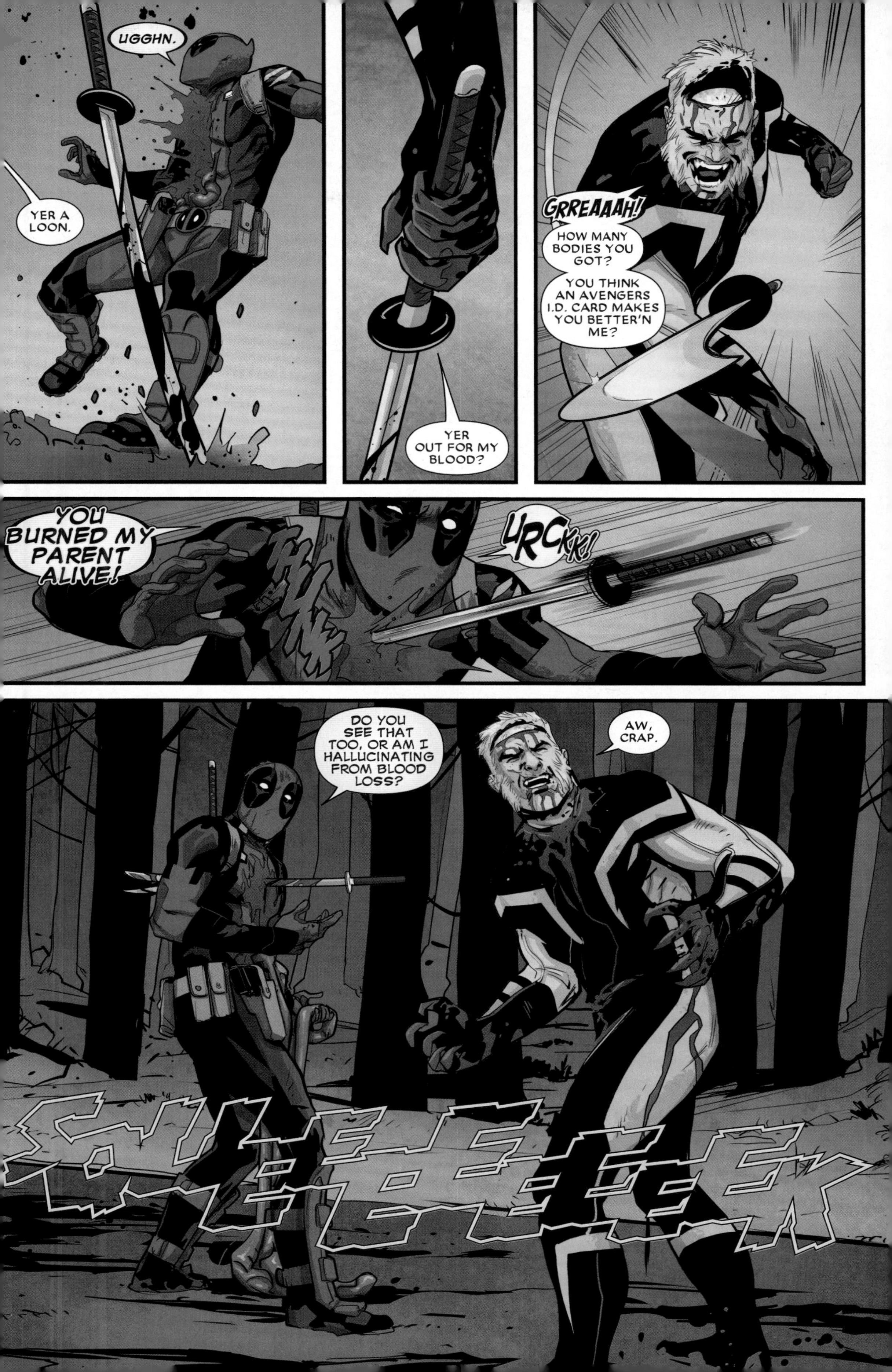
UGGHN.
YER A LOON.
YER OUT FOR MY BLOOD?
GRREAAAH!
HOW MANY BODIES YOU GOT?
YOU THINK AN AVENGERS I.D. CARD MAKES YOU BETTER'N ME?
YOU BURNED MY PARENT ALIVE!
URCKK!
DO YOU SEE THAT TOO, OR AM I HALLUCINATING FROM BLOOD LOSS?
AW, CRAP.

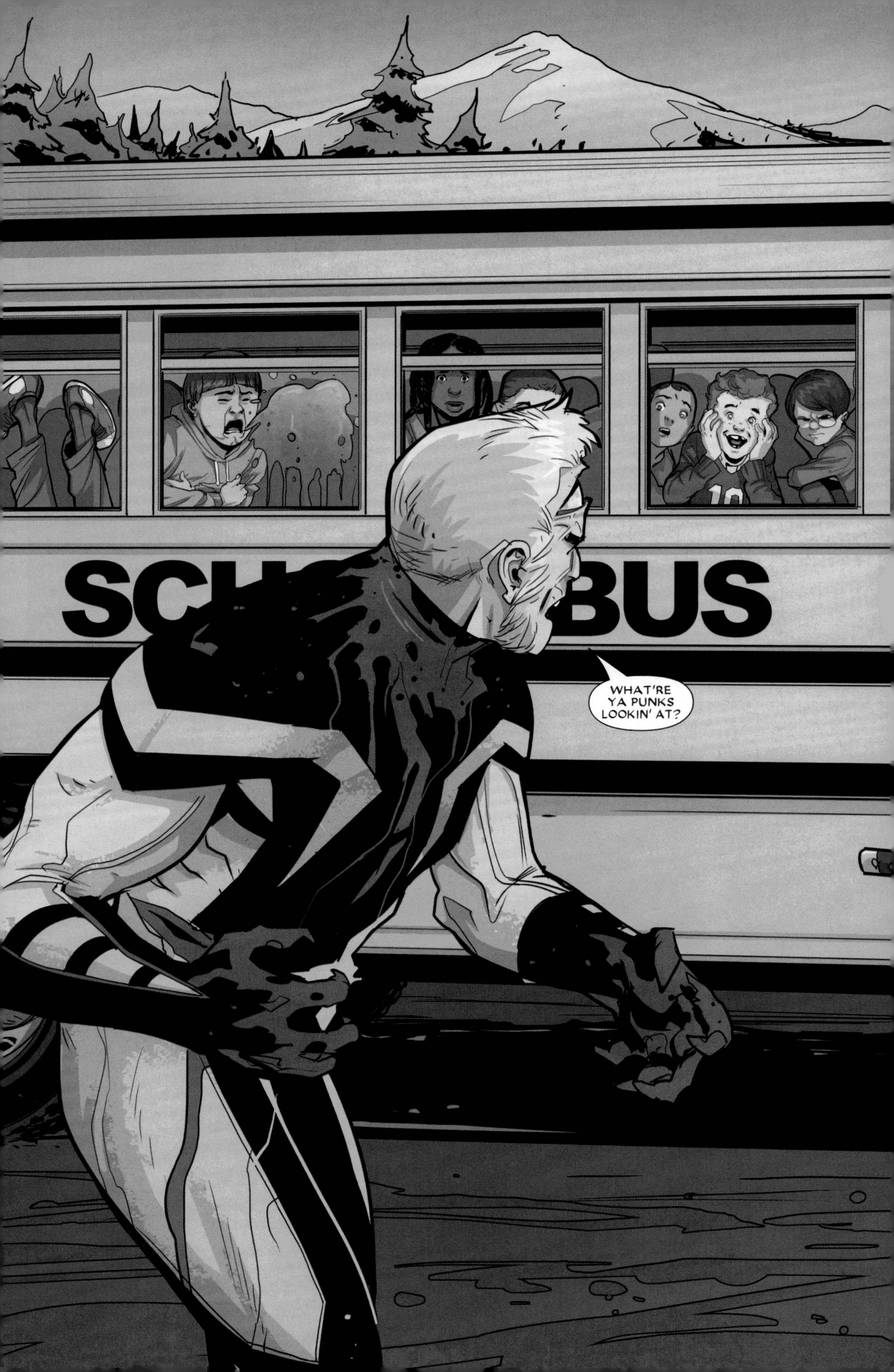
SCH
BUS
WHAT'RE YA PUNKS LOOKIN' AT?

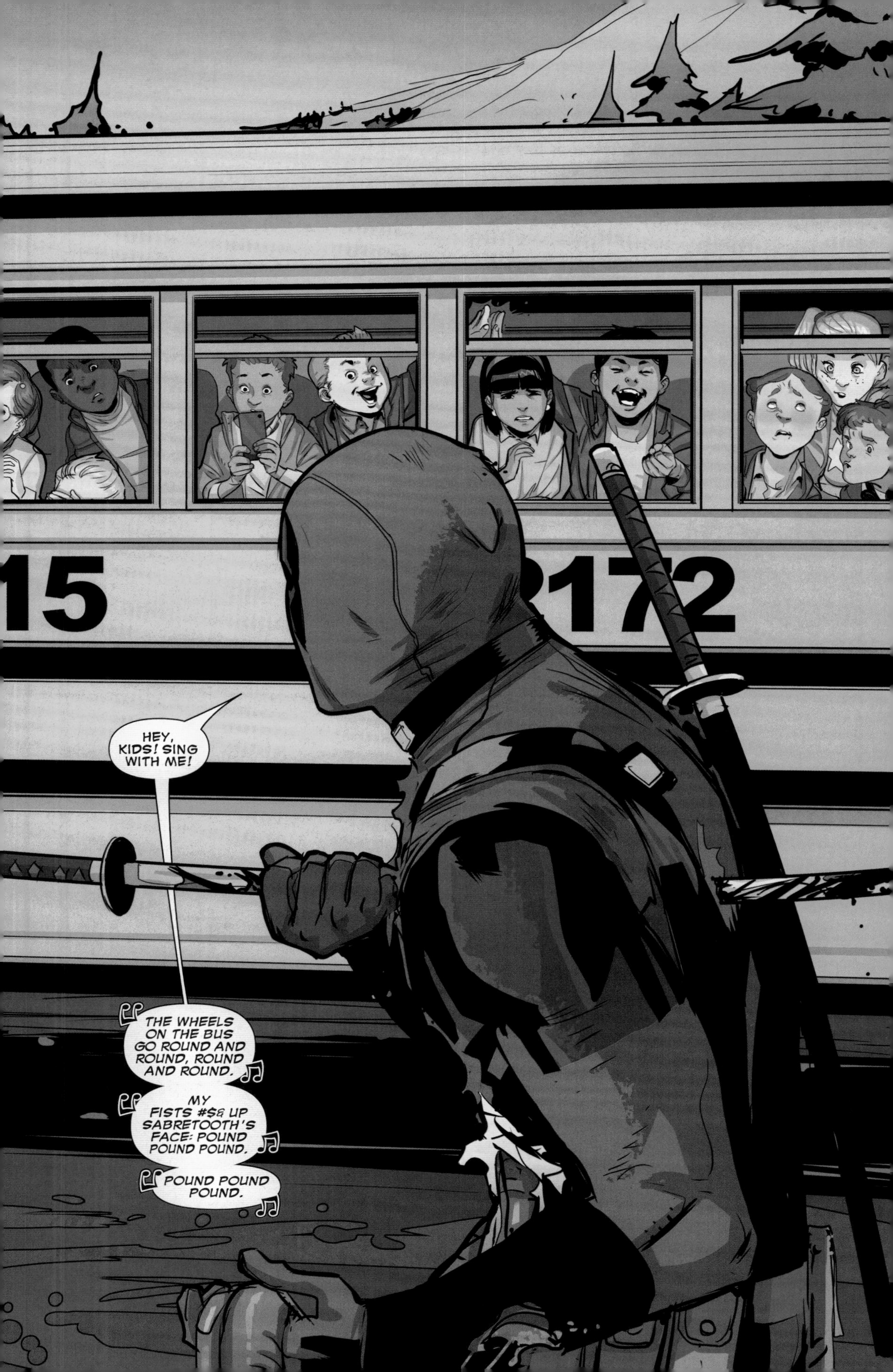
15
2172
HEY, KIDS! SING WITH ME!
THE WHEELS ON THE BUS GO ROUND AND ROUND, ROUND AND ROUND.
MY FISTS #$& UP SABRETOOTH'S FACE: POUND POUND POUND.
POUND POUND POUND.

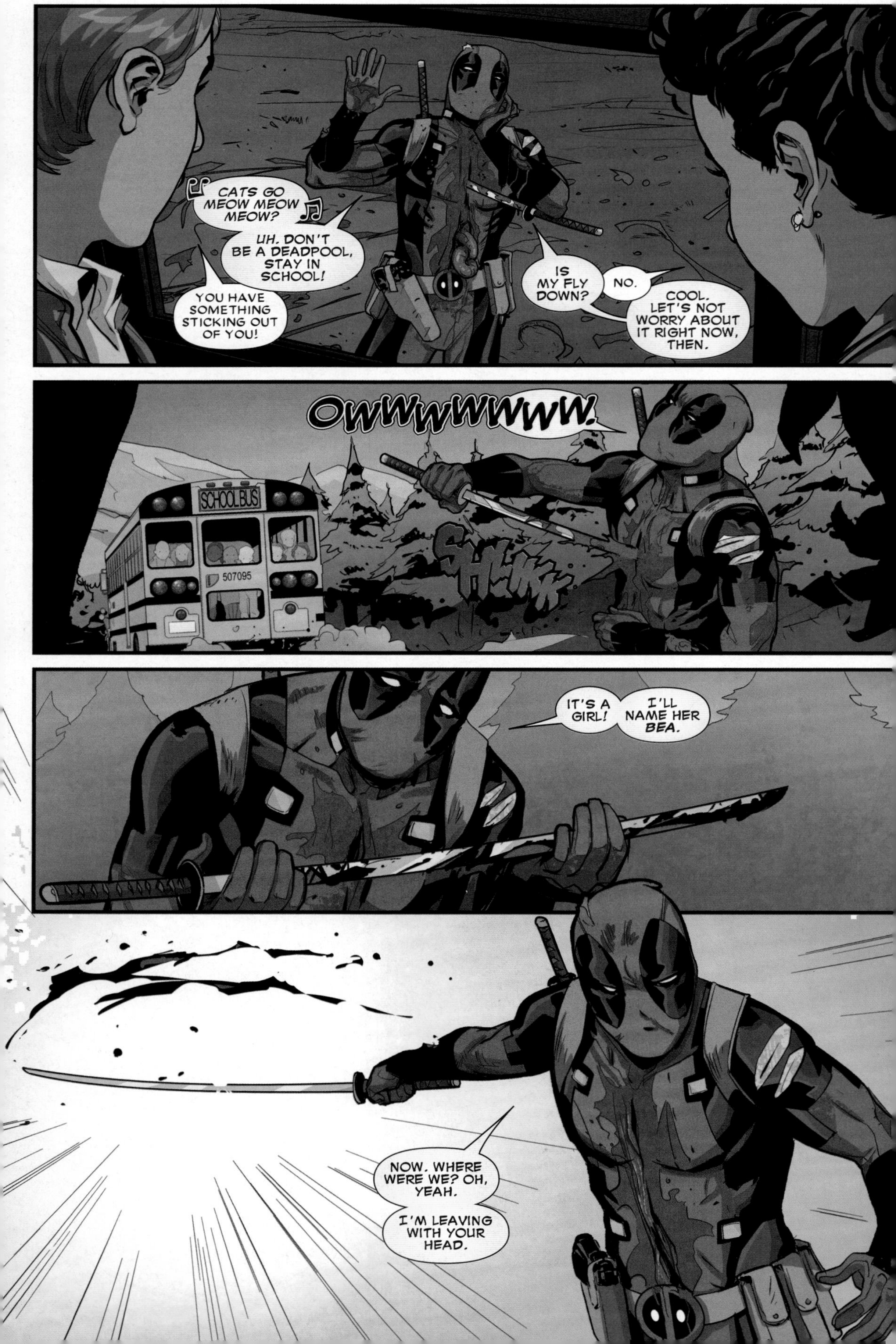

CATS GO MEOW MEOW MEOW?
UH. DON'T BE A DEADPOOL, STAY IN SCHOOL!
YOU HAVE SOMETHING STICKING OUT OF YOU!
IS MY FLY DOWN?
NO.
COOL. LET'S NOT WORRY ABOUT IT RIGHT NOW, THEN.
OWWWWWWW!
SCHOOLBUS
507095
SHLUKK
IT'S A GIRL!
I'LL NAME HER BEA.
NOW. WHERE WERE WE? OH, YEAH.
I'M LEAVING WITH YOUR HEAD.

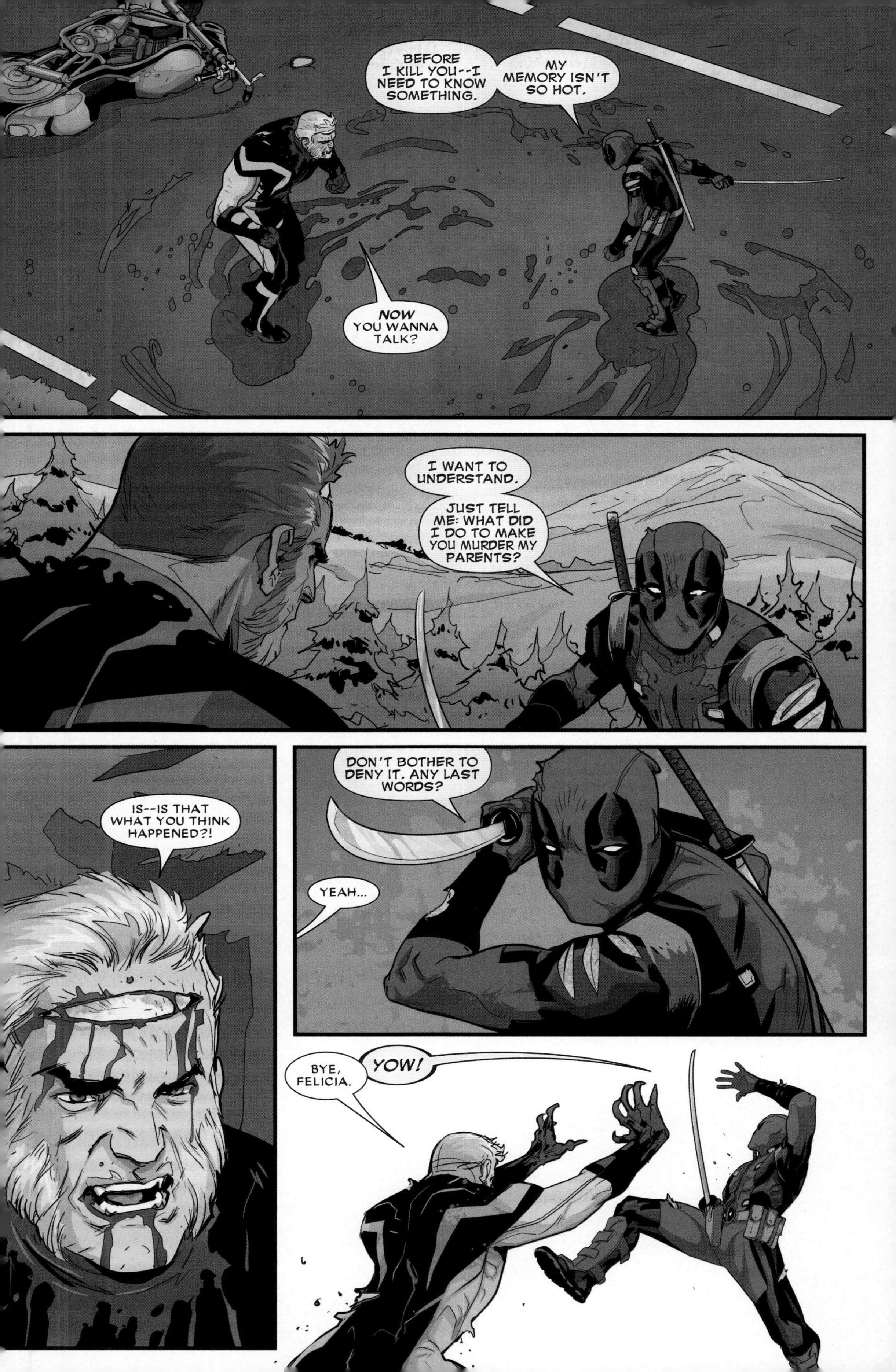
BEFORE I KILL YOU--I NEED TO KNOW SOMETHING.
MY MEMORY ISN'T SO HOT.
NOW YOU WANNA TALK?
I WANT TO UNDERSTAND.
JUST TELL ME: WHAT DID I DO TO MAKE YOU MURDER MY PARENTS?
IS--IS THAT WHAT YOU THINK HAPPENED?!
DON'T BOTHER TO DENY IT. ANY LAST WORDS?
YEAH...
BYE, FELICIA.
YOW!

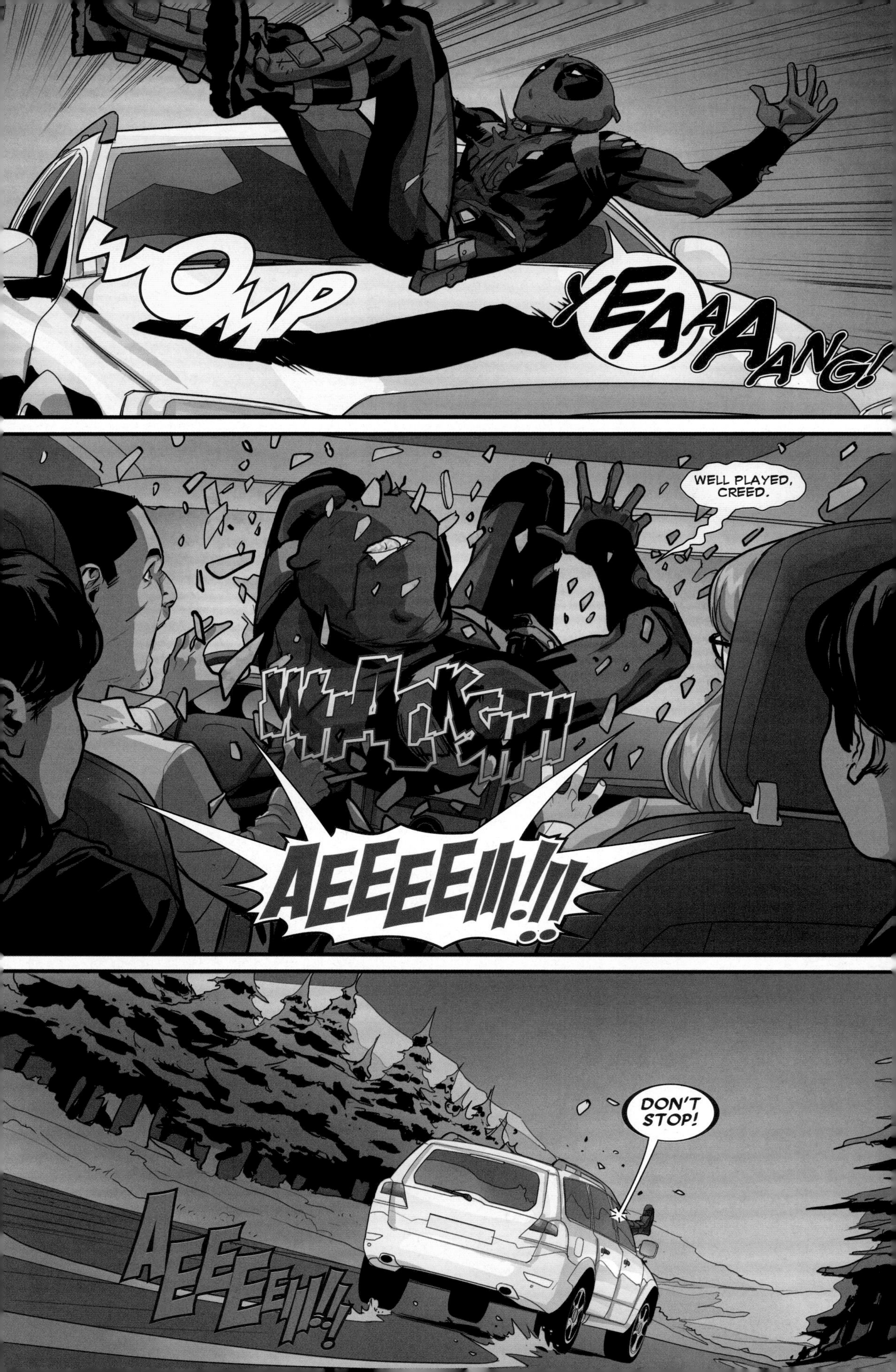
WOMP
YEAAAAANG!
WELL PLAYED, CREED.
WHACKSSHH
AEEEEIIII!!
DON'T STOP!
AEEEEIIII!!

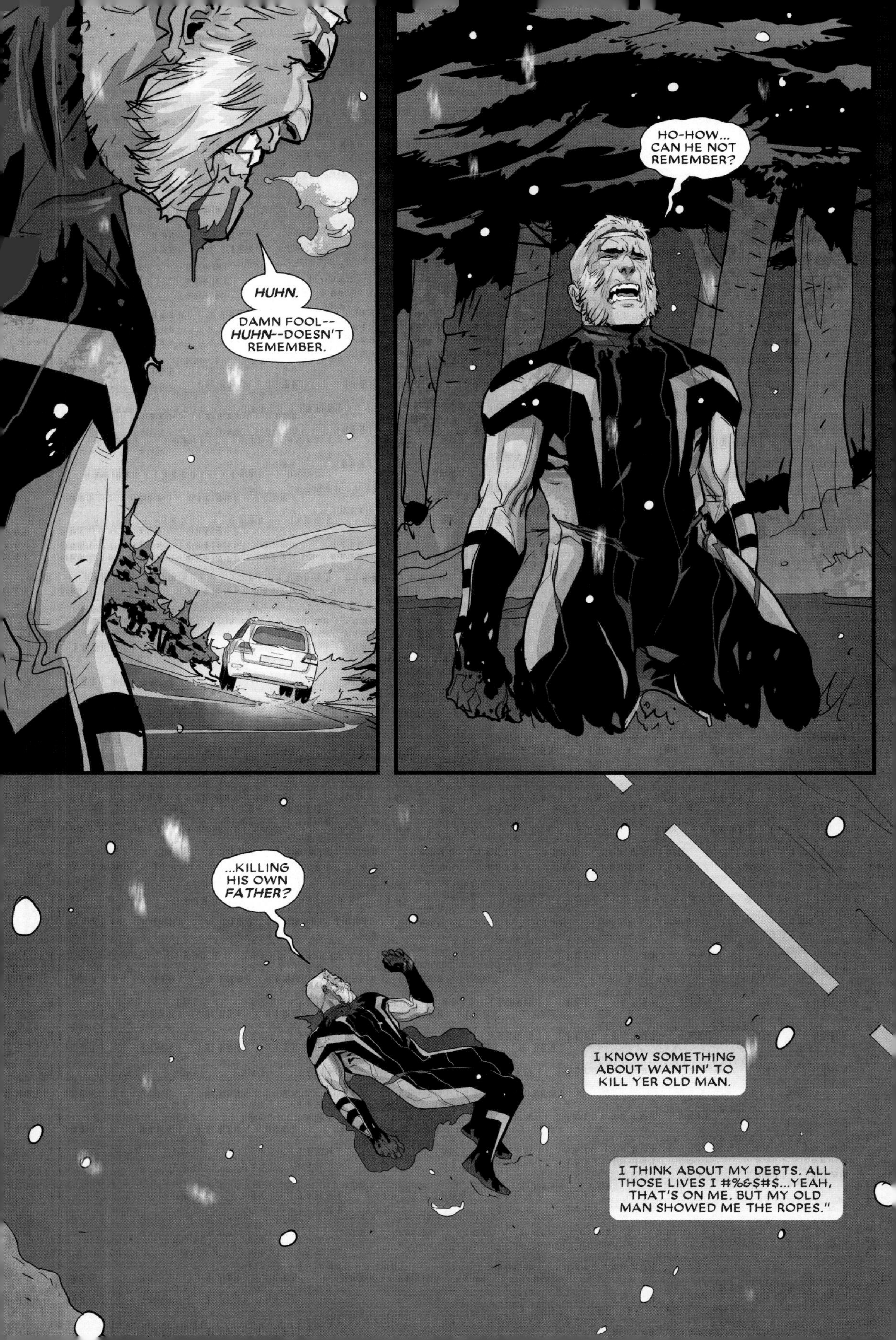
HUHN.
DAMN FOOL--HUHN--DOESN'T REMEMBER.
HO-HOW... CAN HE NOT REMEMBER?
...KILLING HIS OWN FATHER?
I KNOW SOMETHING ABOUT WANTIN' TO KILL YER OLD MAN.
I THINK ABOUT MY DEBTS. ALL THOSE LIVES I #%&$#$...YEAH, THAT'S ON ME. BUT MY OLD MAN SHOWED ME THE ROPES."

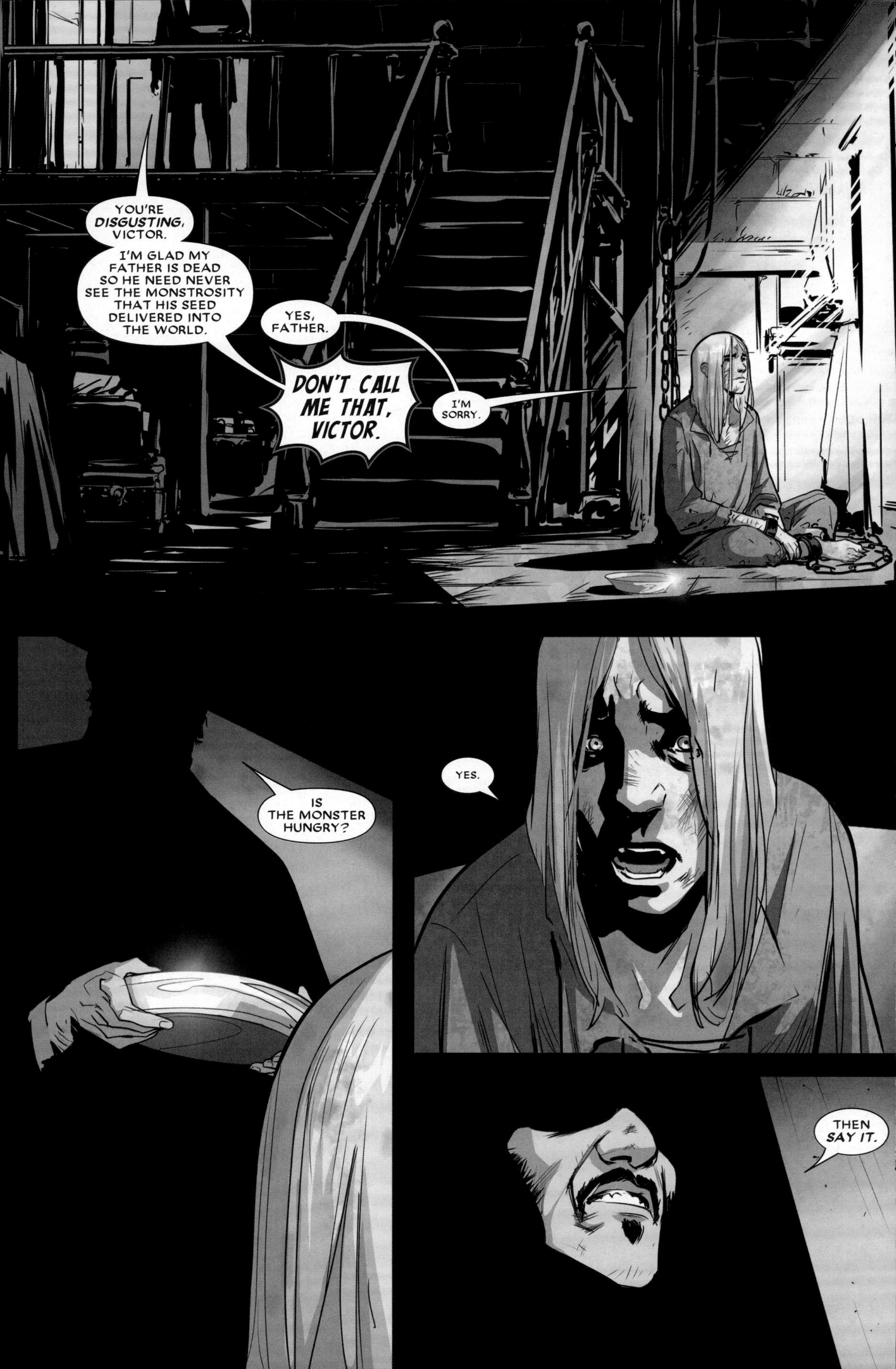

YOU'RE *DISGUSTING*, VICTOR.
I'M GLAD MY FATHER IS DEAD SO HE NEED NEVER SEE THE MONSTROSITY THAT HIS SEED DELIVERED INTO THE WORLD.
YES, FATHER.
DON'T CALL ME THAT, VICTOR.
I'M SORRY.
IS THE MONSTER HUNGRY?
YES.
THEN *SAY IT.*

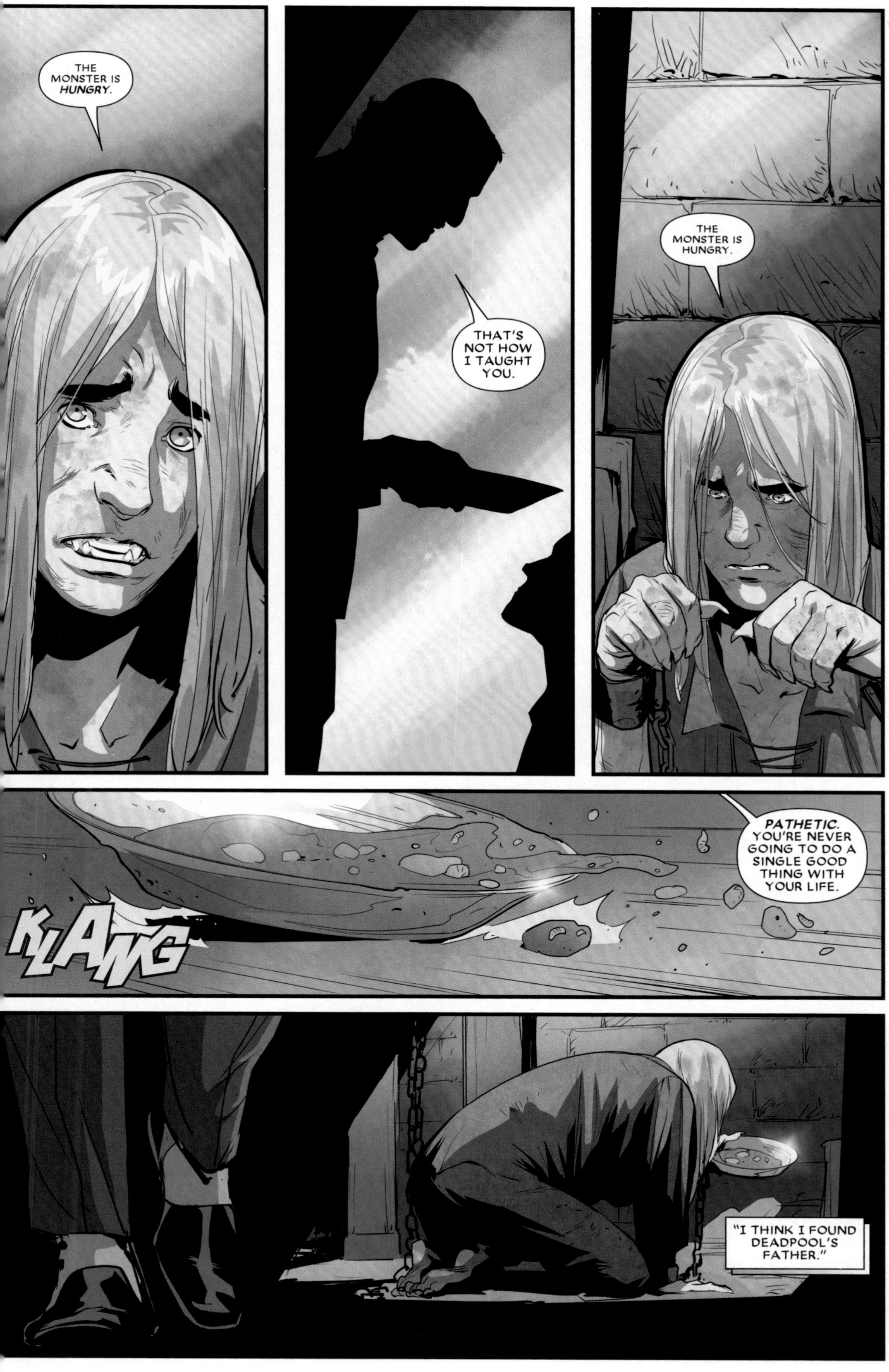
THE MONSTER IS *HUNGRY*.
THAT'S NOT HOW I TAUGHT YOU.
THE MONSTER IS HUNGRY.
PATHETIC. YOU'RE NEVER GOING TO DO A SINGLE GOOD THING WITH YOUR LIFE.
KLANG
"I THINK I FOUND DEADPOOL'S FATHER."

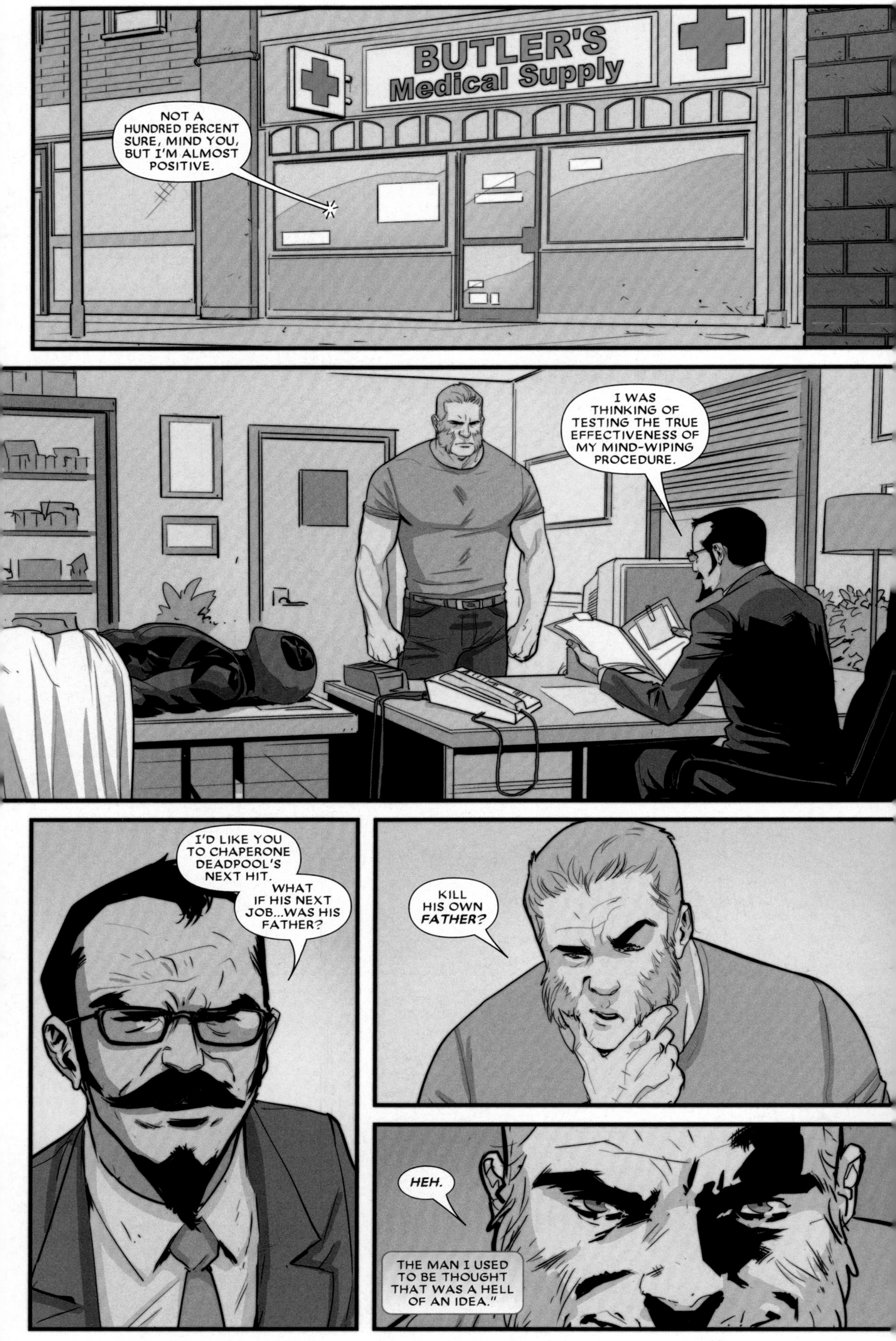
BUTLER'S Medical Supply
NOT A HUNDRED PERCENT SURE, MIND YOU, BUT I'M ALMOST POSITIVE.
I WAS THINKING OF TESTING THE TRUE EFFECTIVENESS OF MY MIND-WIPING PROCEDURE.
I'D LIKE YOU TO CHAPERONE DEADPOOL'S NEXT HIT.
WHAT IF HIS NEXT JOB...WAS HIS FATHER?
KILL HIS OWN *FATHER?*
HEH.
THE MAN I USED TO BE THOUGHT THAT WAS A HELL OF AN IDEA."

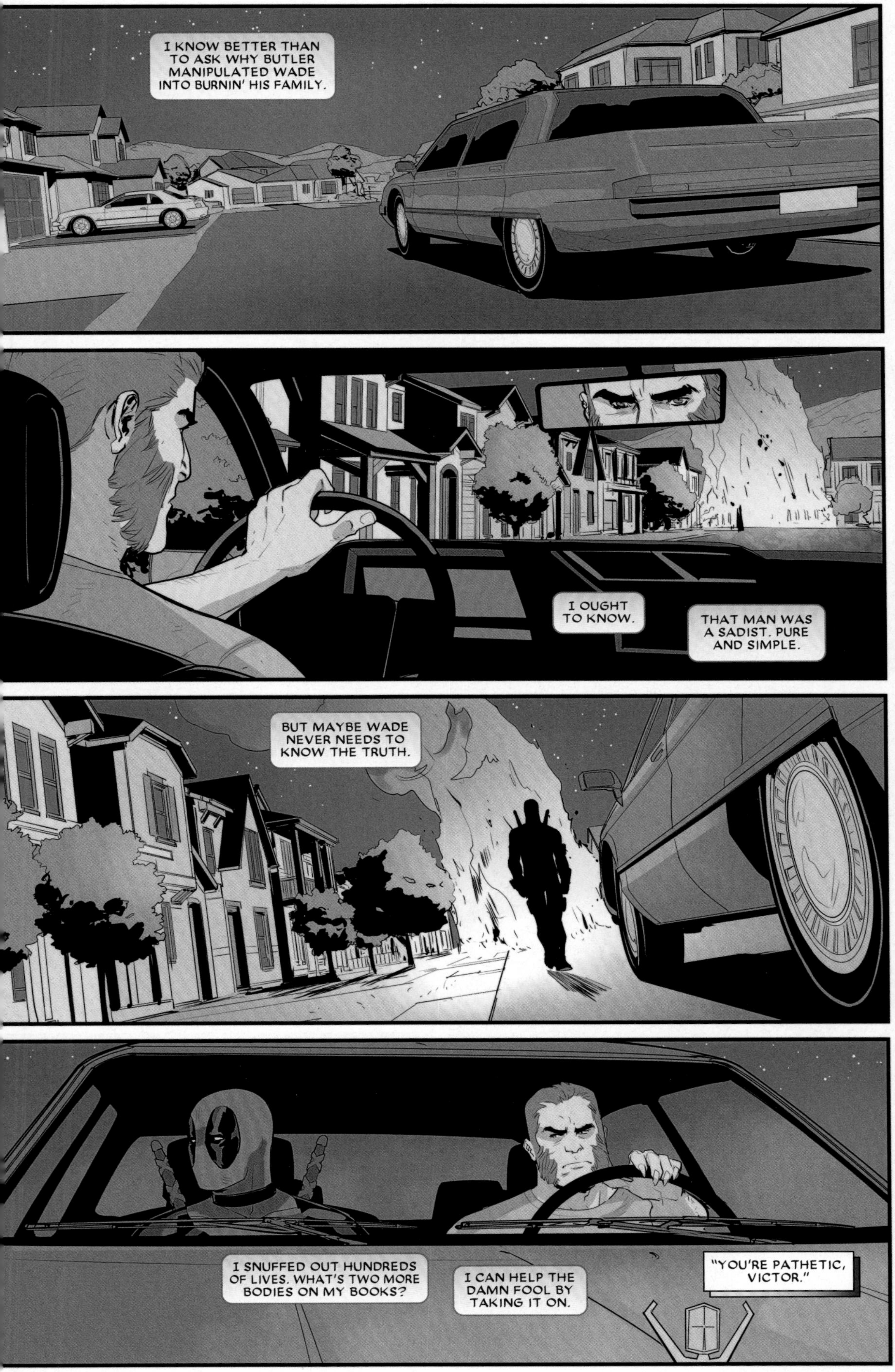
I KNOW BETTER THAN TO ASK WHY BUTLER MANIPULATED WADE INTO BURNIN' HIS FAMILY.
I OUGHT TO KNOW.
THAT MAN WAS A SADIST. PURE AND SIMPLE.
BUT MAYBE WADE NEVER NEEDS TO KNOW THE TRUTH.
I SNUFFED OUT HUNDREDS OF LIVES. WHAT'S TWO MORE BODIES ON MY BOOKS?
I CAN HELP THE DAMN FOOL BY TAKING IT ON.
"YOU'RE PATHETIC, VICTOR."

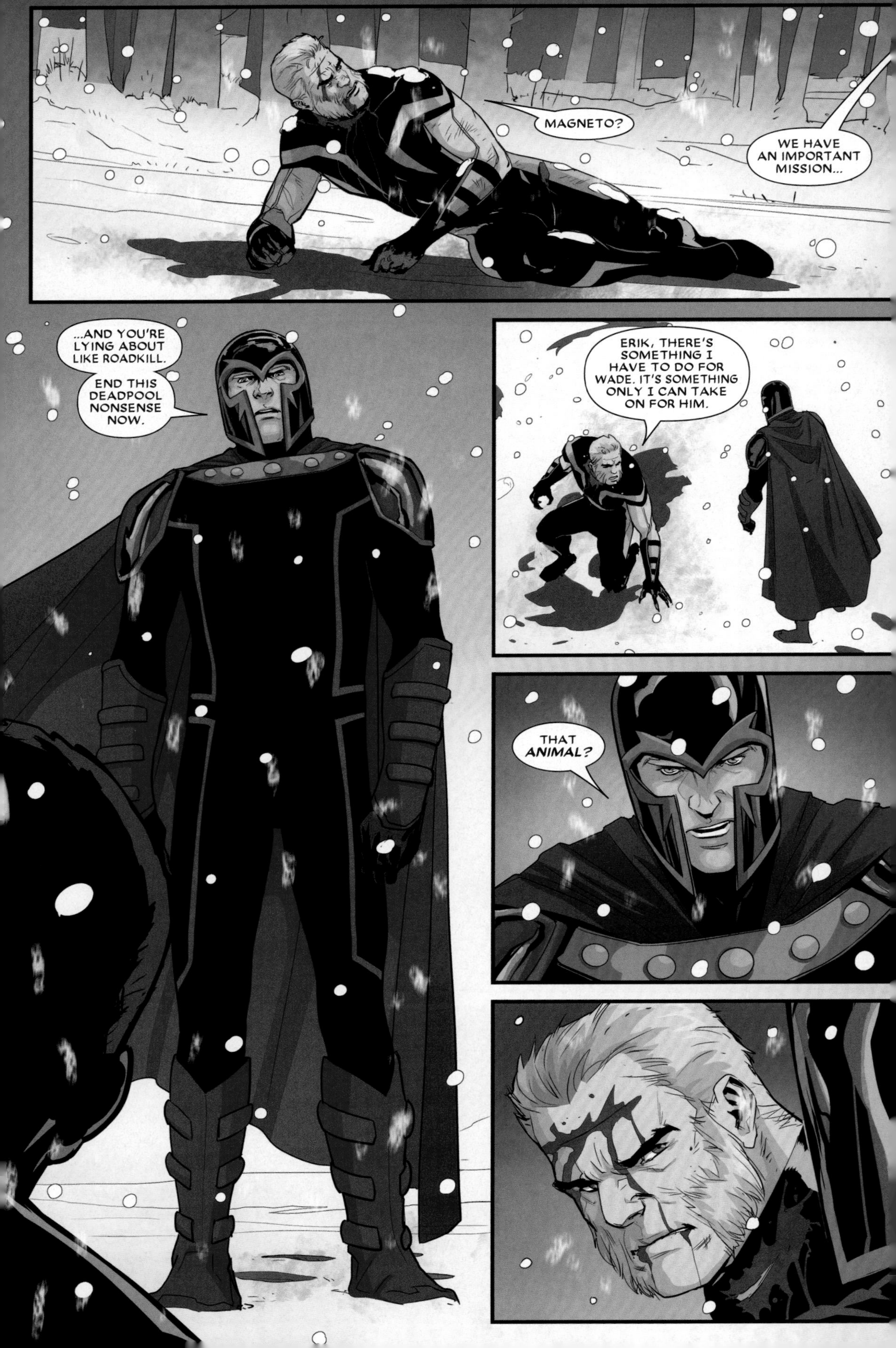
MAGNETO?
WE HAVE AN IMPORTANT MISSION...
...AND YOU'RE LYING ABOUT LIKE ROADKILL.
END THIS DEADPOOL NONSENSE NOW.
ERIK, THERE'S SOMETHING I HAVE TO DO FOR WADE. IT'S SOMETHING ONLY I CAN TAKE ON FOR HIM.
THAT *ANIMAL?*

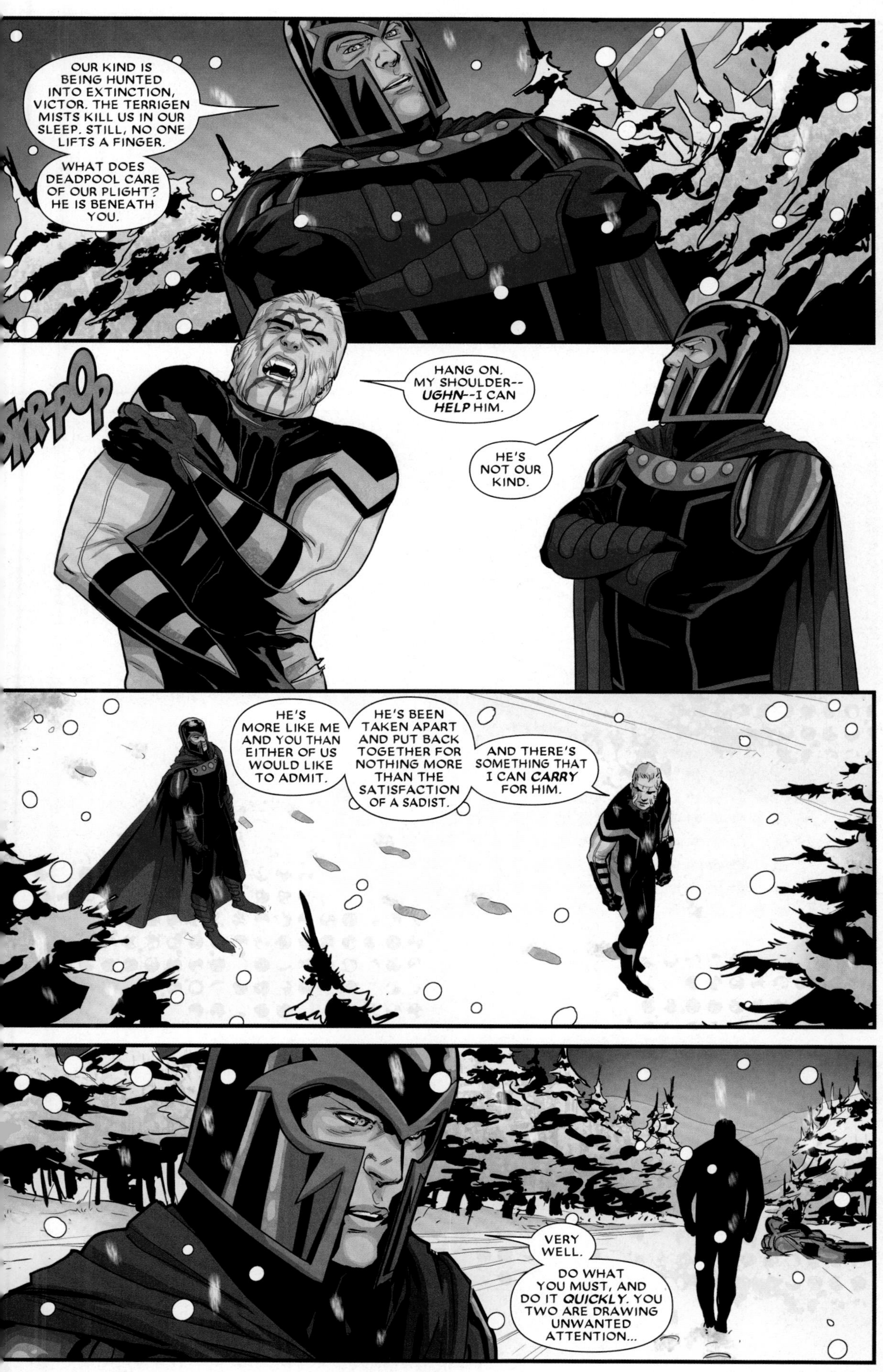
OUR KIND IS BEING HUNTED INTO EXTINCTION, VICTOR. THE TERRIGEN MISTS KILL US IN OUR SLEEP. STILL, NO ONE LIFTS A FINGER.
WHAT DOES DEADPOOL CARE OF OUR PLIGHT? HE IS BENEATH YOU.
SKR-POP
HANG ON. MY SHOULDER-- UGHN--I CAN HELP HIM.
HE'S NOT OUR KIND.
HE'S MORE LIKE ME AND YOU THAN EITHER OF US WOULD LIKE TO ADMIT.
HE'S BEEN TAKEN APART AND PUT BACK TOGETHER FOR NOTHING MORE THAN THE SATISFACTION OF A SADIST.
AND THERE'S SOMETHING THAT I CAN CARRY FOR HIM.
VERY WELL.
DO WHAT YOU MUST, AND DO IT QUICKLY. YOU TWO ARE DRAWING UNWANTED ATTENTION...

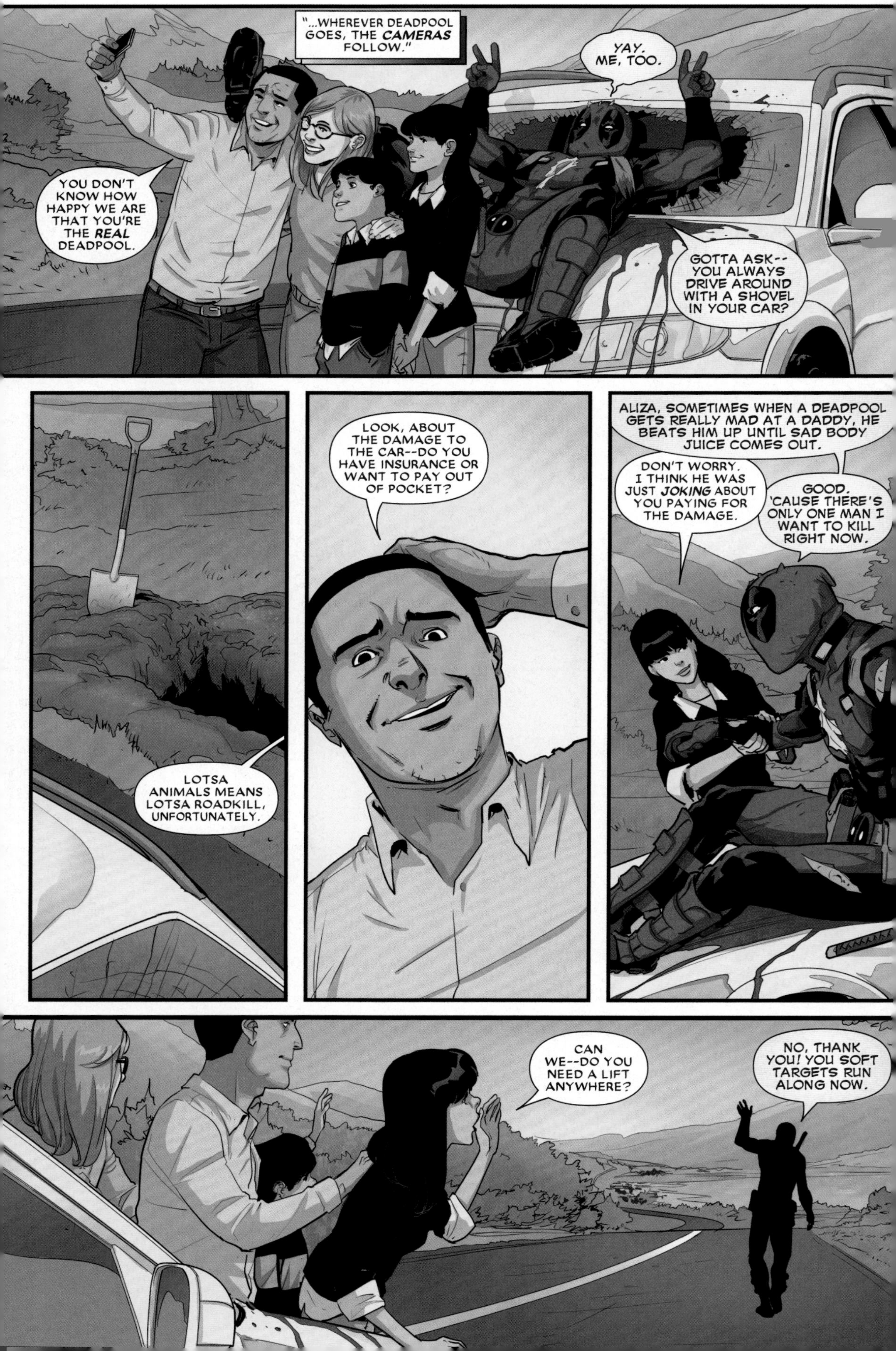
"...WHEREVER DEADPOOL GOES, THE *CAMERAS* FOLLOW."
YOU DON'T KNOW HOW HAPPY WE ARE THAT YOU'RE THE *REAL* DEADPOOL.
YAY. ME, TOO.
GOTTA ASK-- YOU ALWAYS DRIVE AROUND WITH A SHOVEL IN YOUR CAR?
LOTSA ANIMALS MEANS LOTSA ROADKILL, UNFORTUNATELY.
LOOK, ABOUT THE DAMAGE TO THE CAR--DO YOU HAVE INSURANCE OR WANT TO PAY OUT OF POCKET?
ALIZA, SOMETIMES WHEN A DEADPOOL GETS REALLY MAD AT A DADDY, HE BEATS HIM UP UNTIL SAD BODY JUICE COMES OUT.
DON'T WORRY. I THINK HE WAS JUST *JOKING* ABOUT YOU PAYING FOR THE DAMAGE.
GOOD. 'CAUSE THERE'S ONLY ONE MAN I WANT TO KILL RIGHT NOW.
CAN WE--DO YOU NEED A LIFT ANYWHERE?
NO, THANK YOU! YOU SOFT TARGETS RUN ALONG NOW.

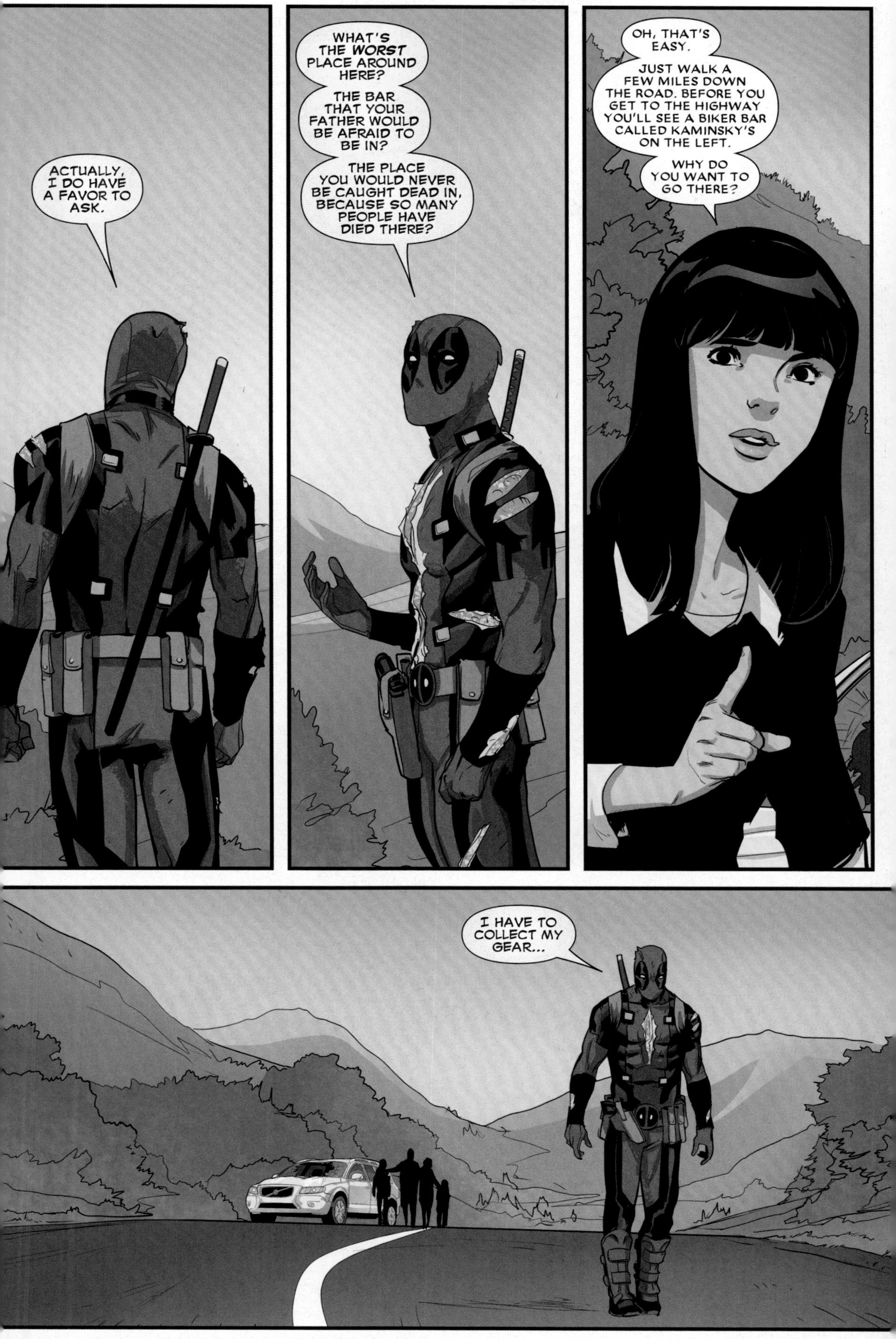
ACTUALLY, I DO HAVE A FAVOR TO ASK.
WHAT'S THE WORST PLACE AROUND HERE?
THE BAR THAT YOUR FATHER WOULD BE AFRAID TO BE IN?
THE PLACE YOU WOULD NEVER BE CAUGHT DEAD IN, BECAUSE SO MANY PEOPLE HAVE DIED THERE?
OH, THAT'S EASY.
JUST WALK A FEW MILES DOWN THE ROAD. BEFORE YOU GET TO THE HIGHWAY YOU'LL SEE A BIKER BAR CALLED KAMINSKY'S ON THE LEFT.
WHY DO YOU WANT TO GO THERE?
I HAVE TO COLLECT MY GEAR...

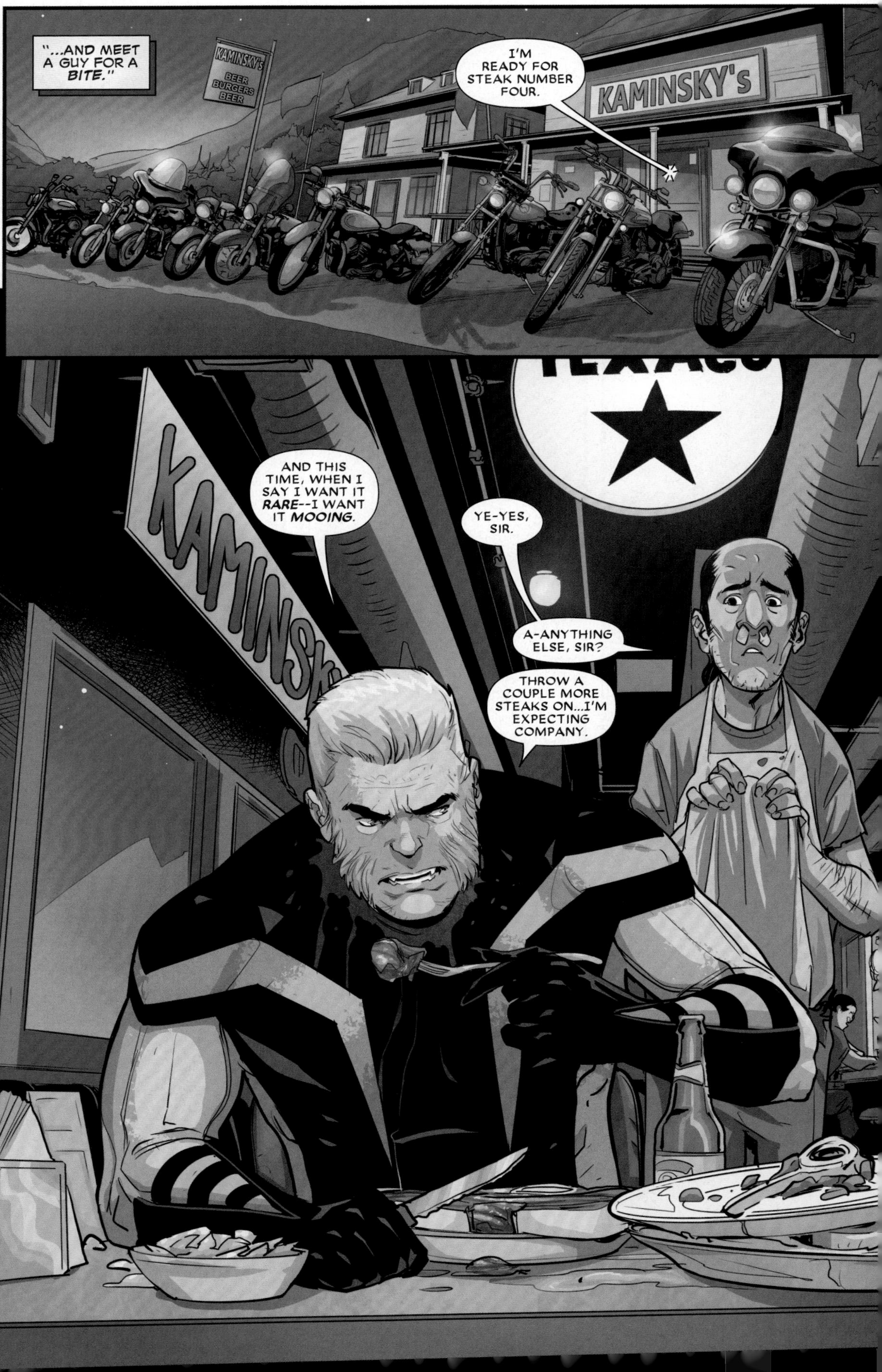
"...AND MEET A GUY FOR A *BITE*."
KAMINSKY'S
BEER BURGERS BEER
I'M READY FOR STEAK NUMBER FOUR.
KAMINSKY'S
AND THIS TIME, WHEN I SAY I WANT IT *RARE*--I WANT IT *MOOING*.
YE-YES, SIR.
A-ANYTHING ELSE, SIR?
THROW A COUPLE MORE STEAKS ON...I'M EXPECTING COMPANY.

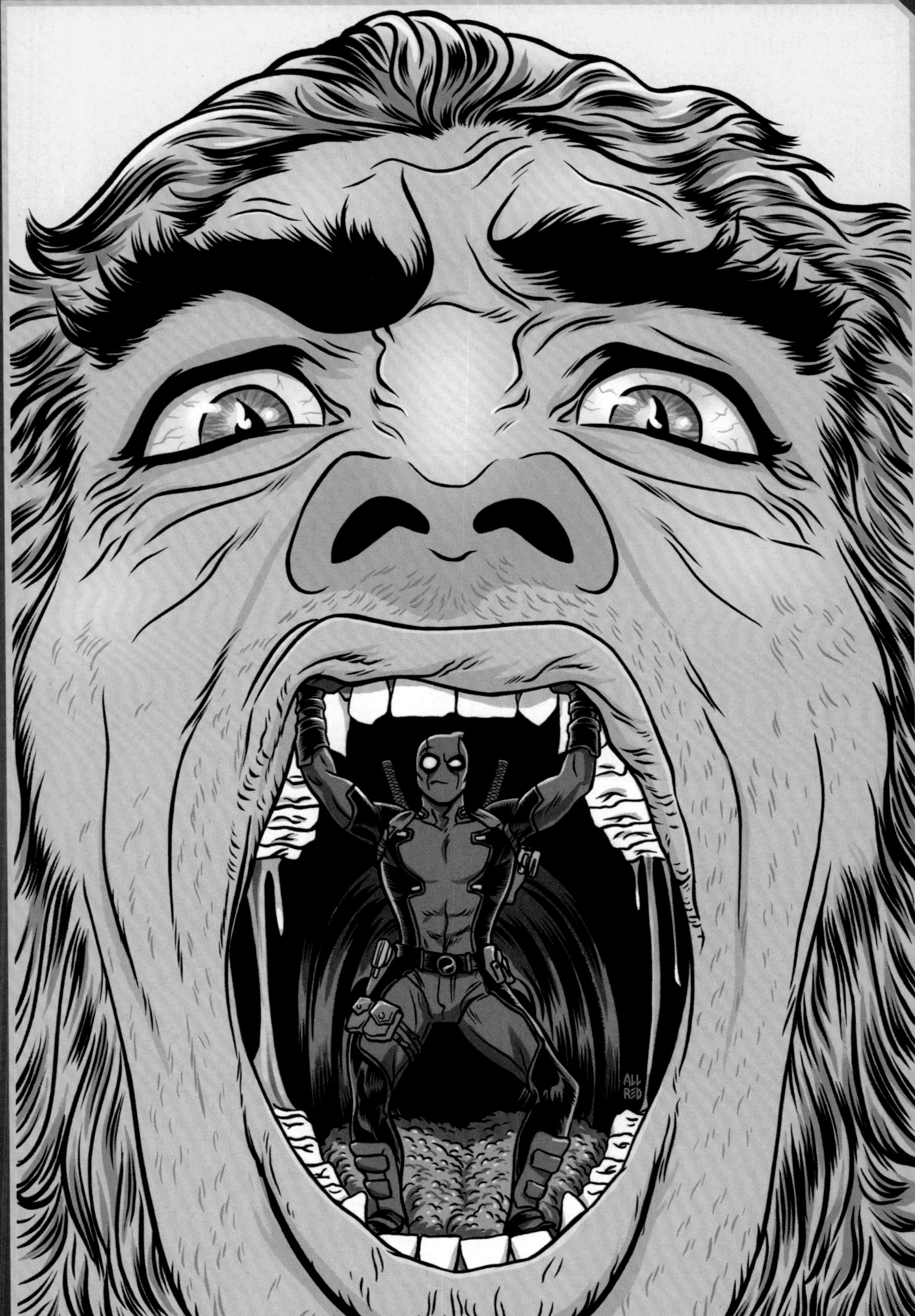
ALL
RED

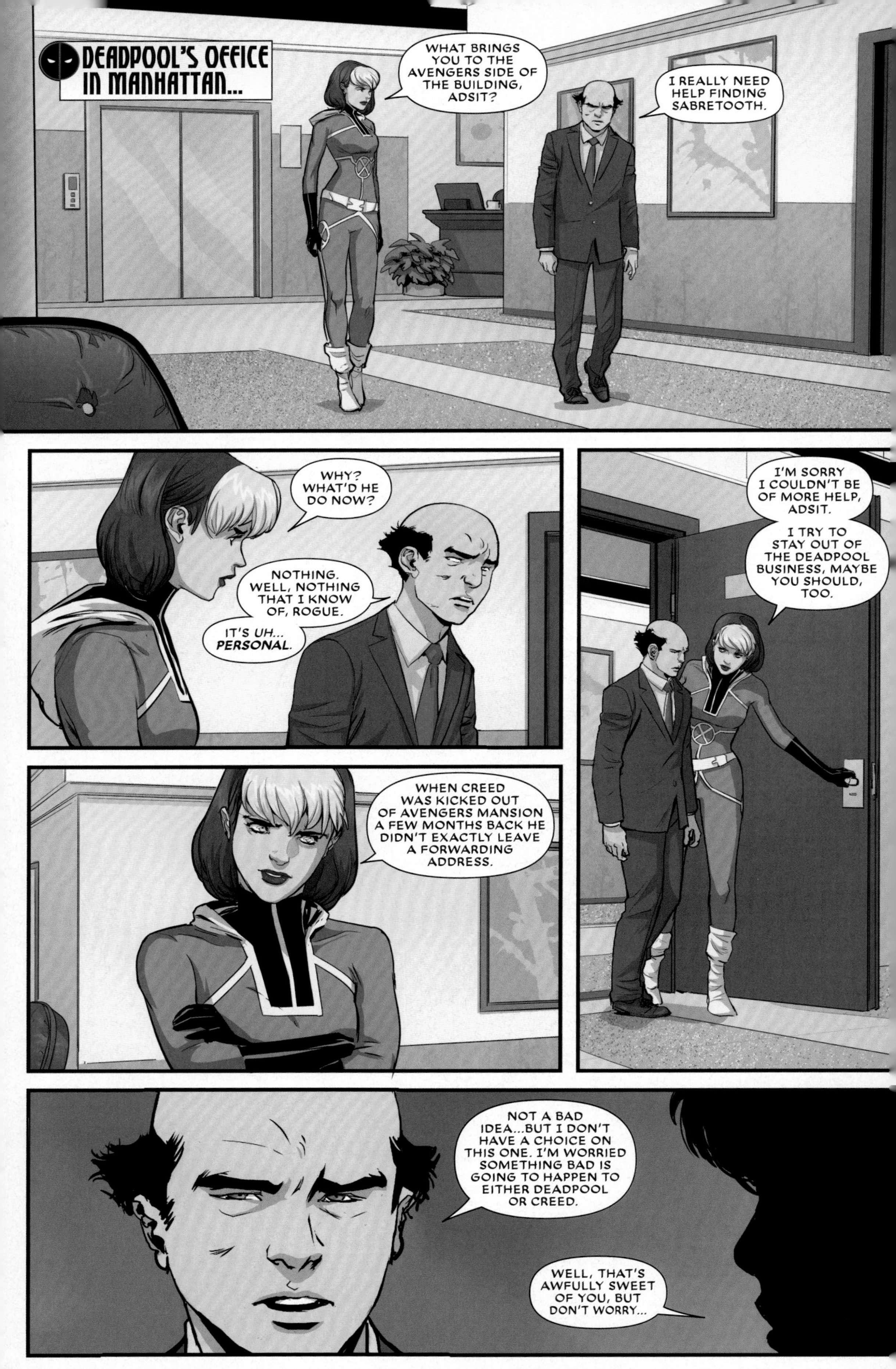
DEADPOOL'S OFFICE IN MANHATTAN...
WHAT BRINGS YOU TO THE AVENGERS SIDE OF THE BUILDING, ADSIT?
I REALLY NEED HELP FINDING SABRETOOTH.
WHY? WHAT'D HE DO NOW?
NOTHING. WELL, NOTHING THAT I KNOW OF, ROGUE.
IT'S UH... PERSONAL.
WHEN CREED WAS KICKED OUT OF AVENGERS MANSION A FEW MONTHS BACK HE DIDN'T EXACTLY LEAVE A FORWARDING ADDRESS.
I'M SORRY I COULDN'T BE OF MORE HELP, ADSIT.
I TRY TO STAY OUT OF THE DEADPOOL BUSINESS, MAYBE YOU SHOULD, TOO.
NOT A BAD IDEA...BUT I DON'T HAVE A CHOICE ON THIS ONE. I'M WORRIED SOMETHING BAD IS GOING TO HAPPEN TO EITHER DEADPOOL OR CREED.
WELL, THAT'S AWFULLY SWEET OF YOU, BUT DON'T WORRY...

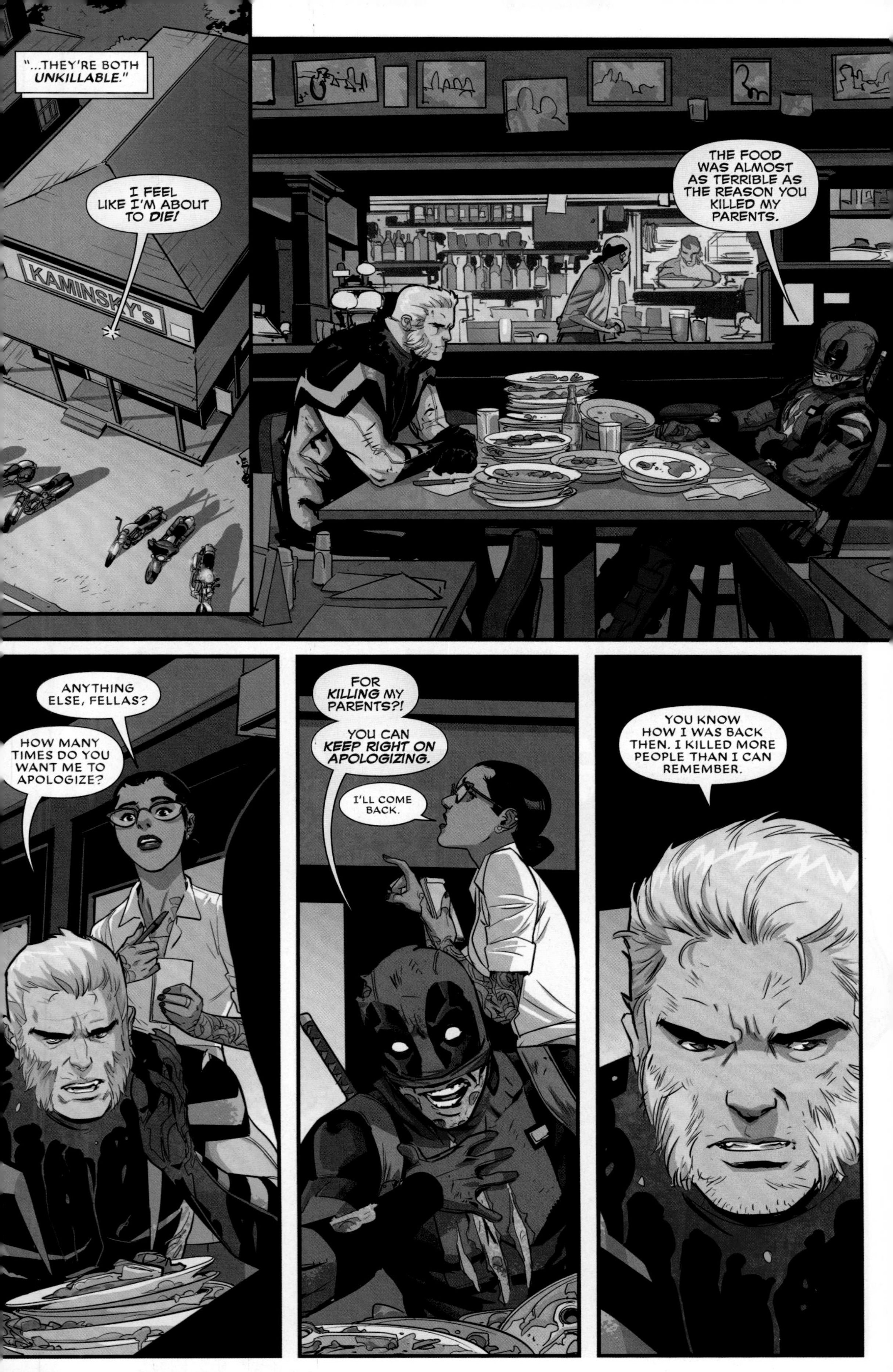
"...THEY'RE BOTH *UNKILLABLE*."
I FEEL LIKE I'M ABOUT TO *DIE!*
KAMINSKY'S
THE FOOD WAS ALMOST AS TERRIBLE AS THE REASON YOU KILLED MY PARENTS.
ANYTHING ELSE, FELLAS?
HOW MANY TIMES DO YOU WANT ME TO APOLOGIZE?
FOR *KILLING* MY PARENTS?!
YOU CAN *KEEP RIGHT ON APOLOGIZING.*
I'LL COME BACK.
YOU KNOW HOW I WAS BACK THEN. I KILLED MORE PEOPLE THAN I CAN REMEMBER.

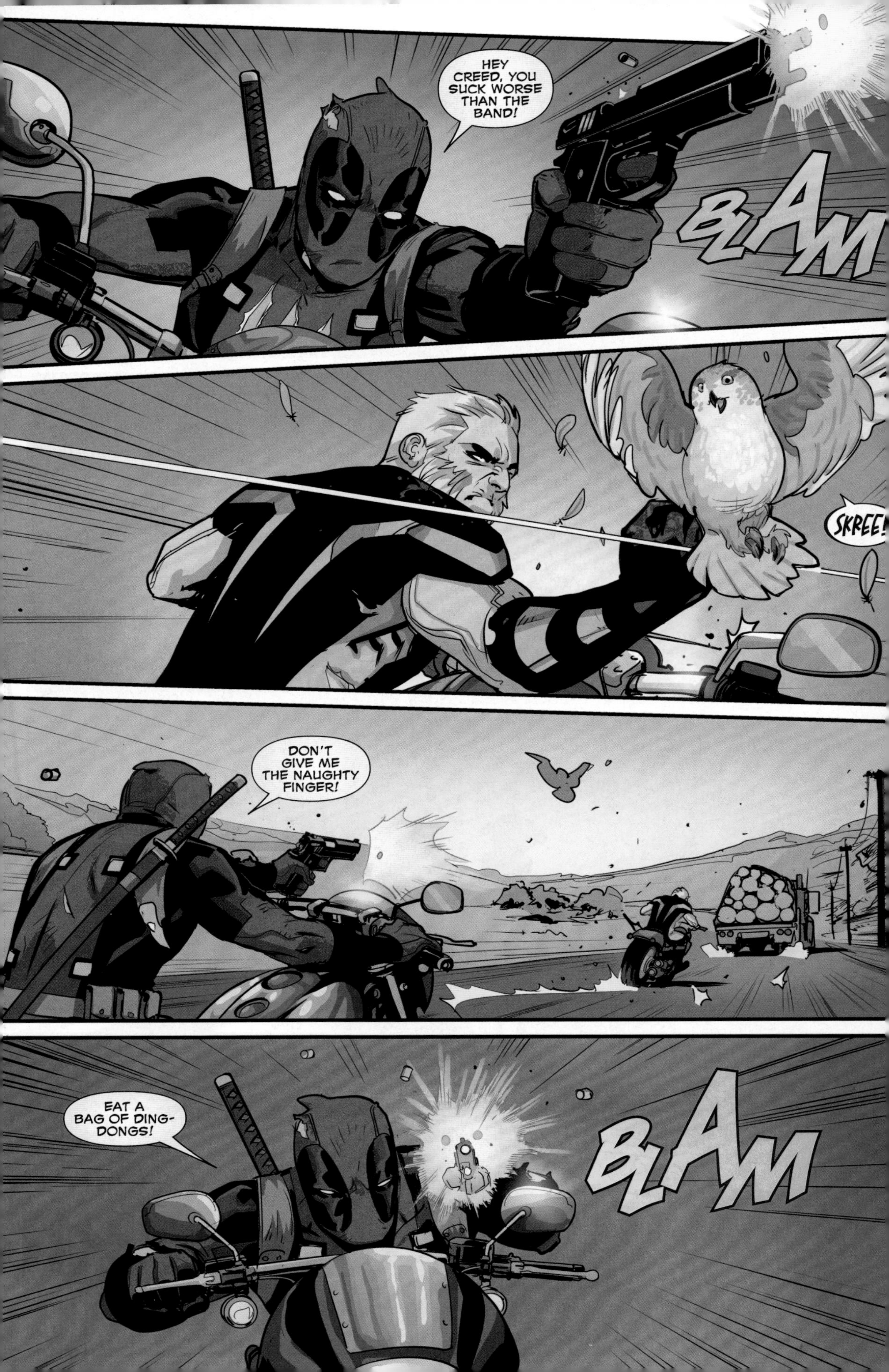
HEY CREED, YOU SUCK WORSE THAN THE BAND!
BLAM
SKREE!
DON'T GIVE ME THE NAUGHTY FINGER!
EAT A BAG OF DING-DONGS!
BLAM

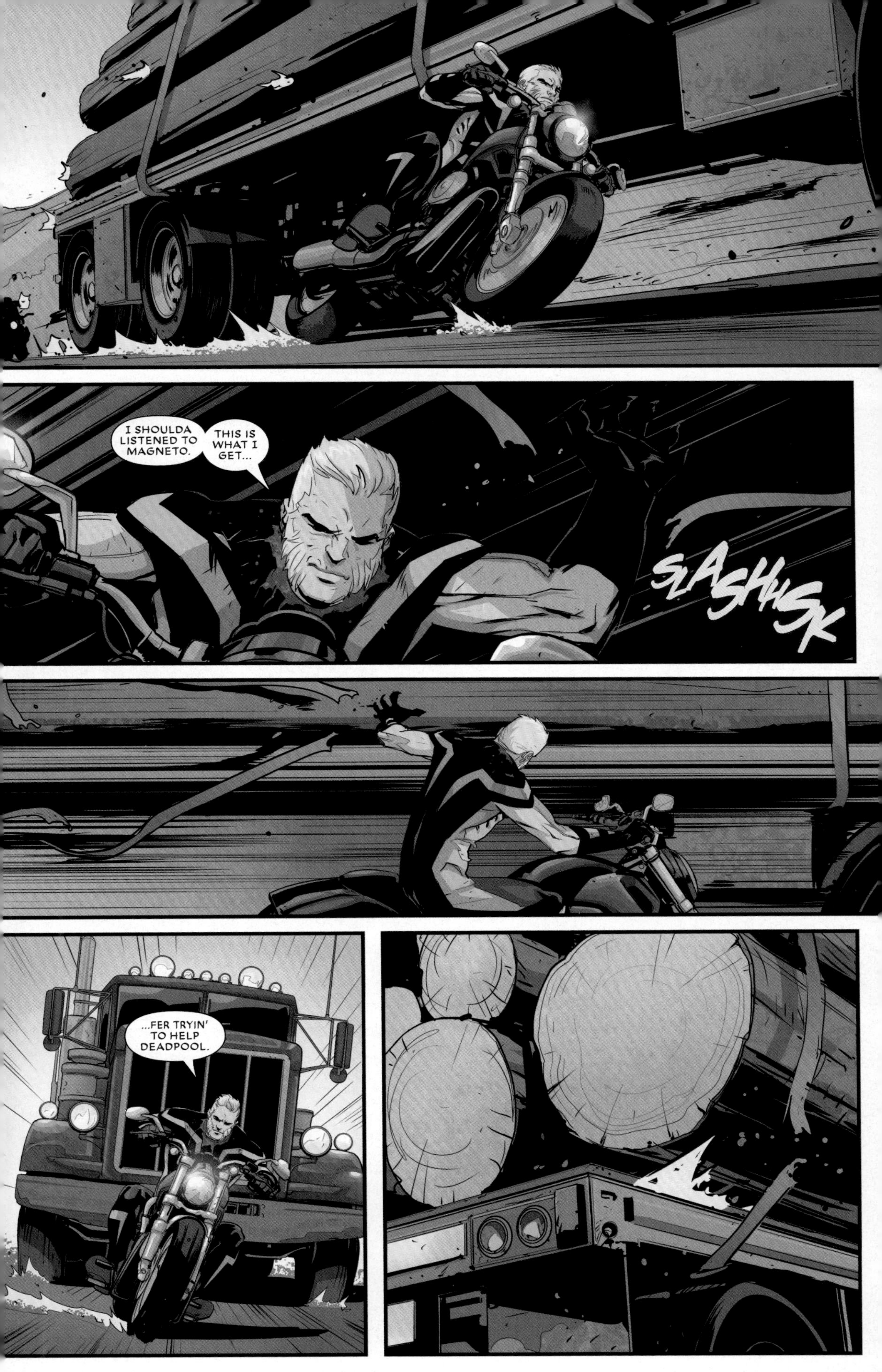
I SHOULDA LISTENED TO MAGNETO.
THIS IS WHAT I GET...
SLASHUSK
...FER TRYIN' TO HELP DEADPOOL.

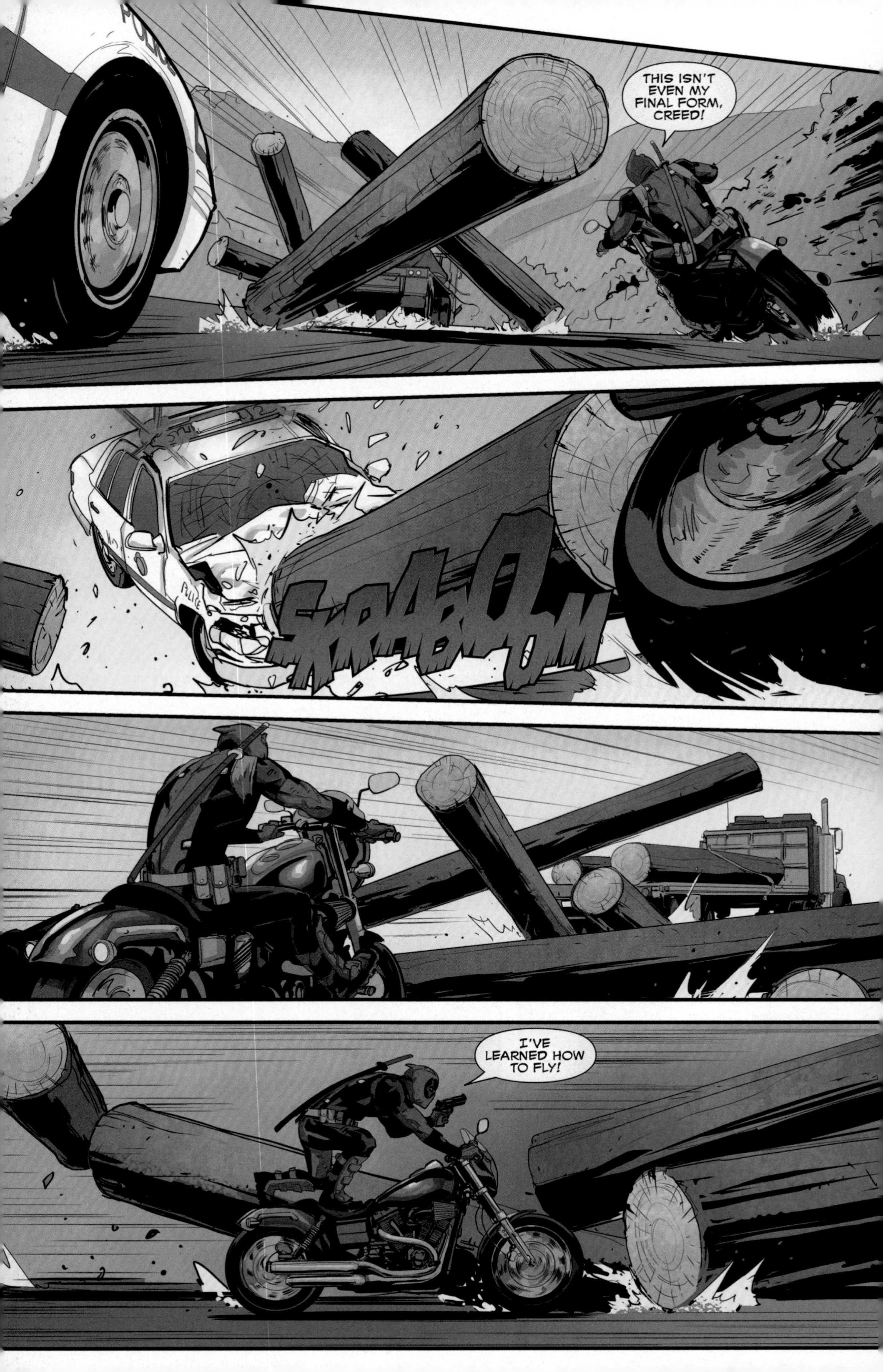
THIS ISN'T EVEN MY FINAL FORM, CREED!
SKRABOOM
I'VE LEARNED HOW TO FLY!

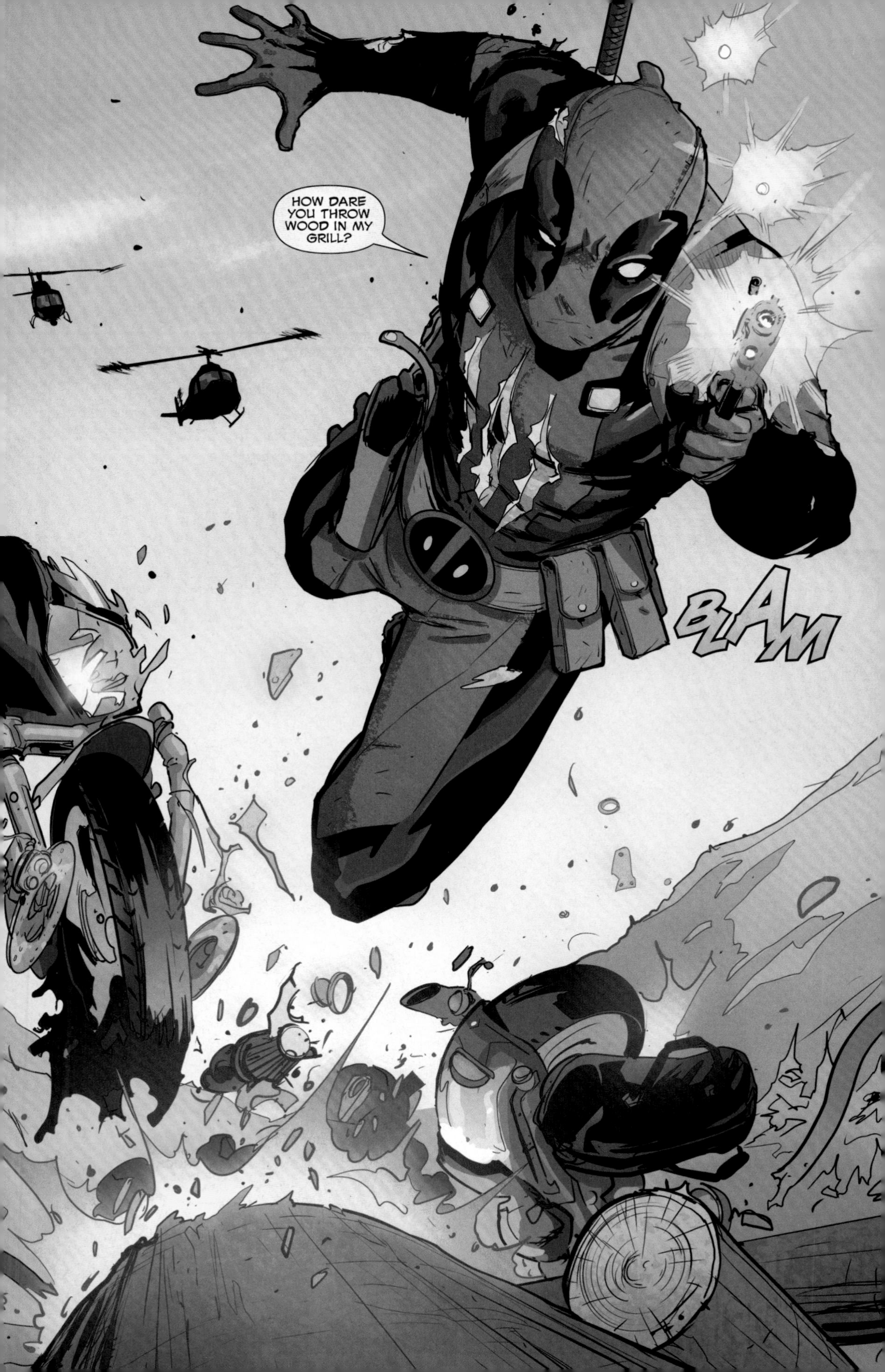
HOW DARE YOU THROW WOOD IN MY GRILL?
BLAM

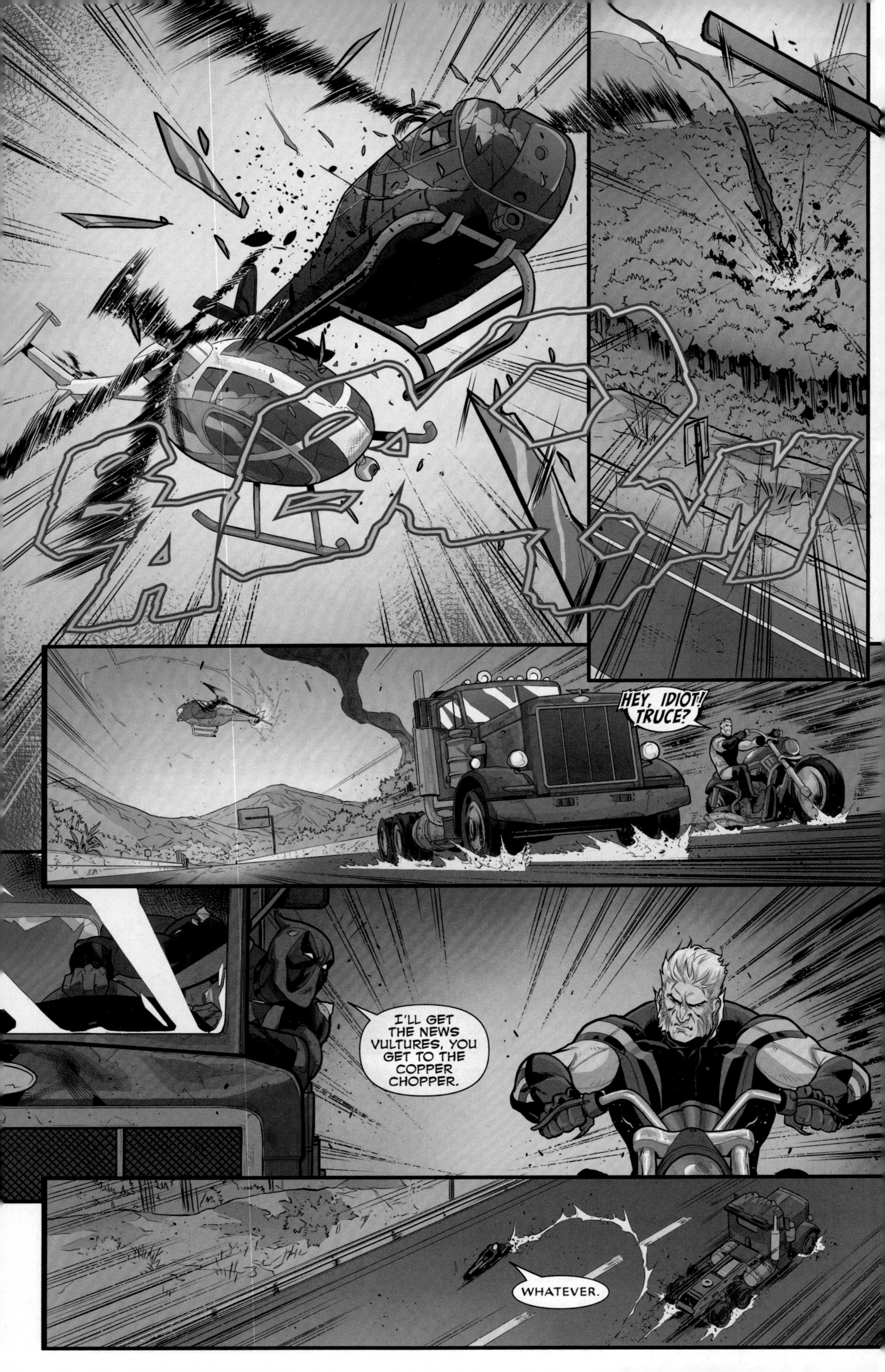
KA-BOOM
HEY, IDIOT! TRUCE?
I'LL GET THE NEWS VULTURES, YOU GET TO THE COPPER CHOPPER.
WHATEVER.

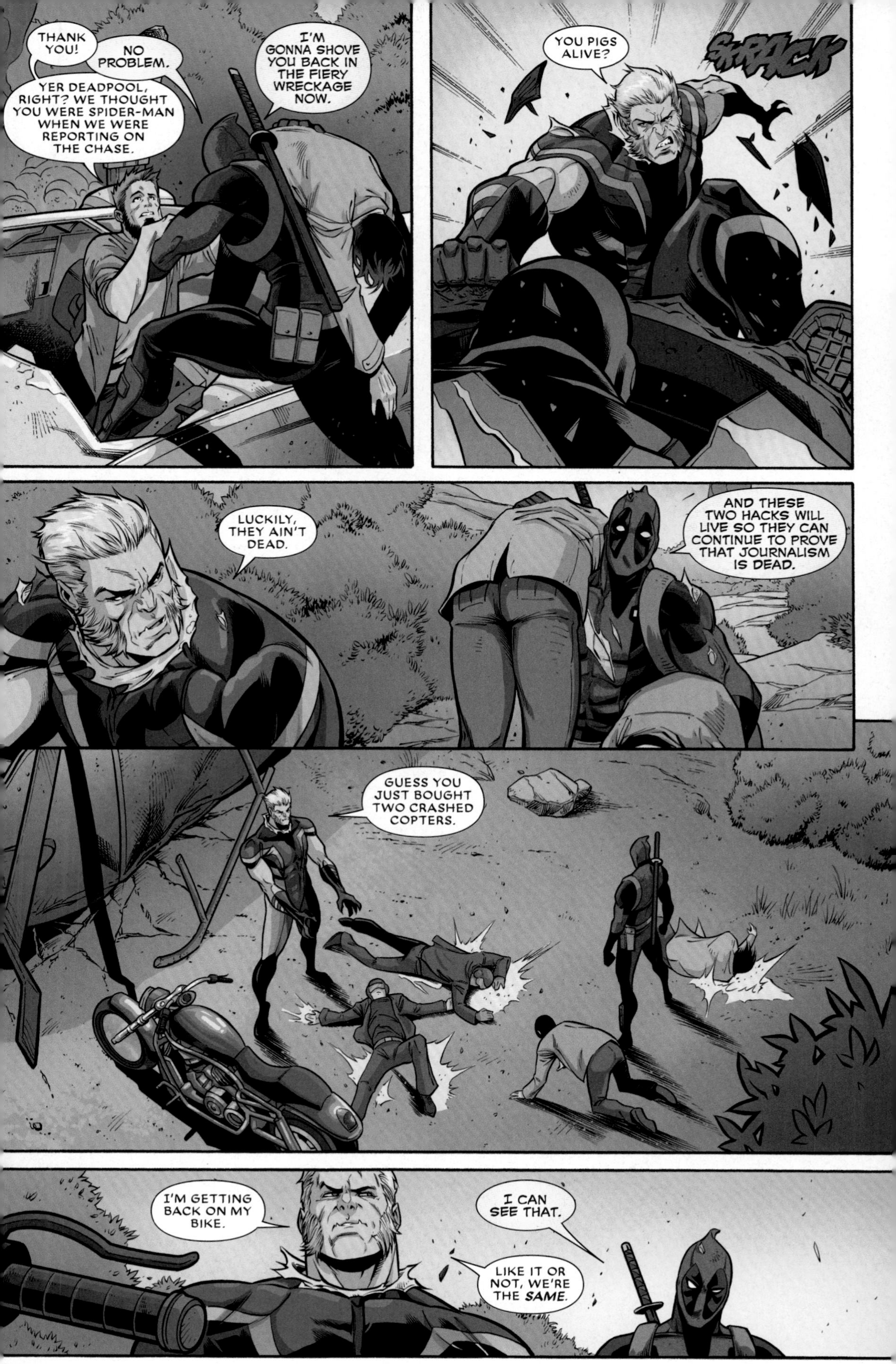
THANK YOU!
NO PROBLEM.
YER DEADPOOL, RIGHT? WE THOUGHT YOU WERE SPIDER-MAN WHEN WE WERE REPORTING ON THE CHASE.
I'M GONNA SHOVE YOU BACK IN THE FIERY WRECKAGE NOW.
YOU PIGS ALIVE?
SKRACK
LUCKILY, THEY AIN'T DEAD.
AND THESE TWO HACKS WILL LIVE SO THEY CAN CONTINUE TO PROVE THAT JOURNALISM IS DEAD.
GUESS YOU JUST BOUGHT TWO CRASHED COPTERS.
I'M GETTING BACK ON MY BIKE.
I CAN SEE THAT.
LIKE IT OR NOT, WE'RE THE SAME.

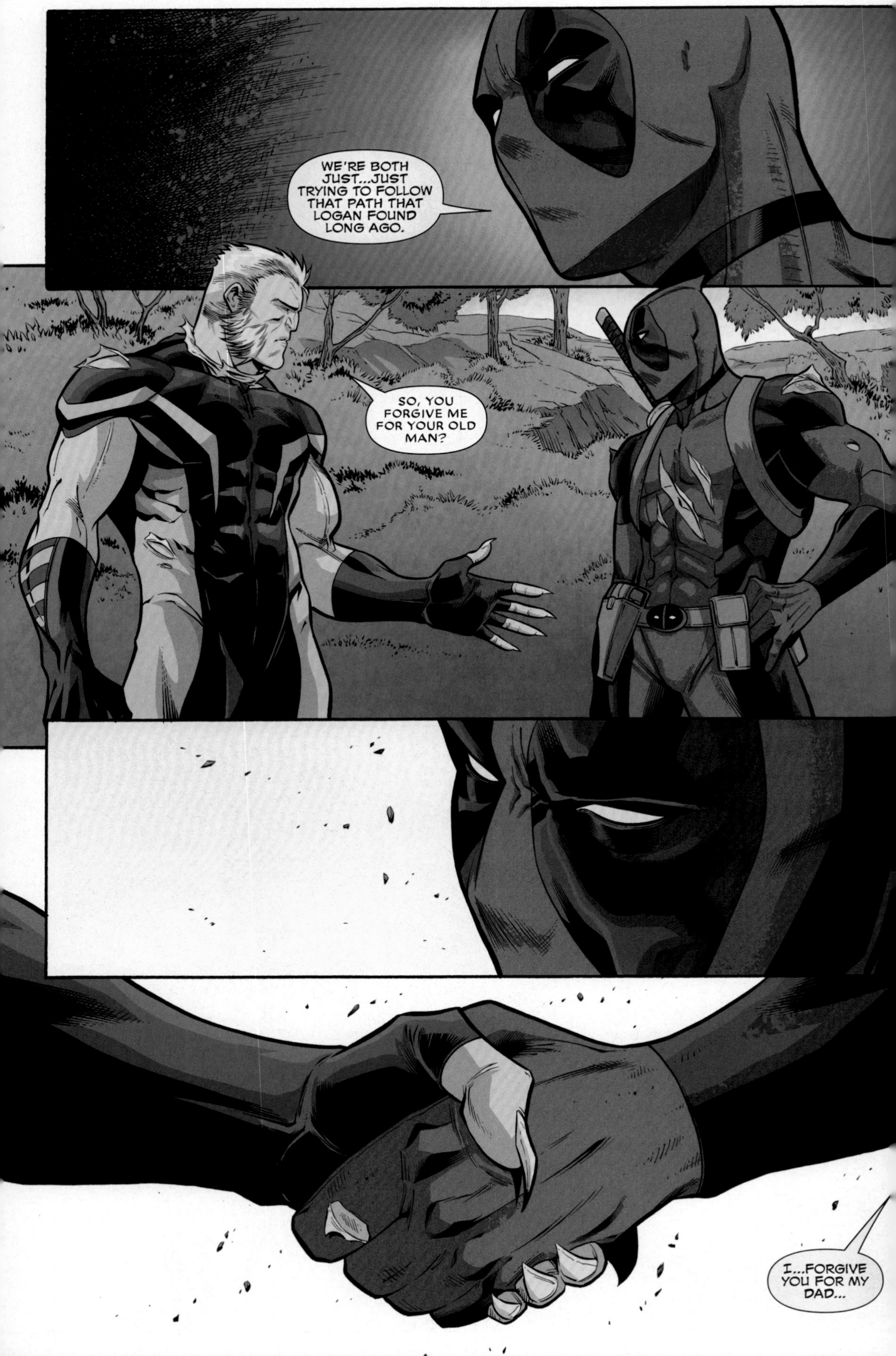
WE'RE BOTH JUST...JUST TRYING TO FOLLOW THAT PATH THAT LOGAN FOUND LONG AGO.
SO, YOU FORGIVE ME FOR YOUR OLD MAN?
I...FORGIVE YOU FOR MY DAD...

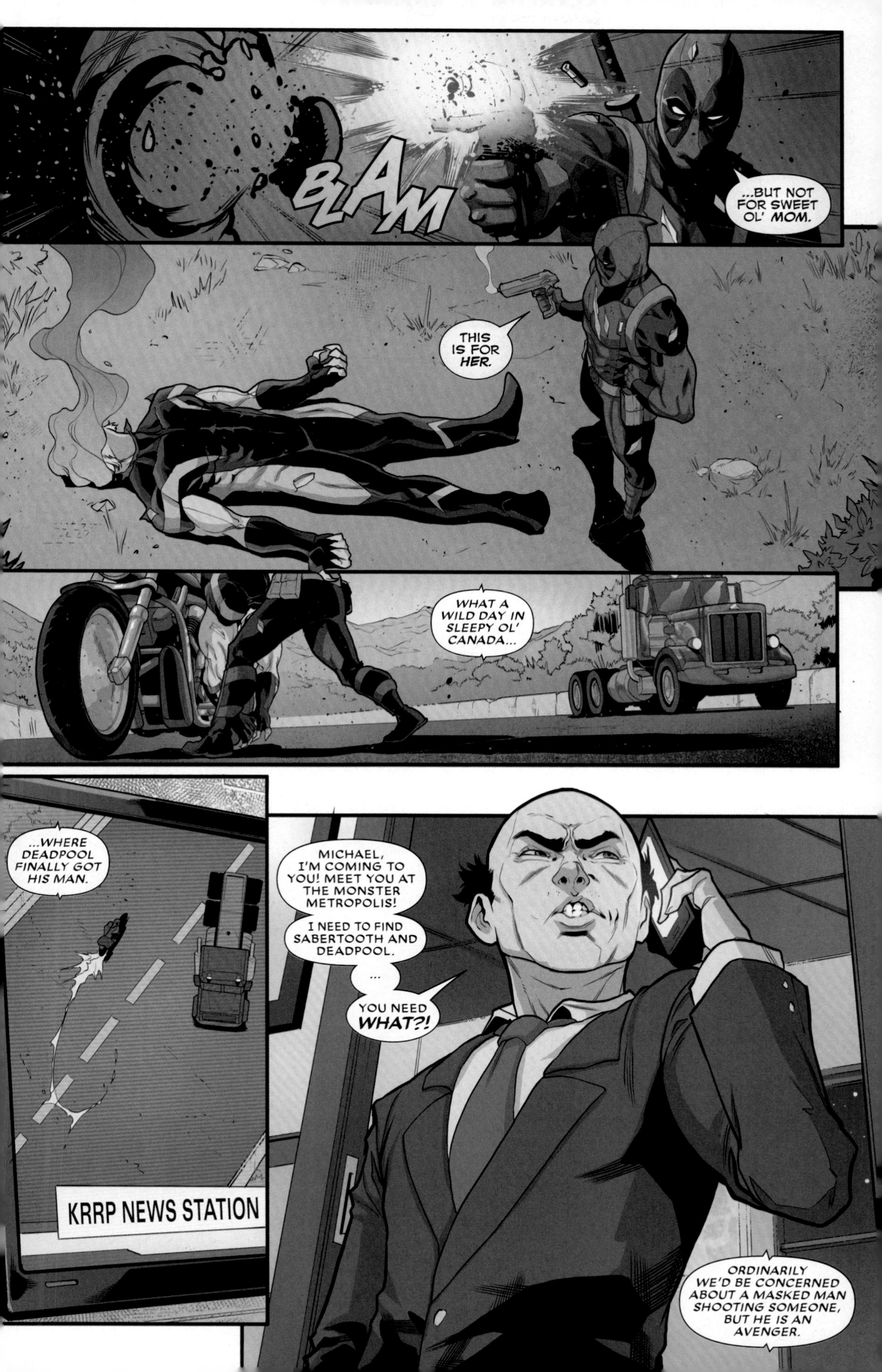
BLAM
...BUT NOT FOR SWEET OL' MOM.
THIS IS FOR HER.
WHAT A WILD DAY IN SLEEPY OL' CANADA...
...WHERE DEADPOOL FINALLY GOT HIS MAN.
KRRP NEWS STATION
MICHAEL, I'M COMING TO YOU! MEET YOU AT THE MONSTER METROPOLIS!
I NEED TO FIND SABERTOOTH AND DEADPOOL.
...
YOU NEED WHAT?!
ORDINARILY WE'D BE CONCERNED ABOUT A MASKED MAN SHOOTING SOMEONE, BUT HE IS AN AVENGER.

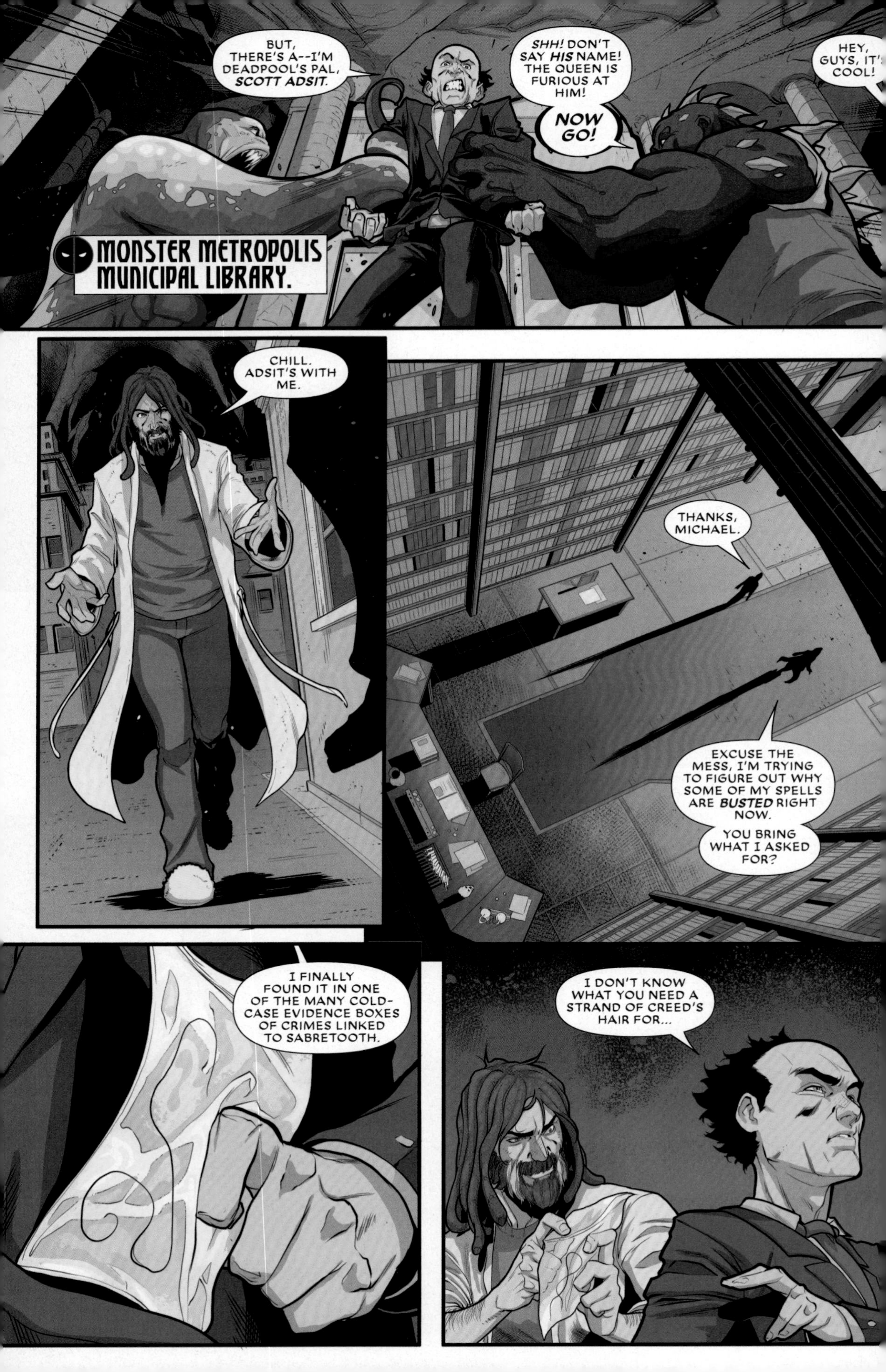
BUT, THERE'S A--I'M DEADPOOL'S PAL, *SCOTT ADSIT*.
SHH! DON'T SAY *HIS* NAME! THE QUEEN IS FURIOUS AT HIM!
NOW GO!
HEY, GUYS, IT'S COOL!
MONSTER METROPOLIS MUNICIPAL LIBRARY.
CHILL. ADSIT'S WITH ME.
THANKS, MICHAEL.
EXCUSE THE MESS, I'M TRYING TO FIGURE OUT WHY SOME OF MY SPELLS ARE *BUSTED* RIGHT NOW.
YOU BRING WHAT I ASKED FOR?
I FINALLY FOUND IT IN ONE OF THE MANY COLD-CASE EVIDENCE BOXES OF CRIMES LINKED TO SABRETOOTH.
I DON'T KNOW WHAT YOU NEED A STRAND OF CREED'S HAIR FOR...

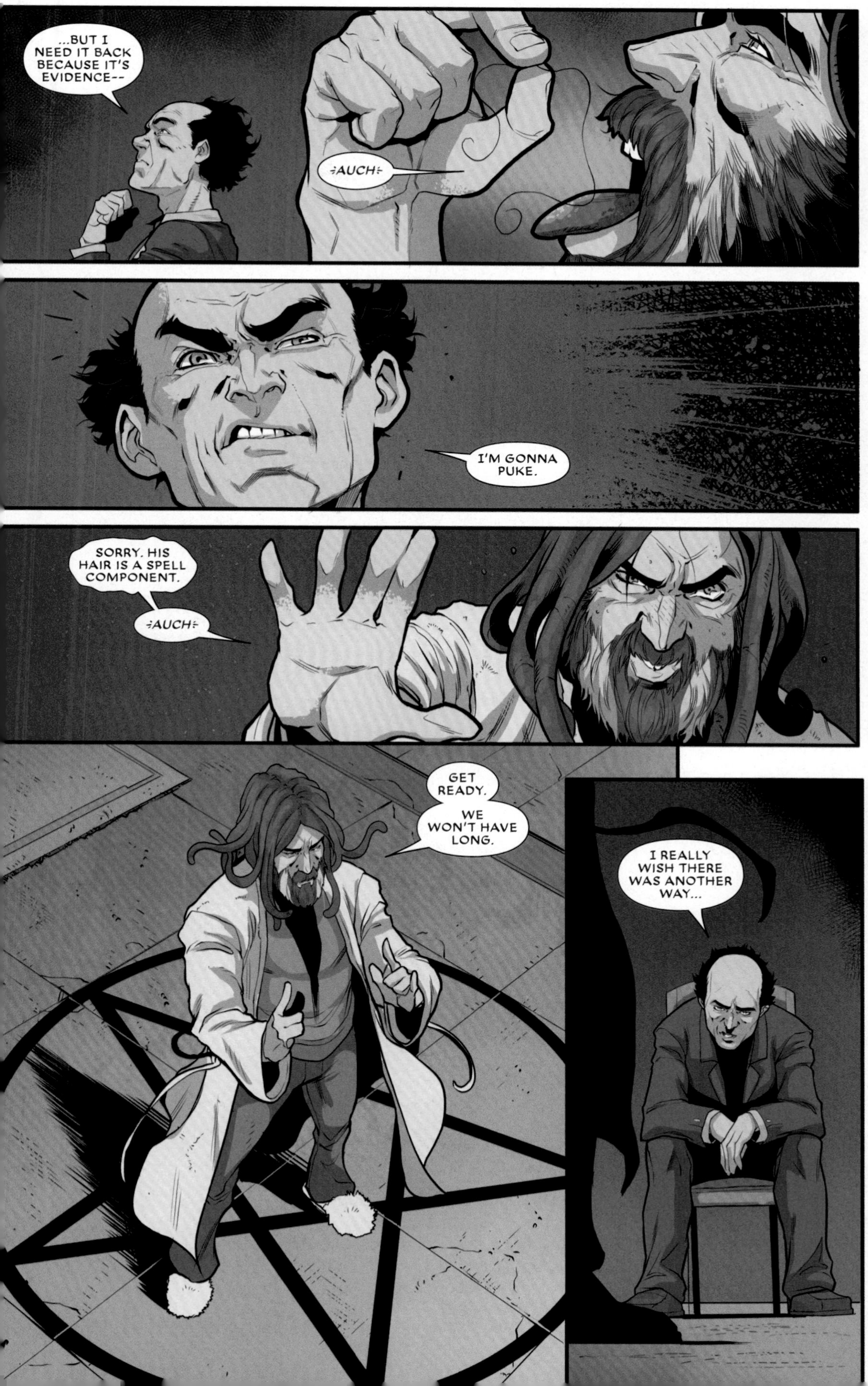
...BUT I NEED IT BACK BECAUSE IT'S EVIDENCE--
AUCH
I'M GONNA PUKE.
SORRY. HIS HAIR IS A SPELL COMPONENT.
AUCH
GET READY.
WE WON'T HAVE LONG.
I REALLY WISH THERE WAS ANOTHER WAY...

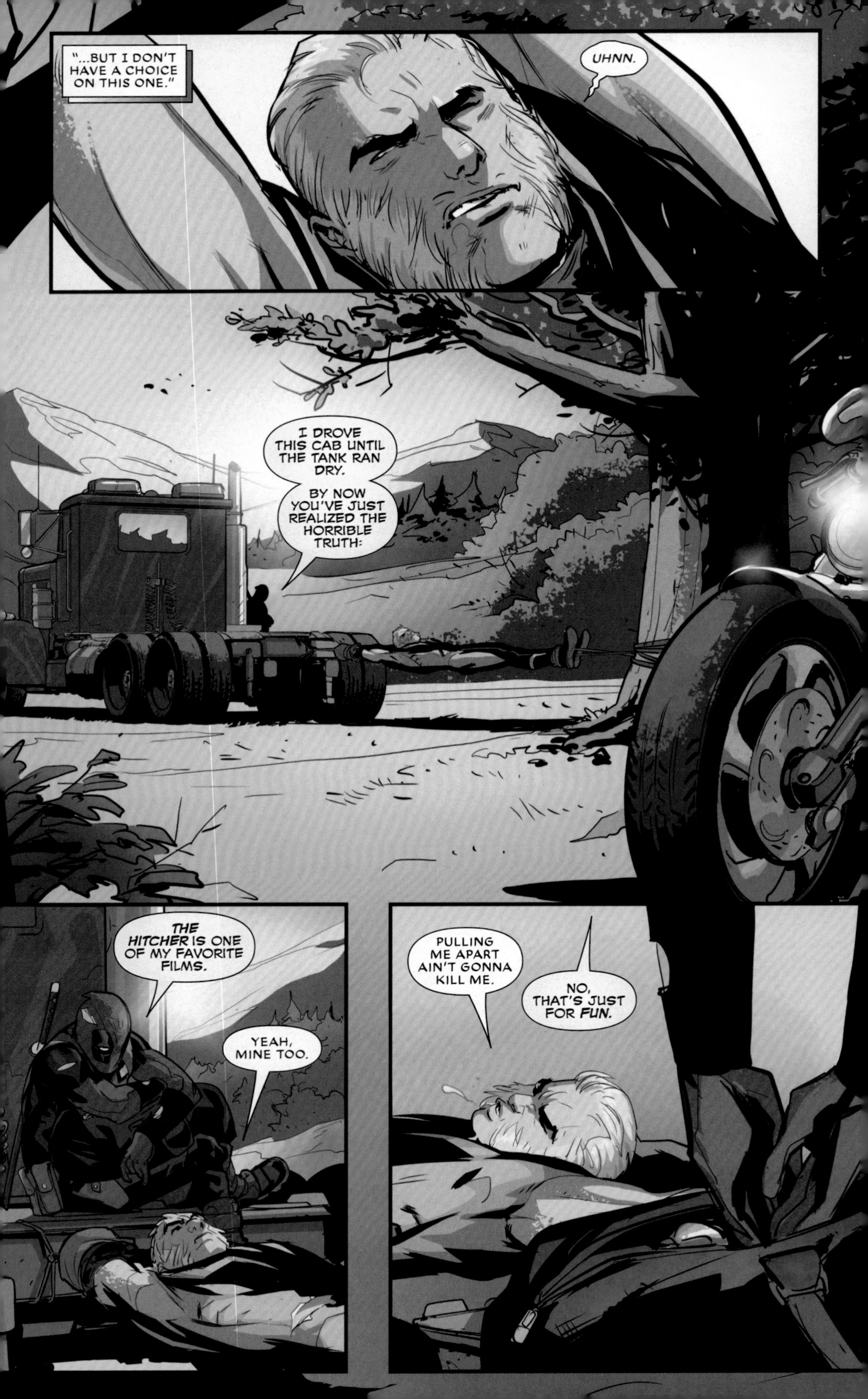
"...BUT I DON'T HAVE A CHOICE ON THIS ONE."
UHNN.
I DROVE THIS CAB UNTIL THE TANK RAN DRY.
BY NOW YOU'VE JUST REALIZED THE HORRIBLE TRUTH:
THE HITCHER IS ONE OF MY FAVORITE FILMS.
YEAH, MINE TOO.
PULLING ME APART AIN'T GONNA KILL ME.
NO, THAT'S JUST FOR *FUN.*

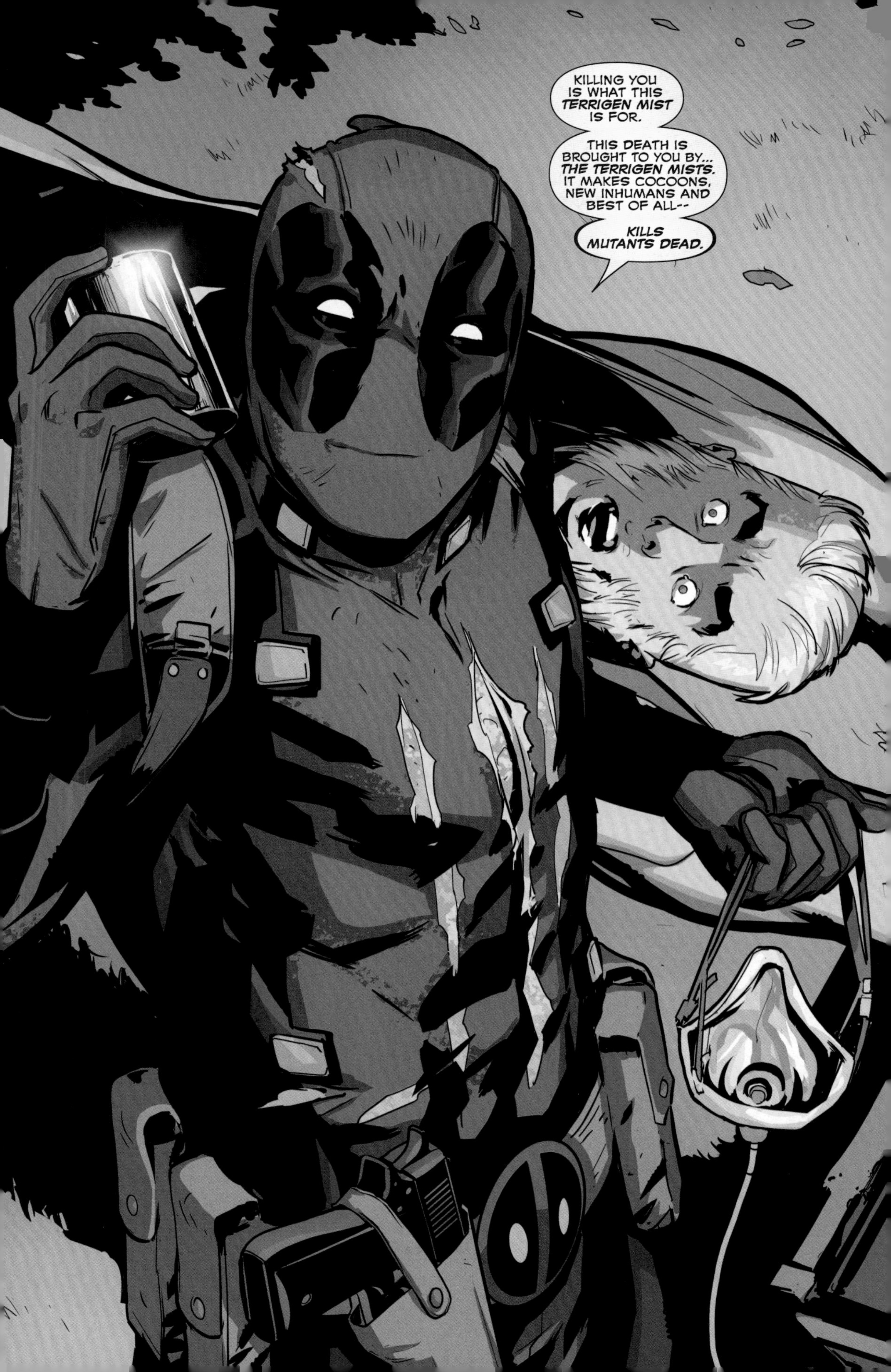
KILLING YOU IS WHAT THIS *TERRIGEN MIST* IS FOR.
THIS DEATH IS BROUGHT TO YOU BY... *THE TERRIGEN MISTS.* IT MAKES COCOONS, NEW INHUMANS AND BEST OF ALL--
KILLS MUTANTS DEAD.

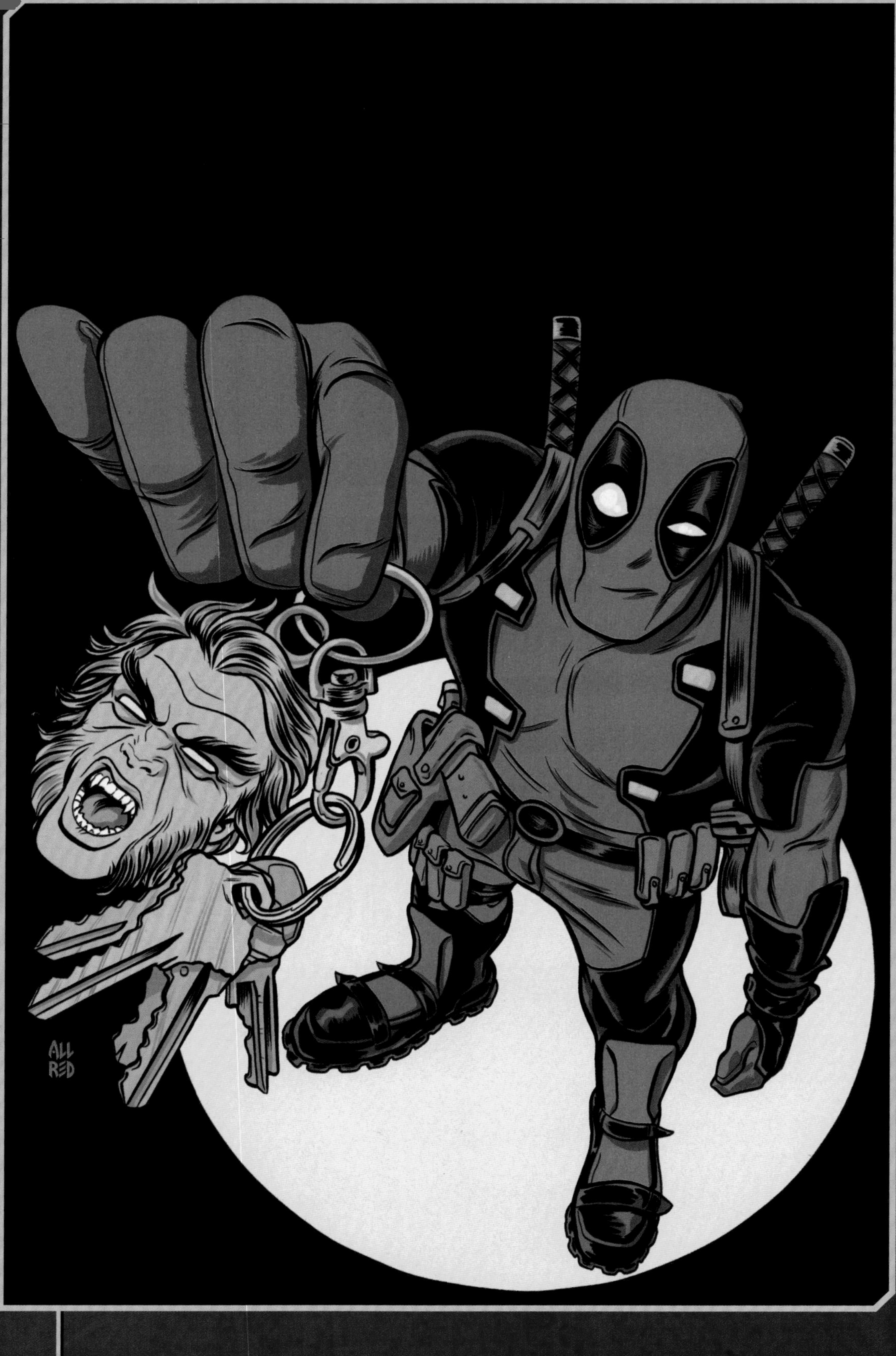
ALL
RED

11 | FAHRENHEIT .357

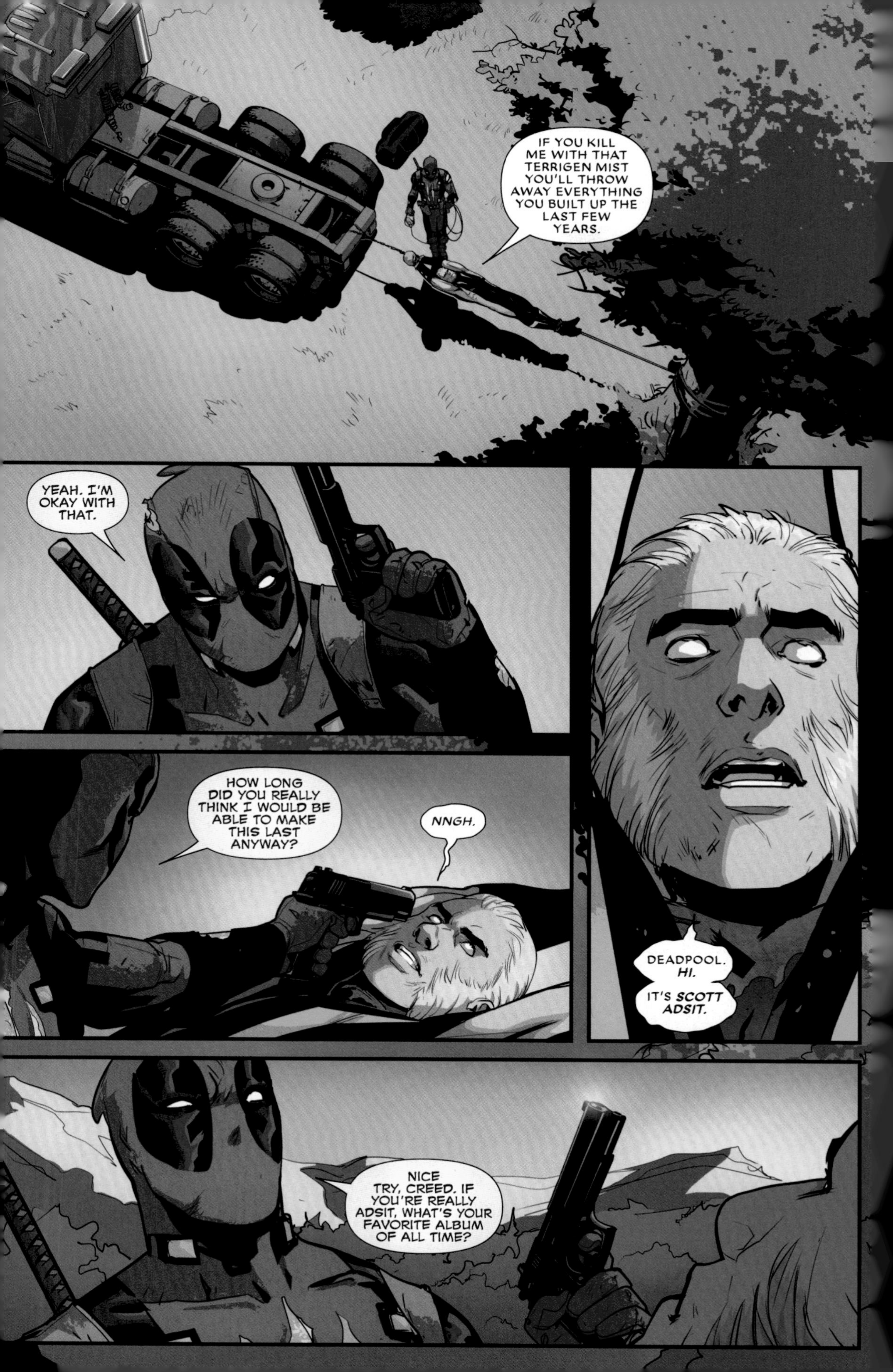
IF YOU KILL ME WITH THAT TERRIGEN MIST YOU'LL THROW AWAY EVERYTHING YOU BUILT UP THE LAST FEW YEARS.
YEAH. I'M OKAY WITH THAT.
HOW LONG DID YOU REALLY THINK I WOULD BE ABLE TO MAKE THIS LAST ANYWAY?
NNGH.
DEADPOOL. HI.
IT'S SCOTT ADSIT.
NICE TRY, CREED. IF YOU'RE REALLY ADSIT, WHAT'S YOUR FAVORITE ALBUM OF ALL TIME?

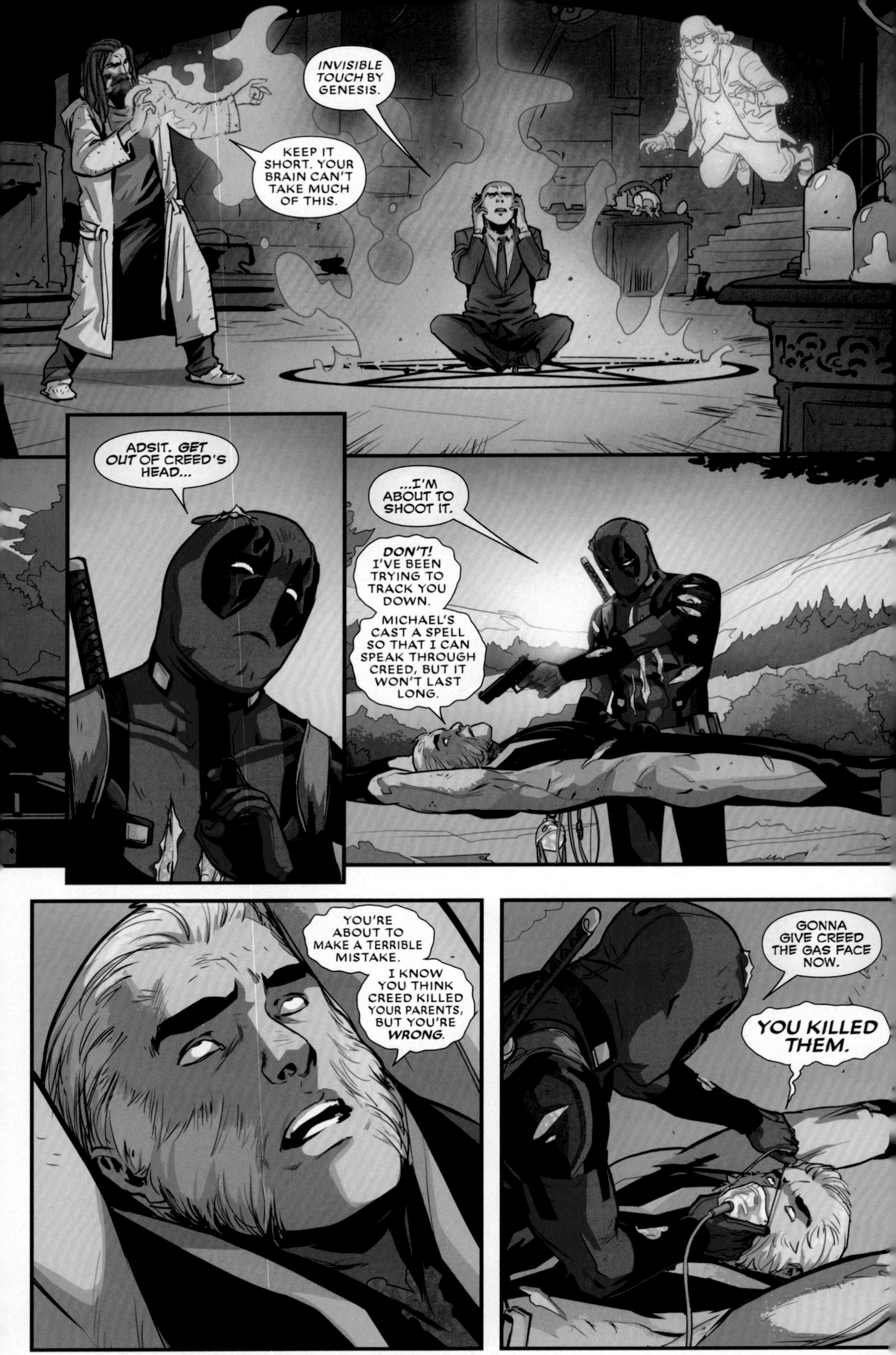
INVISIBLE TOUCH BY GENESIS.
KEEP IT SHORT. YOUR BRAIN CAN'T TAKE MUCH OF THIS.
ADSIT. GET OUT OF CREED'S HEAD...
...I'M ABOUT TO SHOOT IT.
DON'T! I'VE BEEN TRYING TO TRACK YOU DOWN.
MICHAEL'S CAST A SPELL SO THAT I CAN SPEAK THROUGH CREED, BUT IT WON'T LAST LONG.
YOU'RE ABOUT TO MAKE A TERRIBLE MISTAKE.
I KNOW YOU THINK CREED KILLED YOUR PARENTS, BUT YOU'RE WRONG.
GONNA GIVE CREED THE GAS FACE NOW.
YOU KILLED THEM.

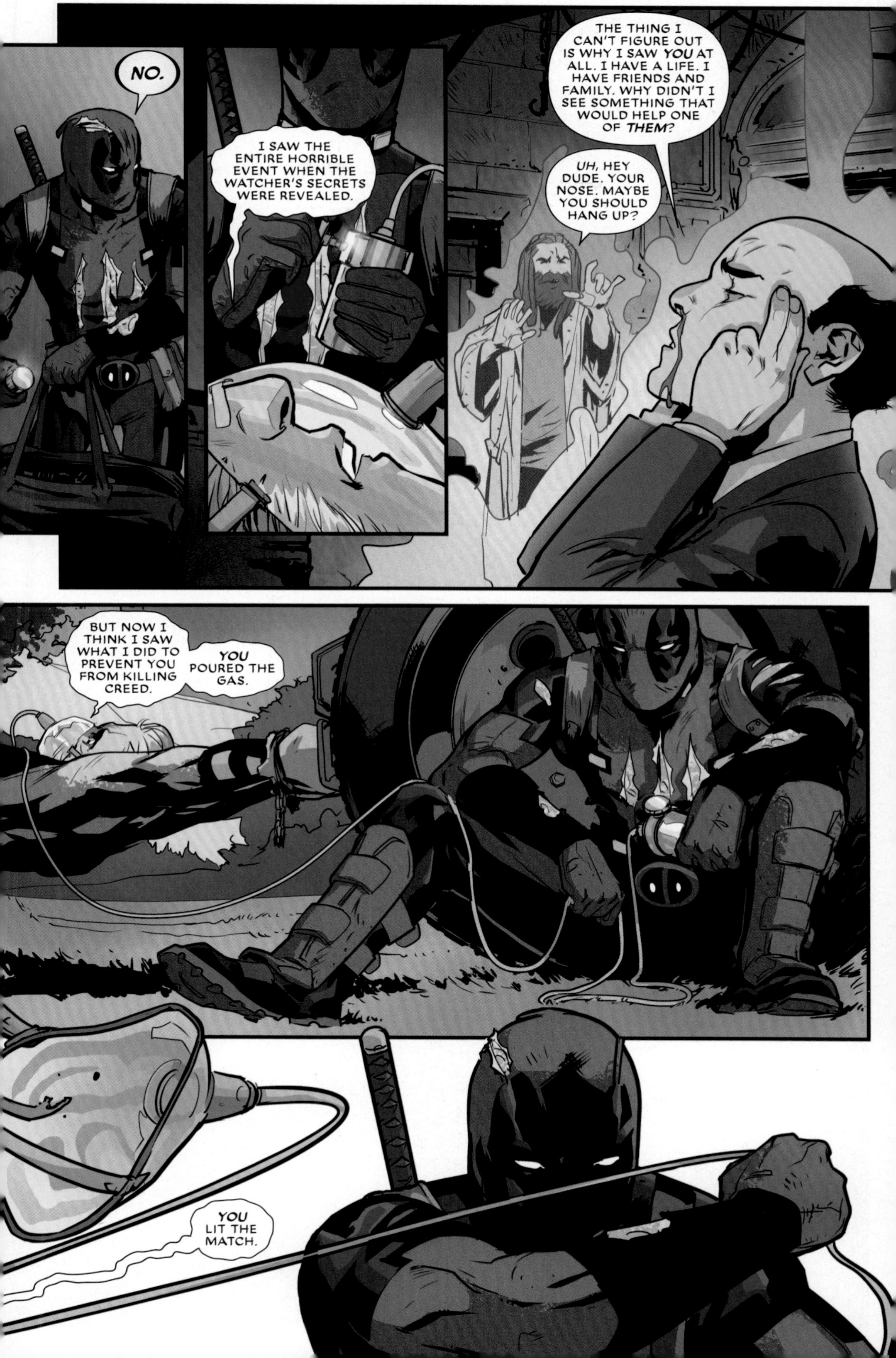
NO.
I SAW THE ENTIRE HORRIBLE EVENT WHEN THE WATCHER'S SECRETS WERE REVEALED.
THE THING I CAN'T FIGURE OUT IS WHY I SAW *YOU* AT ALL. I HAVE A LIFE. I HAVE FRIENDS AND FAMILY. WHY DIDN'T I SEE SOMETHING THAT WOULD HELP ONE OF *THEM*?
UH, HEY DUDE. YOUR NOSE. MAYBE YOU SHOULD HANG UP?
BUT NOW I THINK I SAW WHAT I DID TO PREVENT YOU FROM KILLING CREED.
YOU POURED THE GAS.
YOU LIT THE MATCH.

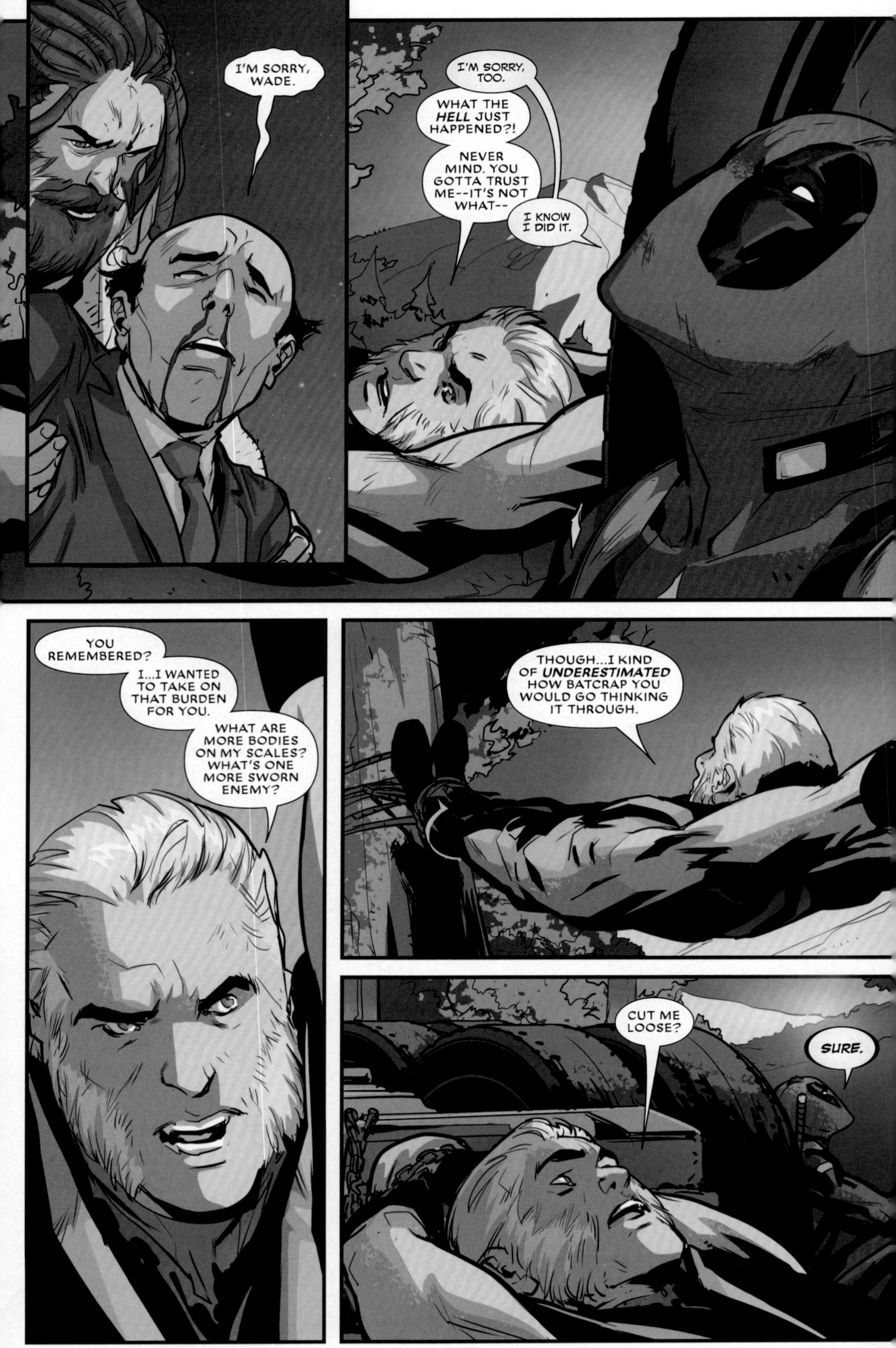

I'M SORRY, WADE.
I'M SORRY, TOO.
WHAT THE *HELL* JUST HAPPENED?!
NEVER MIND. YOU GOTTA TRUST ME--IT'S NOT WHAT--
I KNOW I DID IT.
YOU REMEMBERED?
I...I WANTED TO TAKE ON THAT BURDEN FOR YOU.
WHAT ARE MORE BODIES ON MY SCALES? WHAT'S ONE MORE SWORN ENEMY?
THOUGH...I KIND OF *UNDERESTIMATED* HOW BATCRAP YOU WOULD GO THINKING IT THROUGH.
CUT ME LOOSE?
SURE.

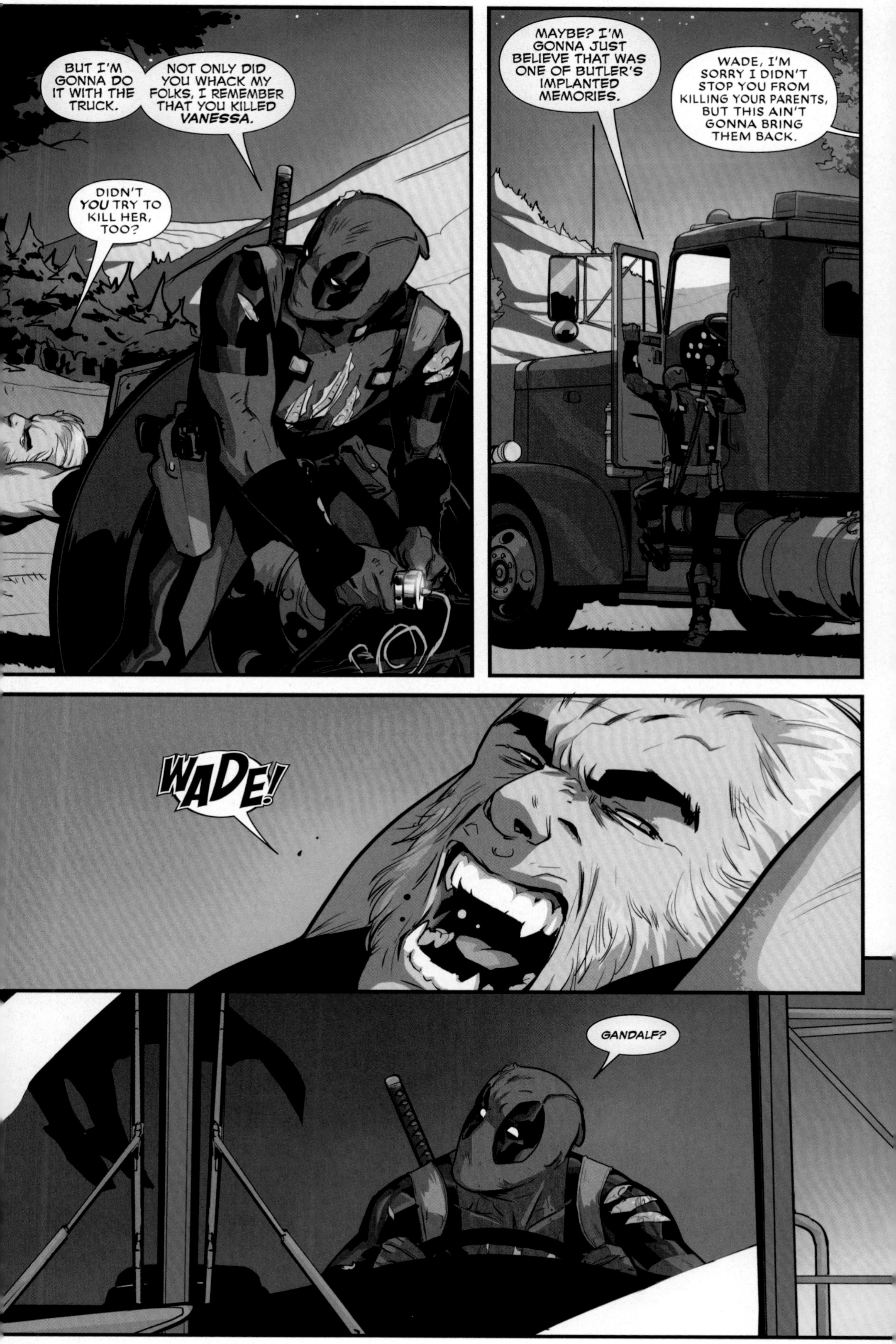
BUT I'M GONNA DO IT WITH THE TRUCK.
NOT ONLY DID YOU WHACK MY FOLKS, I REMEMBER THAT YOU KILLED VANESSA.
DIDN'T YOU TRY TO KILL HER, TOO?
MAYBE? I'M GONNA JUST BELIEVE THAT WAS ONE OF BUTLER'S IMPLANTED MEMORIES.
WADE, I'M SORRY I DIDN'T STOP YOU FROM KILLING YOUR PARENTS, BUT THIS AIN'T GONNA BRING THEM BACK.
WADE!
GANDALF?

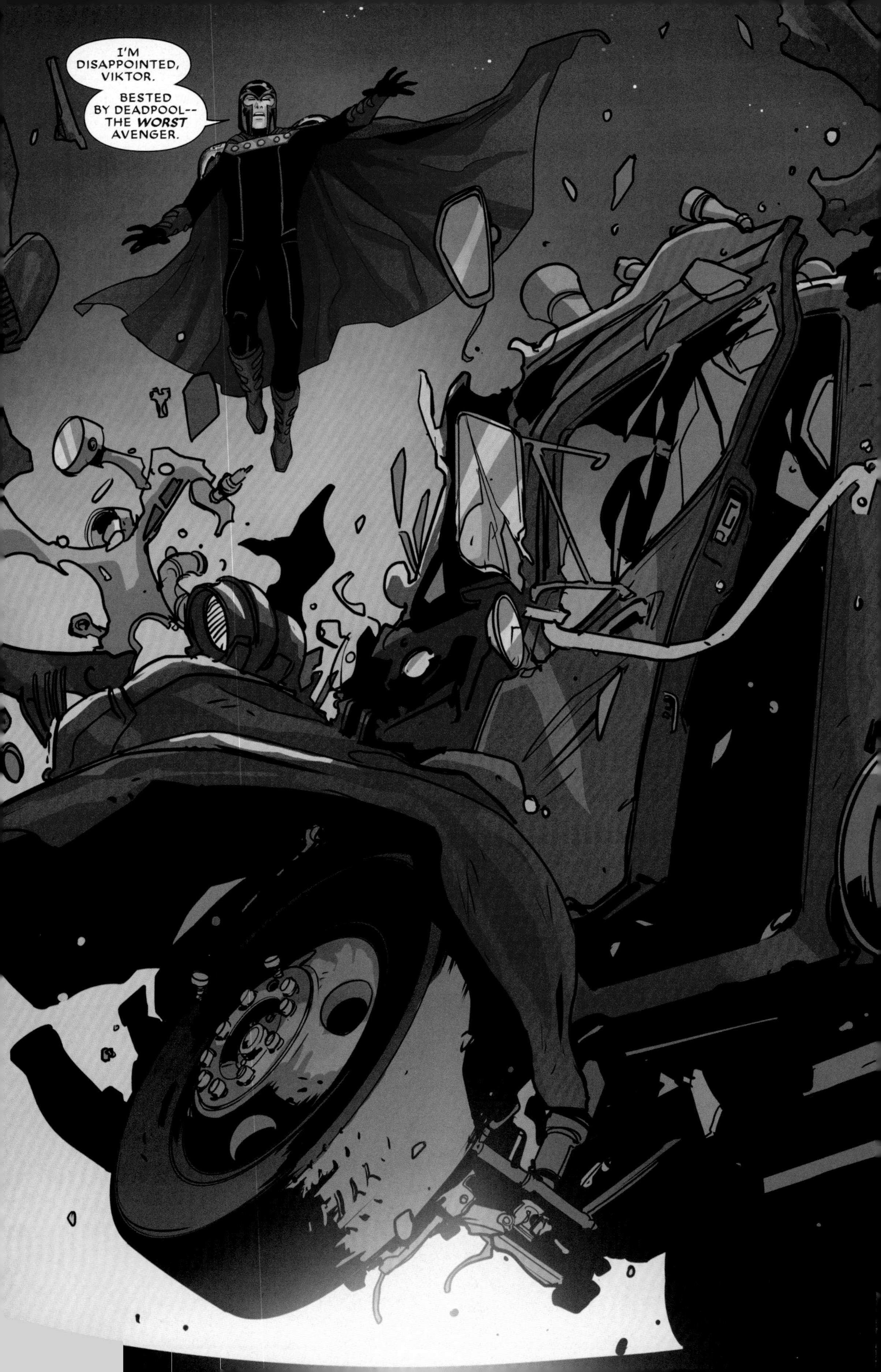
I'M DISAPPOINTED, VIKTOR.
BESTED BY DEADPOOL-- THE *WORST* AVENGER.

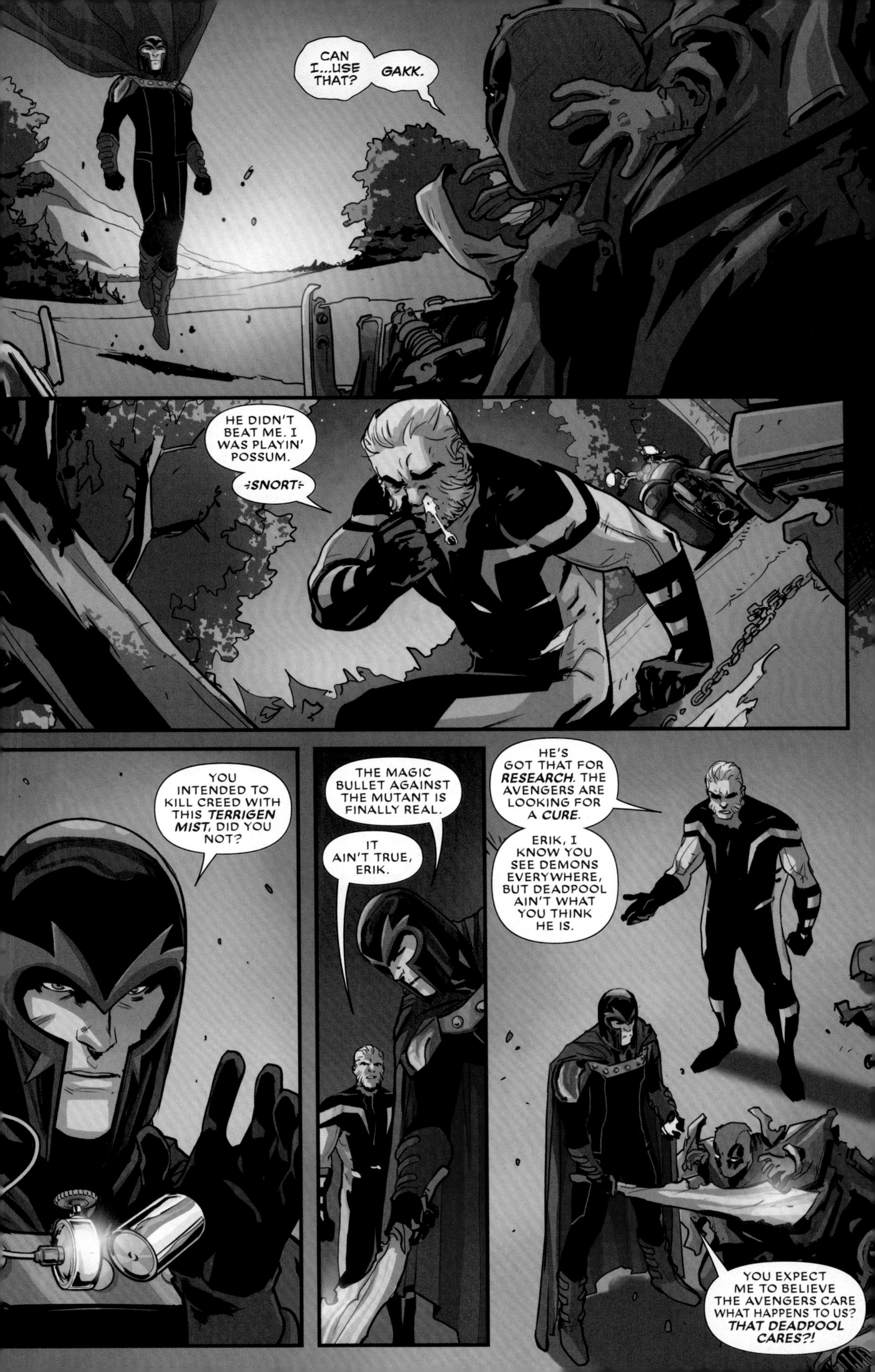
CAN I...USE THAT?
GAKK.
HE DIDN'T BEAT ME. I WAS PLAYIN' POSSUM.
SNORT
YOU INTENDED TO KILL CREED WITH THIS TERRIGEN MIST, DID YOU NOT?
THE MAGIC BULLET AGAINST THE MUTANT IS FINALLY REAL.
IT AIN'T TRUE, ERIK.
HE'S GOT THAT FOR RESEARCH. THE AVENGERS ARE LOOKING FOR A CURE.
ERIK, I KNOW YOU SEE DEMONS EVERYWHERE, BUT DEADPOOL AIN'T WHAT YOU THINK HE IS.
YOU EXPECT ME TO BELIEVE THE AVENGERS CARE WHAT HAPPENS TO US? THAT DEADPOOL CARES?!

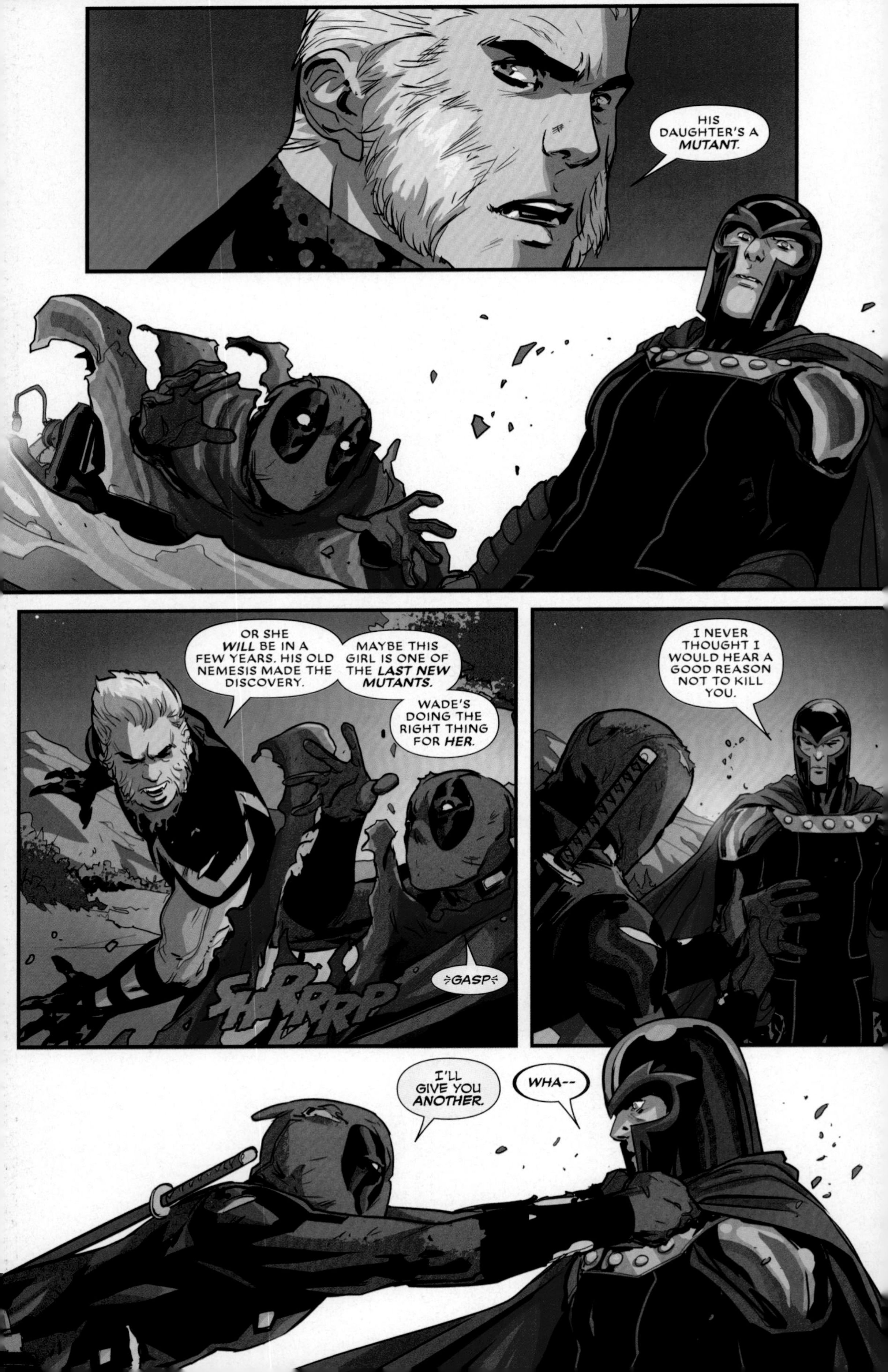
HIS DAUGHTER'S A MUTANT.
OR SHE WILL BE IN A FEW YEARS. HIS OLD NEMESIS MADE THE DISCOVERY.
MAYBE THIS GIRL IS ONE OF THE LAST NEW MUTANTS.
WADE'S DOING THE RIGHT THING FOR HER.
SHRRRP
GASP
I NEVER THOUGHT I WOULD HEAR A GOOD REASON NOT TO KILL YOU.
I'LL GIVE YOU ANOTHER.
WHA--

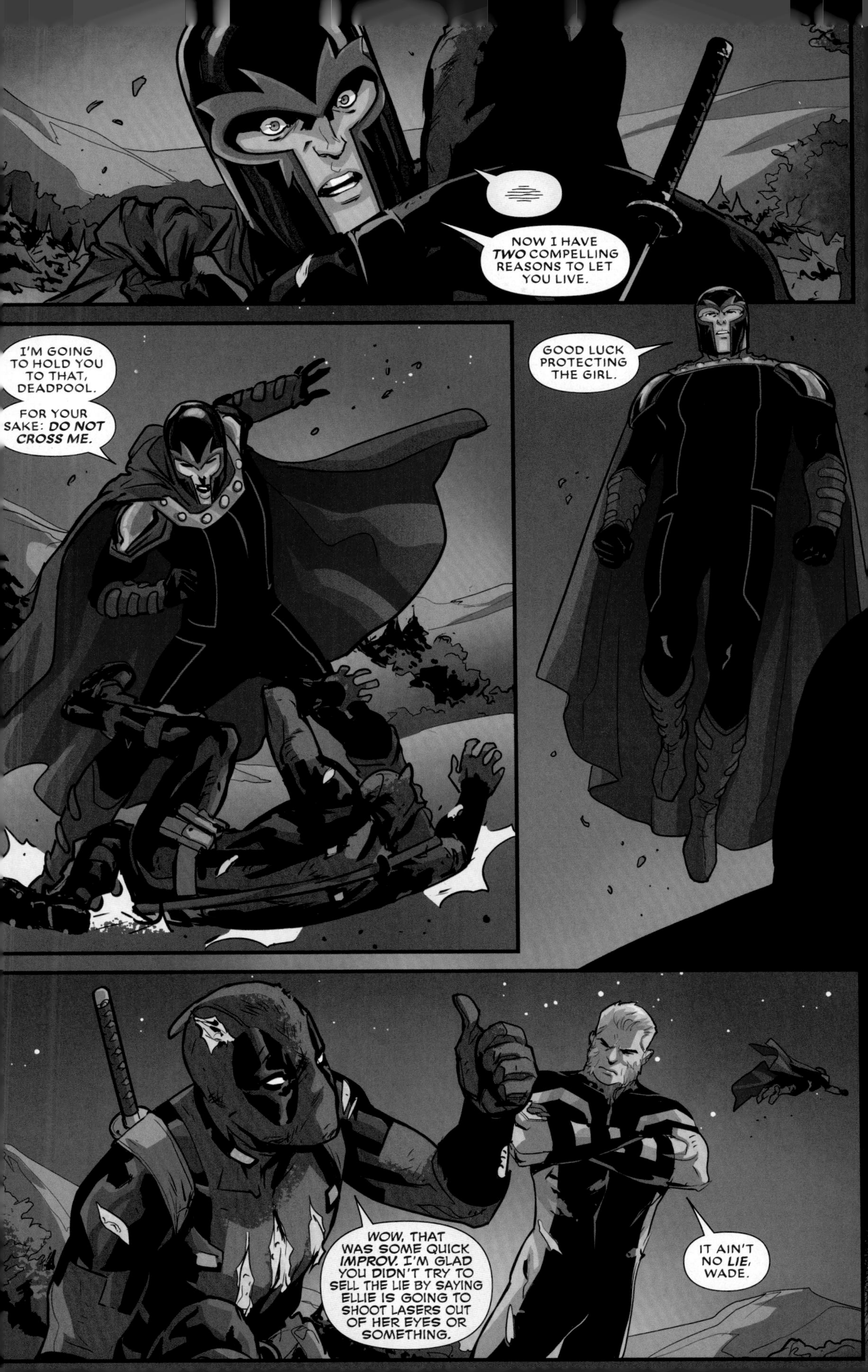
NOW I HAVE TWO COMPELLING REASONS TO LET YOU LIVE.
I'M GOING TO HOLD YOU TO THAT, DEADPOOL.
FOR YOUR SAKE: DO NOT CROSS ME.
GOOD LUCK PROTECTING THE GIRL.
WOW, THAT WAS SOME QUICK IMPROV. I'M GLAD YOU DIDN'T TRY TO SELL THE LIE BY SAYING ELLIE IS GOING TO SHOOT LASERS OUT OF HER EYES OR SOMETHING.
IT AIN'T NO LIE, WADE.

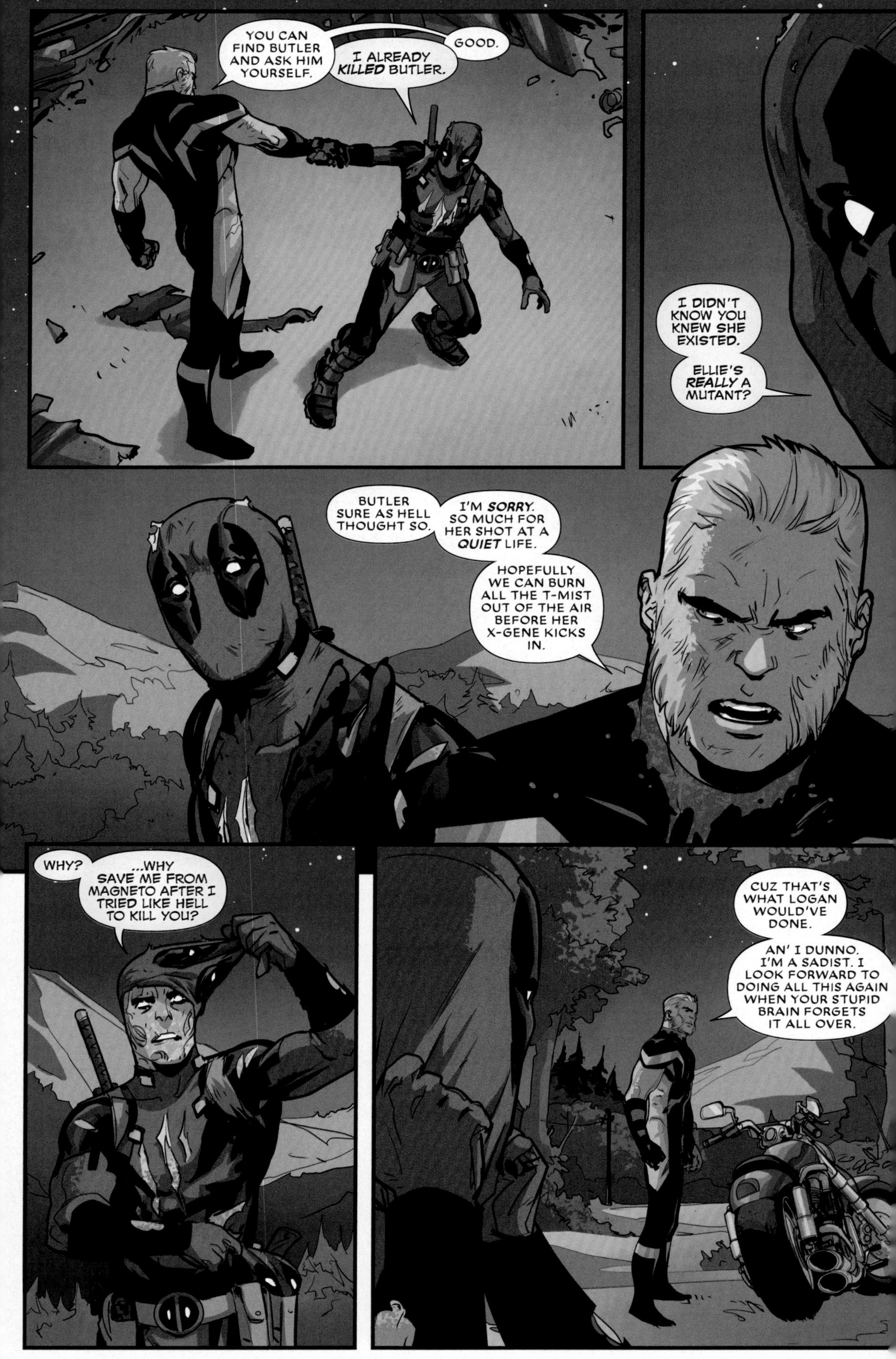

YOU CAN FIND BUTLER AND ASK HIM YOURSELF.
GOOD.
I ALREADY KILLED BUTLER.
I DIDN'T KNOW YOU KNEW SHE EXISTED.
ELLIE'S REALLY A MUTANT?
BUTLER SURE AS HELL THOUGHT SO.
I'M SORRY. SO MUCH FOR HER SHOT AT A QUIET LIFE.
HOPEFULLY WE CAN BURN ALL THE T-MIST OUT OF THE AIR BEFORE HER X-GENE KICKS IN.
WHY?
...WHY SAVE ME FROM MAGNETO AFTER I TRIED LIKE HELL TO KILL YOU?
CUZ THAT'S WHAT LOGAN WOULD'VE DONE.
AN' I DUNNO. I'M A SADIST. I LOOK FORWARD TO DOING ALL THIS AGAIN WHEN YOUR STUPID BRAIN FORGETS IT ALL OVER.

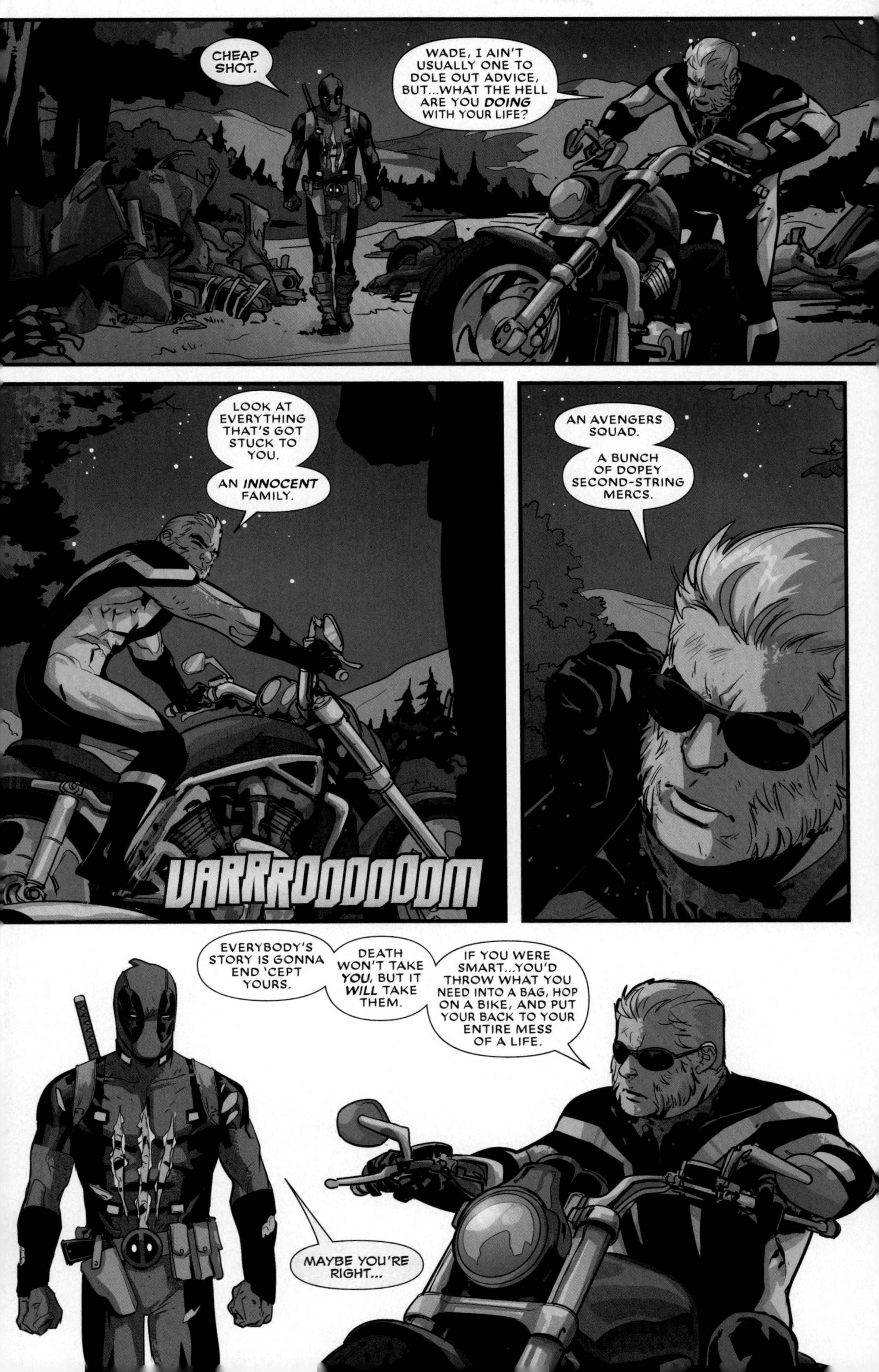
CHEAP SHOT.
WADE, I AIN'T USUALLY ONE TO DOLE OUT ADVICE, BUT...WHAT THE HELL ARE YOU *DOING* WITH YOUR LIFE?
LOOK AT EVERYTHING THAT'S GOT STUCK TO YOU.
AN *INNOCENT* FAMILY.
VARRROOOOOOOM
AN AVENGERS SQUAD.
A BUNCH OF DOPEY SECOND-STRING MERCS.
EVERYBODY'S STORY IS GONNA END 'CEPT YOURS.
DEATH WON'T TAKE *YOU*, BUT IT *WILL* TAKE THEM.
IF YOU WERE SMART...YOU'D THROW WHAT YOU NEED INTO A BAG, HOP ON A BIKE, AND PUT YOUR BACK TO YOUR ENTIRE MESS OF A LIFE.
MAYBE YOU'RE RIGHT...

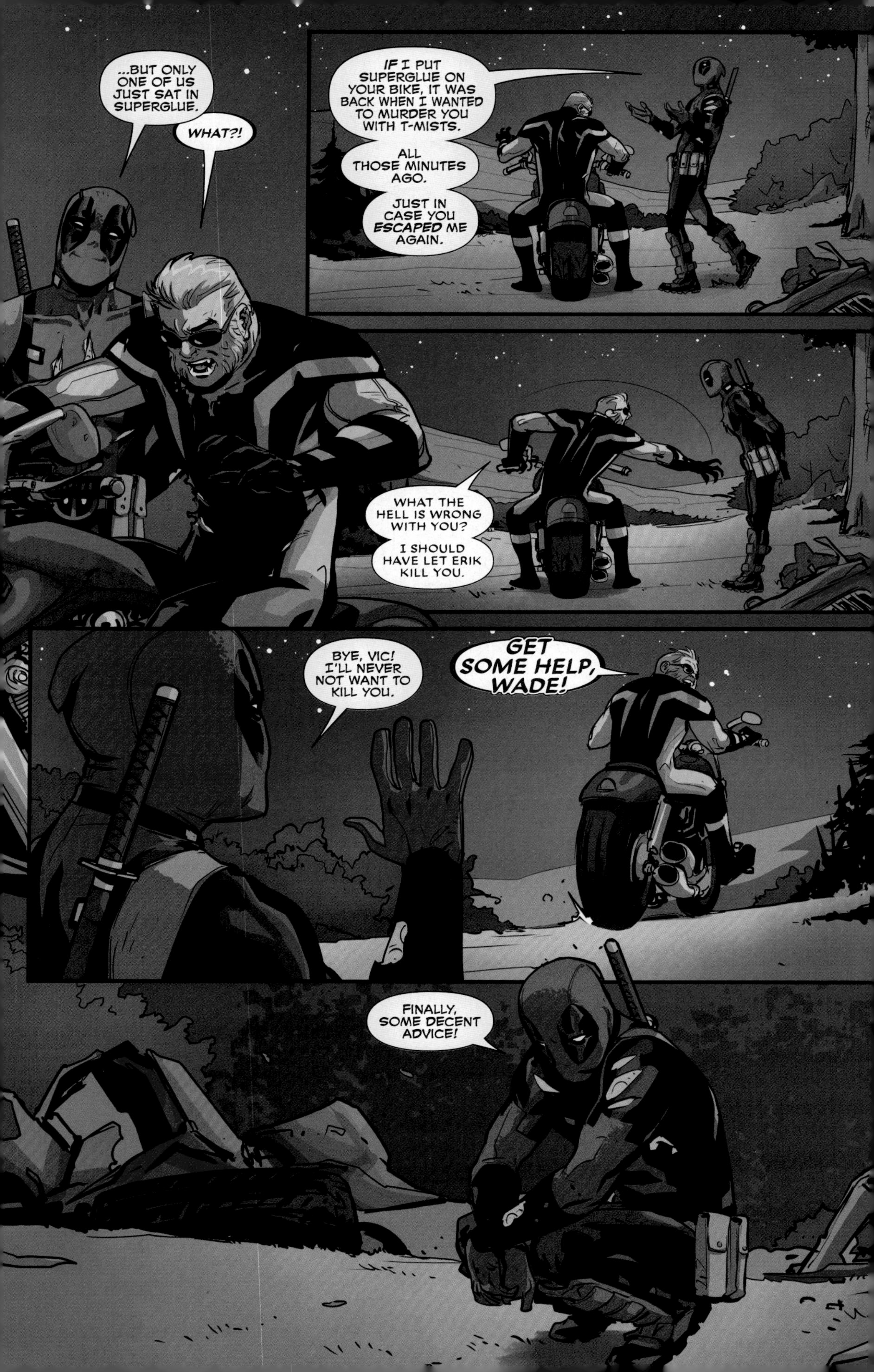
...BUT ONLY ONE OF US JUST SAT IN SUPERGLUE.
WHAT?!
IF I PUT SUPERGLUE ON YOUR BIKE, IT WAS BACK WHEN I WANTED TO MURDER YOU WITH T-MISTS.
ALL THOSE MINUTES AGO.
JUST IN CASE YOU ESCAPED ME AGAIN.
WHAT THE HELL IS WRONG WITH YOU?
I SHOULD HAVE LET ERIK KILL YOU.
BYE, VIC! I'LL NEVER NOT WANT TO KILL YOU.
GET SOME HELP, WADE!
FINALLY, SOME DECENT ADVICE!

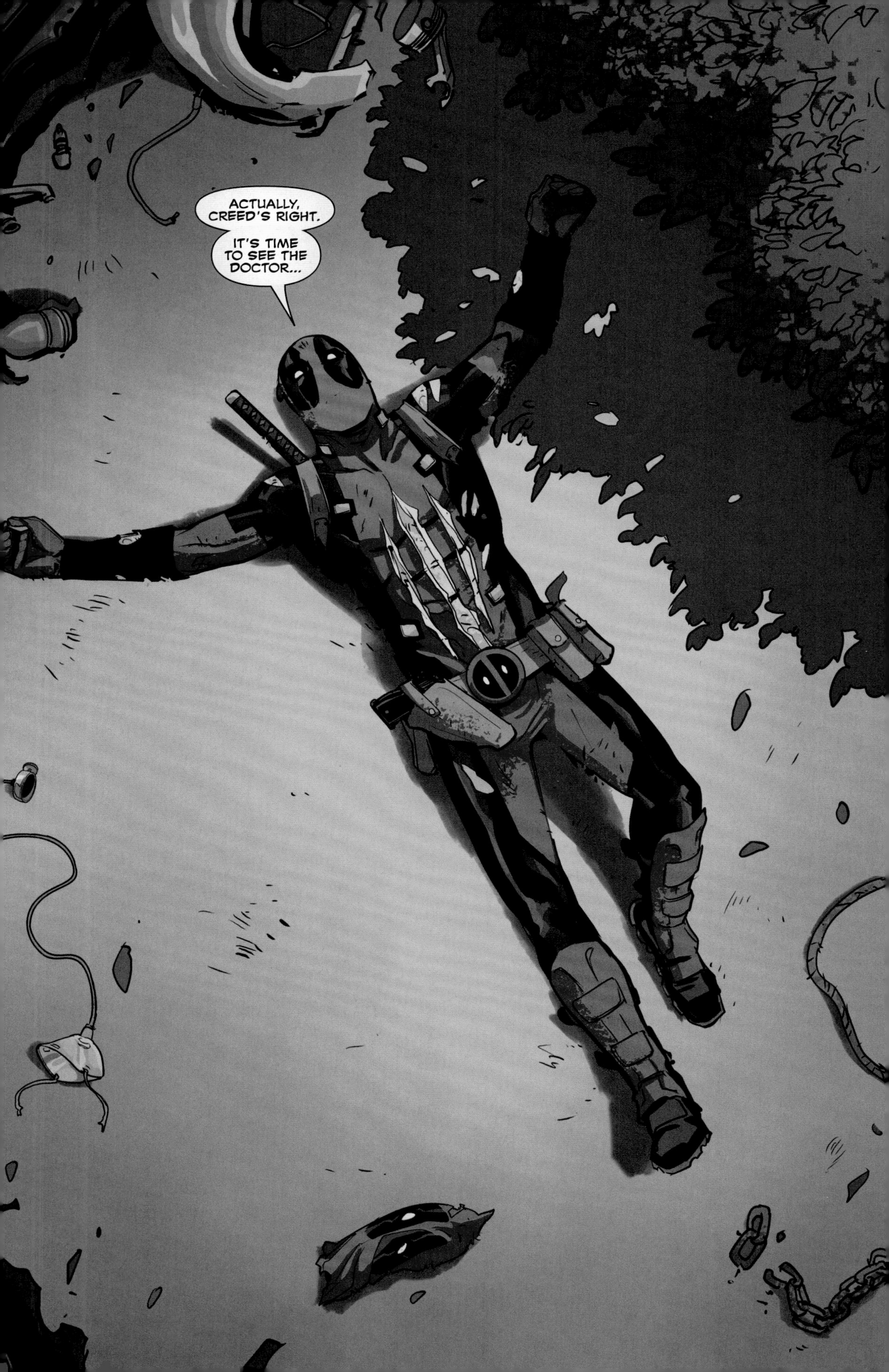
ACTUALLY, CREED'S RIGHT.
IT'S TIME TO SEE THE DOCTOR...

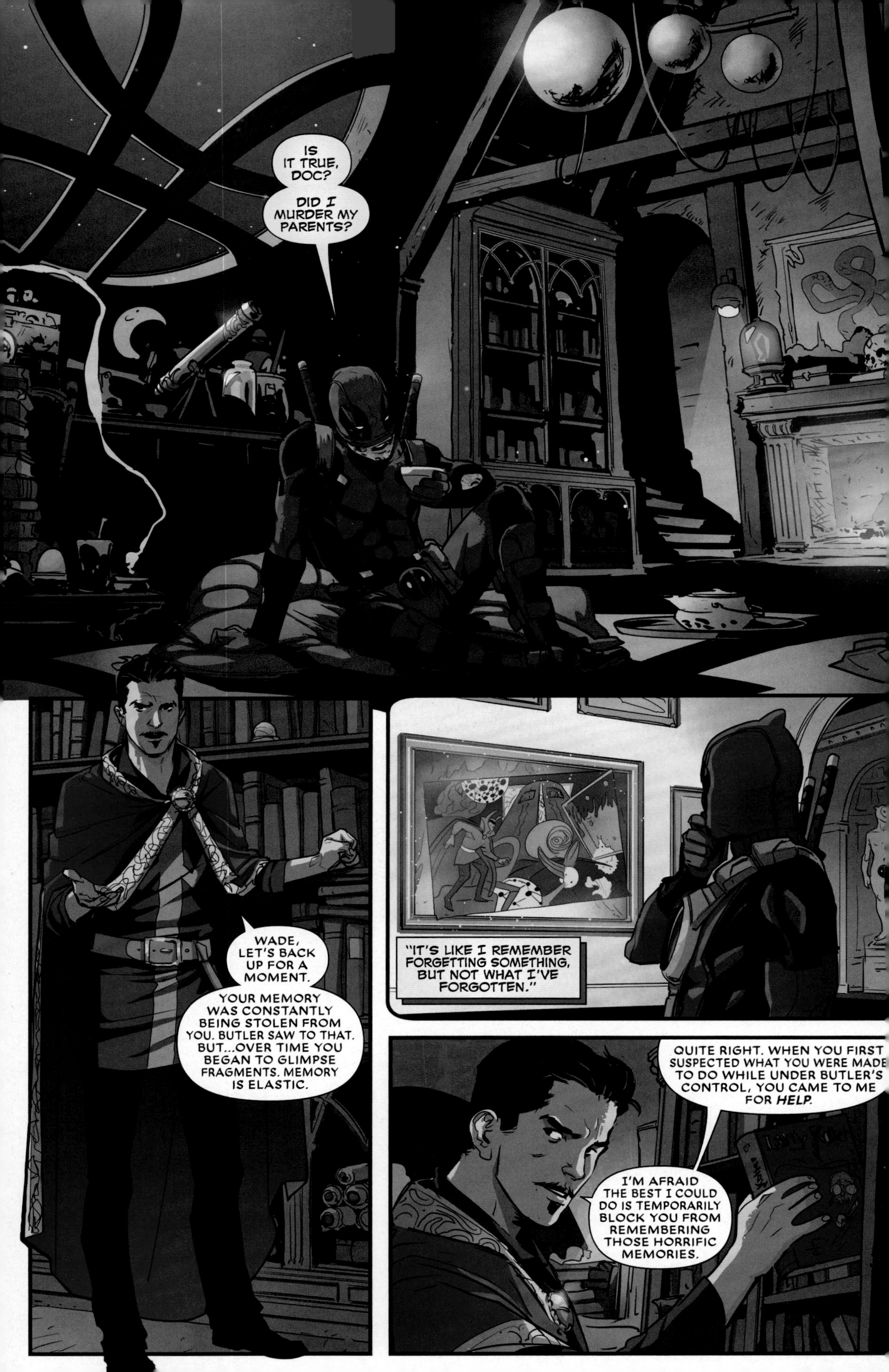

IS IT TRUE, DOC?
DID I MURDER MY PARENTS?
WADE, LET'S BACK UP FOR A MOMENT.
YOUR MEMORY WAS CONSTANTLY BEING STOLEN FROM YOU. BUTLER SAW TO THAT. BUT...OVER TIME YOU BEGAN TO GLIMPSE FRAGMENTS. MEMORY IS ELASTIC.
"IT'S LIKE I REMEMBER FORGETTING SOMETHING, BUT NOT WHAT I'VE FORGOTTEN."
QUITE RIGHT. WHEN YOU FIRST SUSPECTED WHAT YOU WERE MADE TO DO WHILE UNDER BUTLER'S CONTROL, YOU CAME TO ME FOR *HELP*.
I'M AFRAID THE BEST I COULD DO IS TEMPORARILY BLOCK YOU FROM REMEMBERING THOSE HORRIFIC MEMORIES.

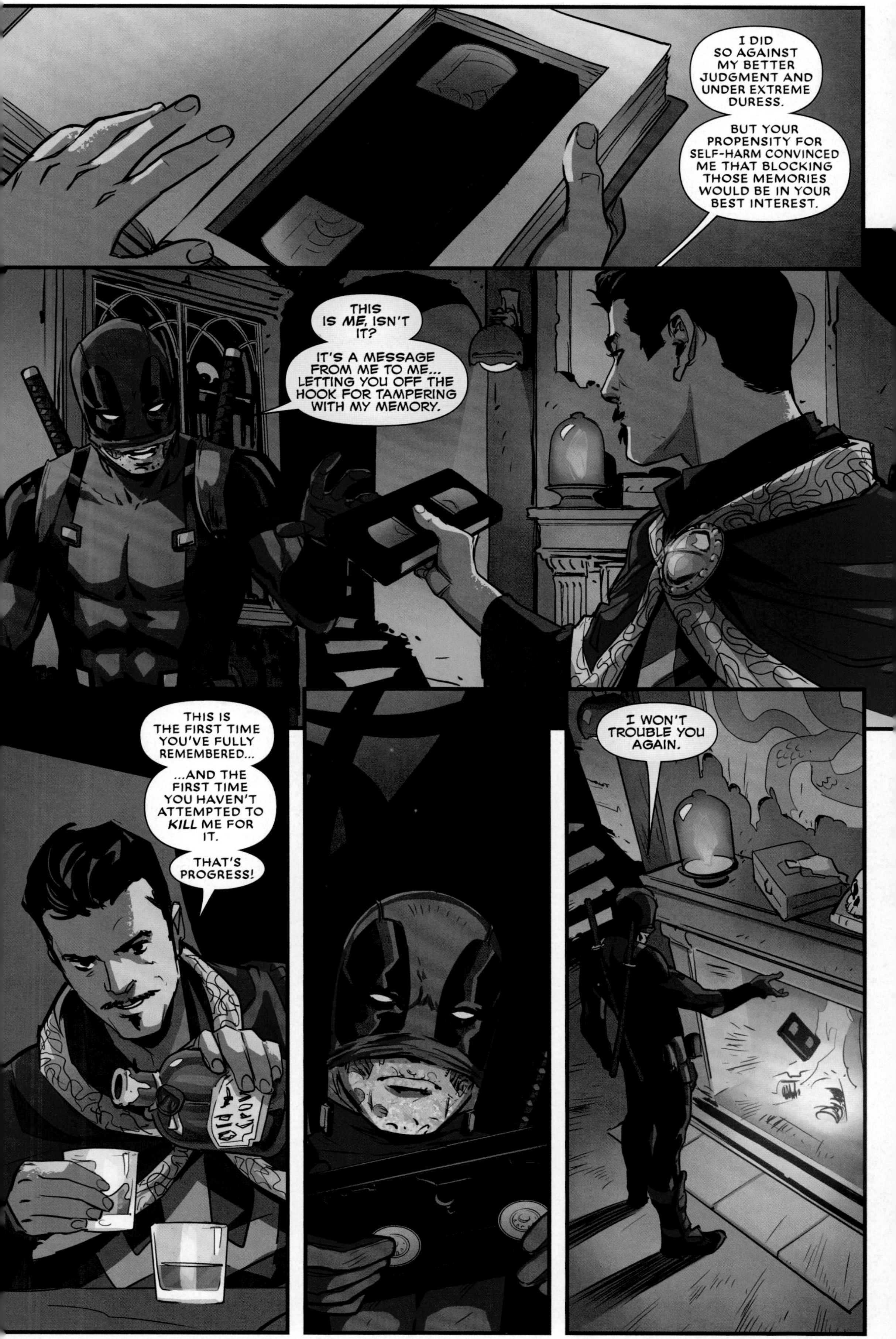
I DID SO AGAINST MY BETTER JUDGMENT AND UNDER EXTREME DURESS.
BUT YOUR PROPENSITY FOR SELF-HARM CONVINCED ME THAT BLOCKING THOSE MEMORIES WOULD BE IN YOUR BEST INTEREST.
THIS IS *ME*, ISN'T IT?
IT'S A MESSAGE FROM ME TO ME... LETTING YOU OFF THE HOOK FOR TAMPERING WITH MY MEMORY.
THIS IS THE FIRST TIME YOU'VE FULLY REMEMBERED...
...AND THE FIRST TIME YOU HAVEN'T ATTEMPTED TO *KILL* ME FOR IT.
THAT'S PROGRESS!
I WON'T TROUBLE YOU AGAIN.

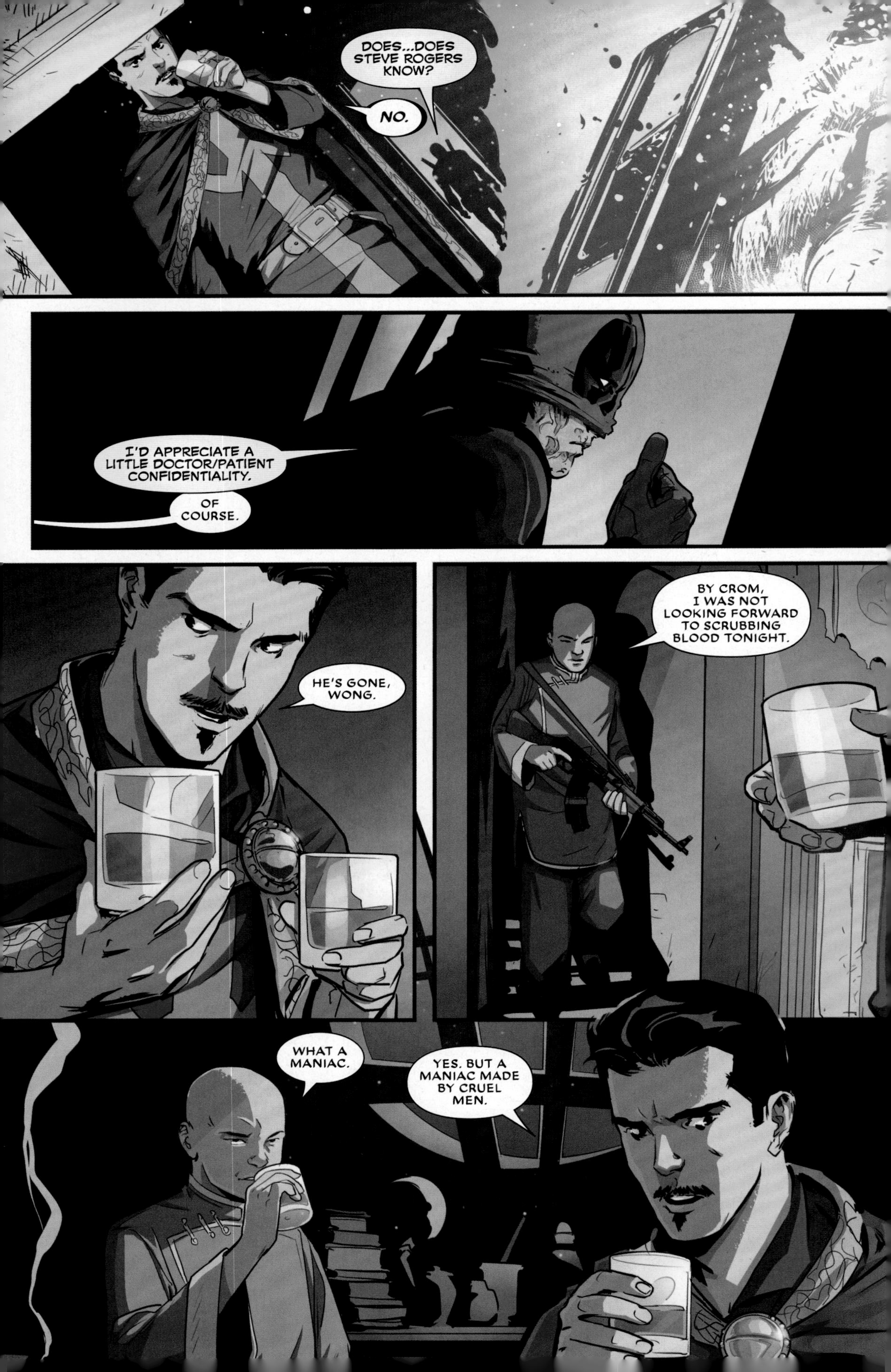
DOES...DOES STEVE ROGERS KNOW?
NO.
I'D APPRECIATE A LITTLE DOCTOR/PATIENT CONFIDENTIALITY.
OF COURSE.
HE'S GONE, WONG.
BY CROM, I WAS NOT LOOKING FORWARD TO SCRUBBING BLOOD TONIGHT.
WHAT A MANIAC.
YES. BUT A MANIAC MADE BY CRUEL MEN.

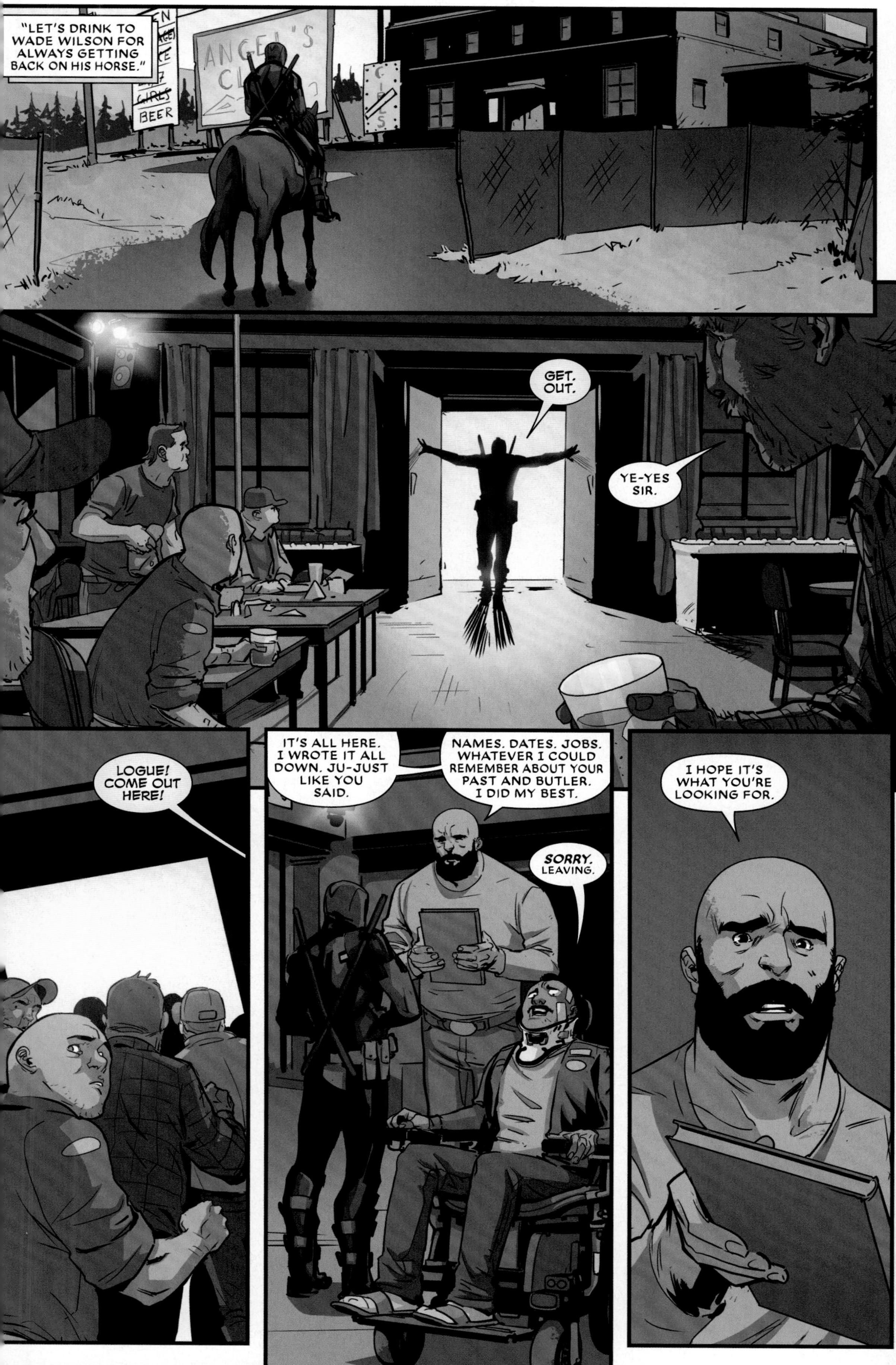
"LET'S DRINK TO WADE WILSON FOR ALWAYS GETTING BACK ON HIS HORSE."
ANGEL'S CL
GIRLS
BEER
GET. OUT.
YE-YES SIR.
LOGUE! COME OUT HERE!
IT'S ALL HERE. I WROTE IT ALL DOWN. JU-JUST LIKE YOU SAID.
NAMES. DATES. JOBS. WHATEVER I COULD REMEMBER ABOUT YOUR PAST AND BUTLER. I DID MY BEST.
SORRY. LEAVING.
I HOPE IT'S WHAT YOU'RE LOOKING FOR.

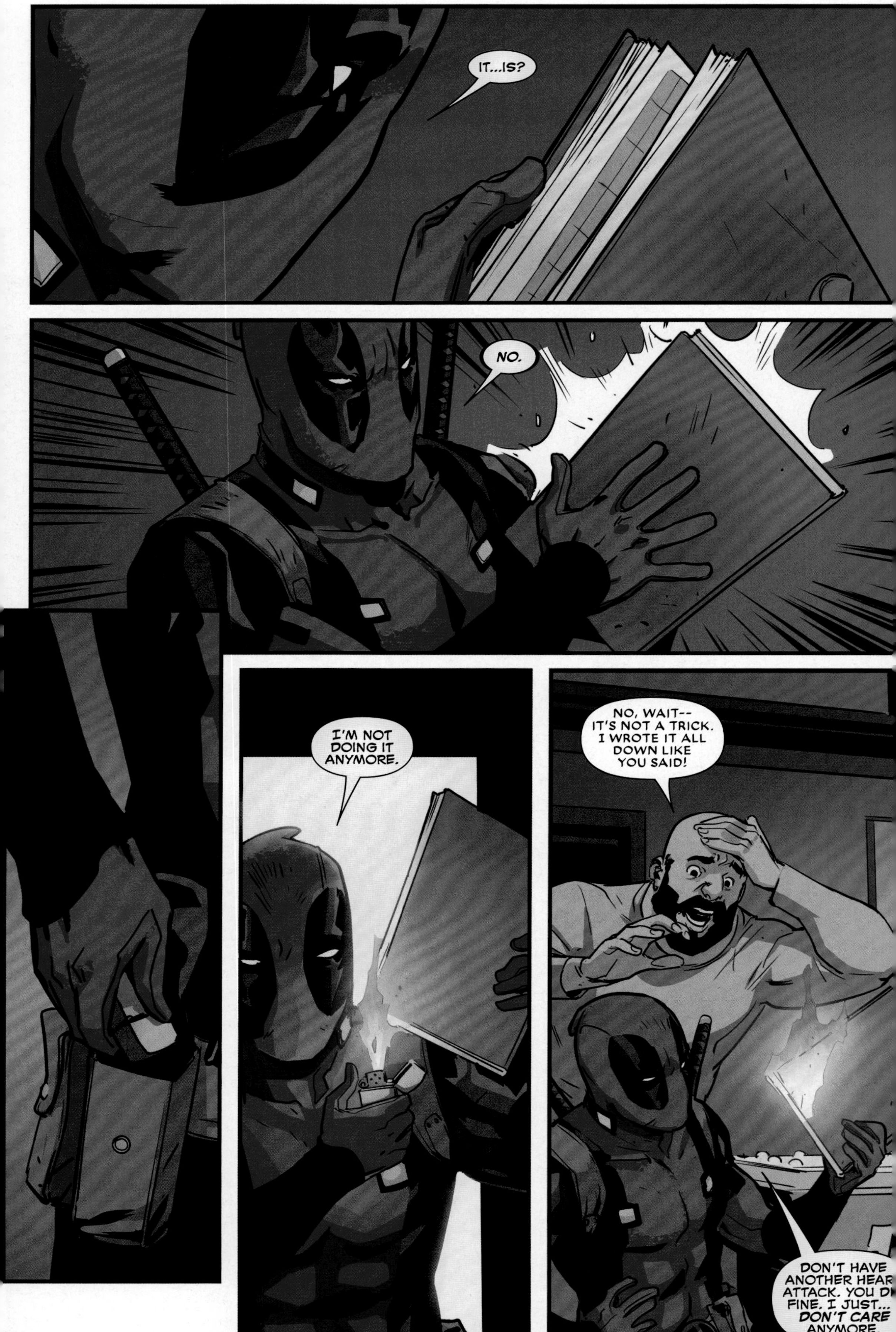
IT...IS?
NO.
I'M NOT DOING IT ANYMORE.
NO, WAIT-- IT'S NOT A TRICK. I WROTE IT ALL DOWN LIKE YOU SAID!
DON'T HAVE ANOTHER HEAR ATTACK. YOU D FINE. I JUST... DON'T CARE ANYMORE.

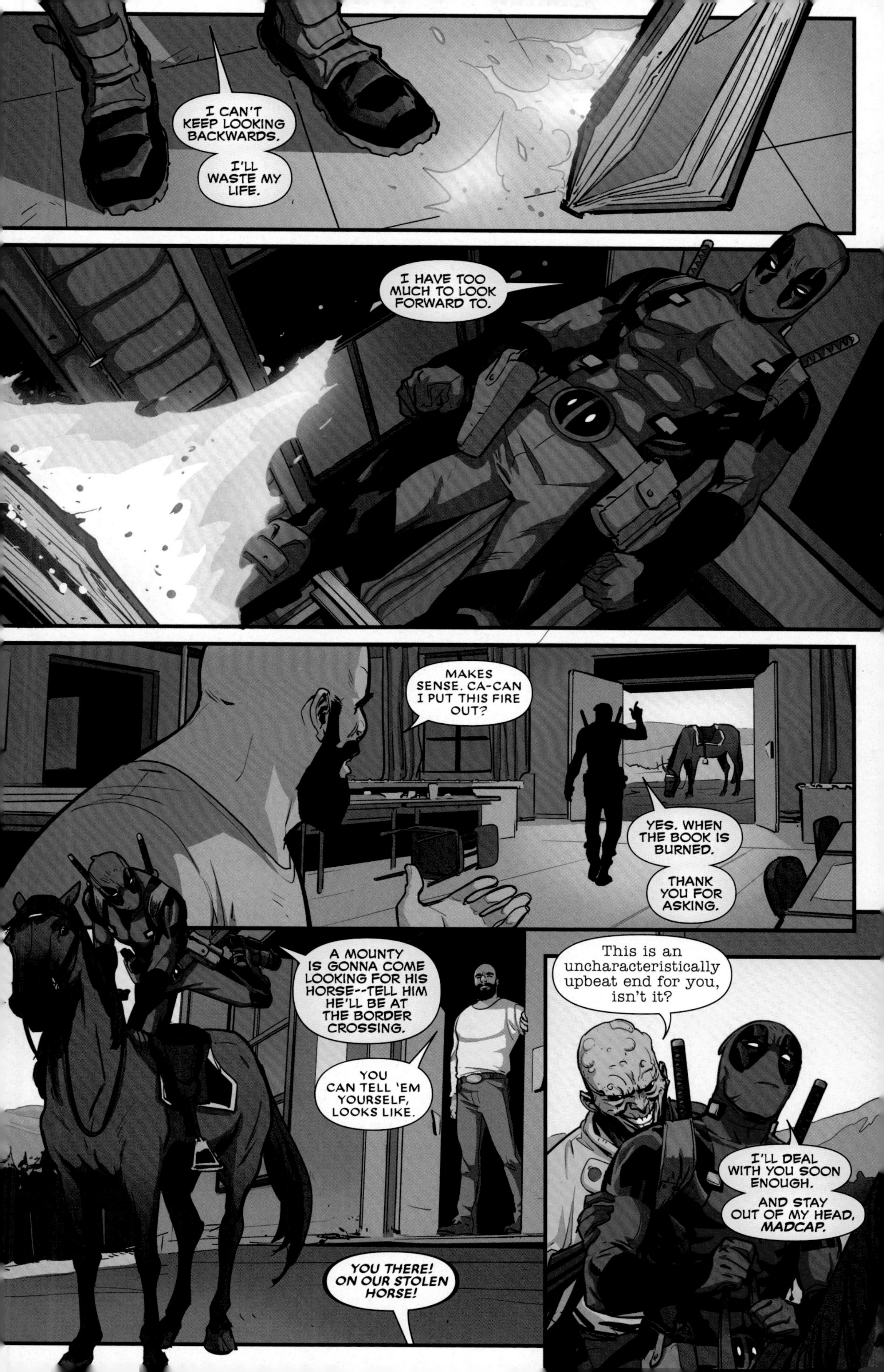
I CAN'T KEEP LOOKING BACKWARDS.
I'LL WASTE MY LIFE.
I HAVE TOO MUCH TO LOOK FORWARD TO.
MAKES SENSE. CA-CAN I PUT THIS FIRE OUT?
YES. WHEN THE BOOK IS BURNED.
THANK YOU FOR ASKING.
A MOUNTY IS GONNA COME LOOKING FOR HIS HORSE--TELL HIM HE'LL BE AT THE BORDER CROSSING.
YOU CAN TELL 'EM YOURSELF, LOOKS LIKE.
YOU THERE! ON OUR STOLEN HORSE!
This is an uncharacteristically upbeat end for you, isn't it?
I'LL DEAL WITH YOU SOON ENOUGH.
AND STAY OUT OF MY HEAD, MADCAP.

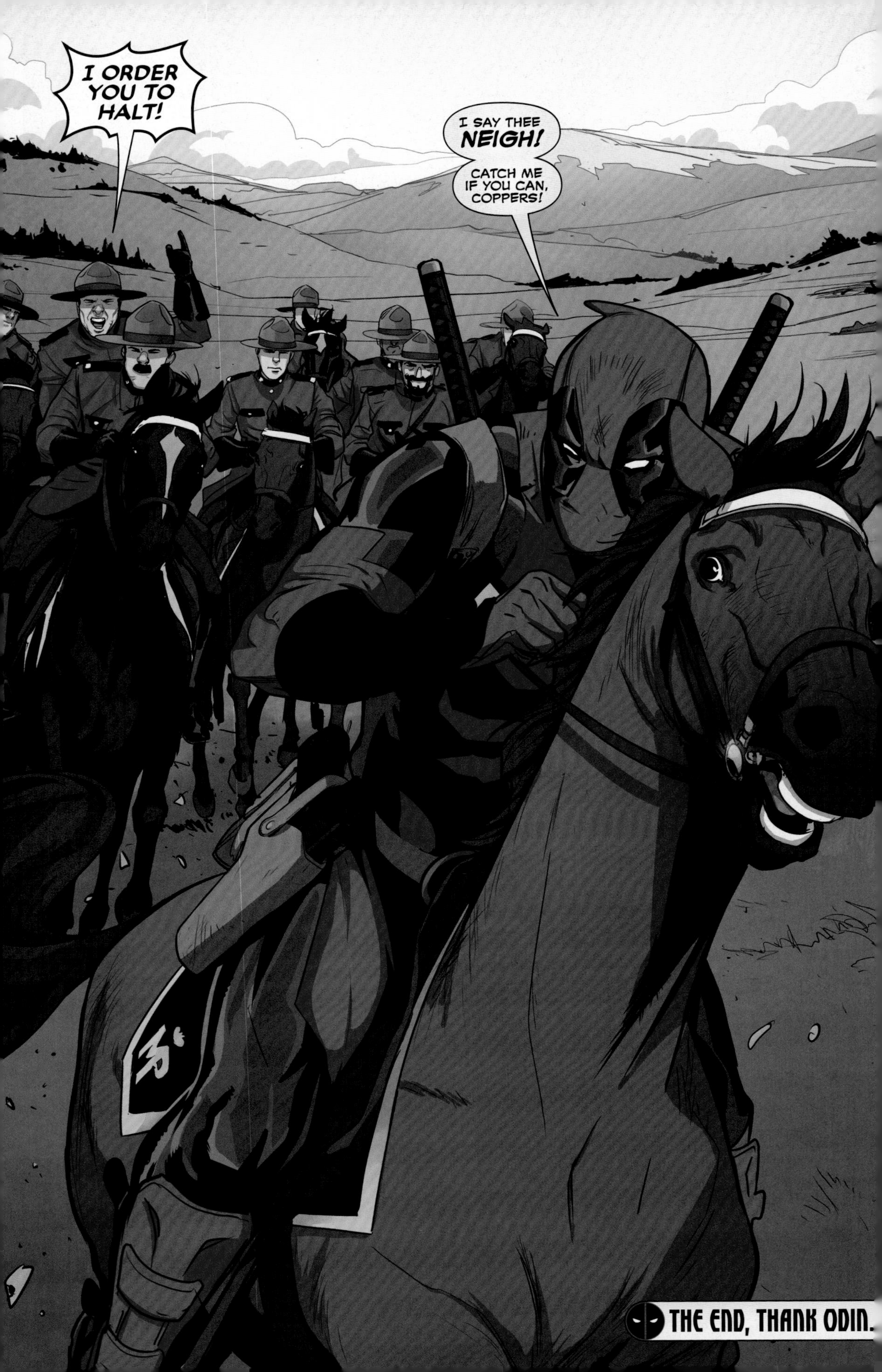
I ORDER YOU TO HALT!
I SAY THEE NEIGH!
CATCH ME IF YOU CAN, COPPERS!
THE END, THANK ODIN.

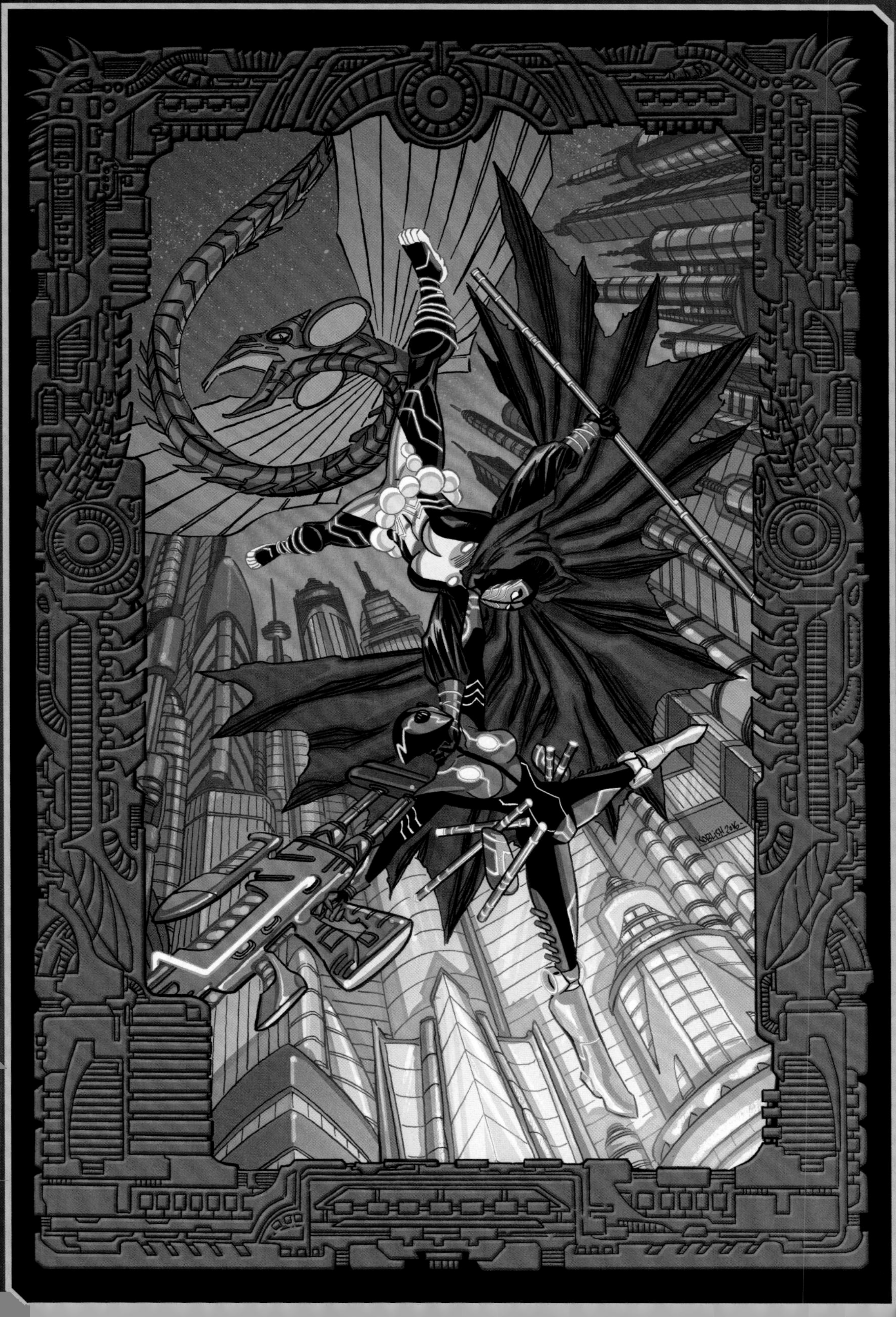
KOBLISH 2016

POSSIBLY THE MOST SKILLED MERCENARY OF THE CENTURY, AND DEFINITELY THE MOST DANGEROUS, WARDA WILSON WREAKS HAVOK ACROSS THE WORLD OF 2099, REBELLING AGAINST SOCIETY AND DOING THINGS HER OWN WAY. DAUGHTER OF A FAST-TALKING MERCENARY WITH A HEALING FACTOR AND A DEMONIC SUCCUBUS QUEEN, WARDA HAS NEVER FIT IN ANYWHERE...SO SHE MAKES HER HOME ON THE OUTSIDE, LIVING BY HER OWN RULES. CALL HER THE MERC WITH THE MOUTH...CALL HER THE REGENERATIN' DEGENERATE...CALL HER...

DEADPOOL

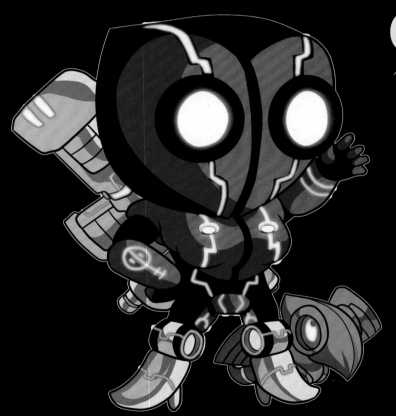

LI'L DEADPOOL 2099 ART BY
IRENE Y. LEE 2099

WASSUP TO ALL MY POOLIES! IT'S ME, WARDA WILSON-- DEADPOOL!

I KNOW, I KNOW--YOU'RE USED TO READING ABOUT MY PATHETIC, SORRY EXCUSE FOR A FATHER, *WADE WILSON*. WELL, I AIN'T HIM.

I'VE GOT THAT OLD BEARDY MOTHERSHOCKER LOCKED AWAY TO *ROT*... AT LEAST UNTIL HE FINALLY BREAKS AND TELLS ME WHAT HAPPENED TO MY DEMONIC MOTHER, *SHIKLAH*.

UNTIL THEN, IMMA KEEP RAISING HELL AND CAUSING TROUBLE WITH MY VERY OWN PERSONAL GANG OF HENCHES, *THE BOBS*.

OH--AND THERE'S ALSO THIS GREY-SUITED 'POOL-LOOKING CHUMP POUNDING HER WAY THROUGH THE STREETS LOOKING FOR ME.

WHATEVER. I'M NOT WORRIED. I'M DEADPOOL. WHAT COULD STOP ME?

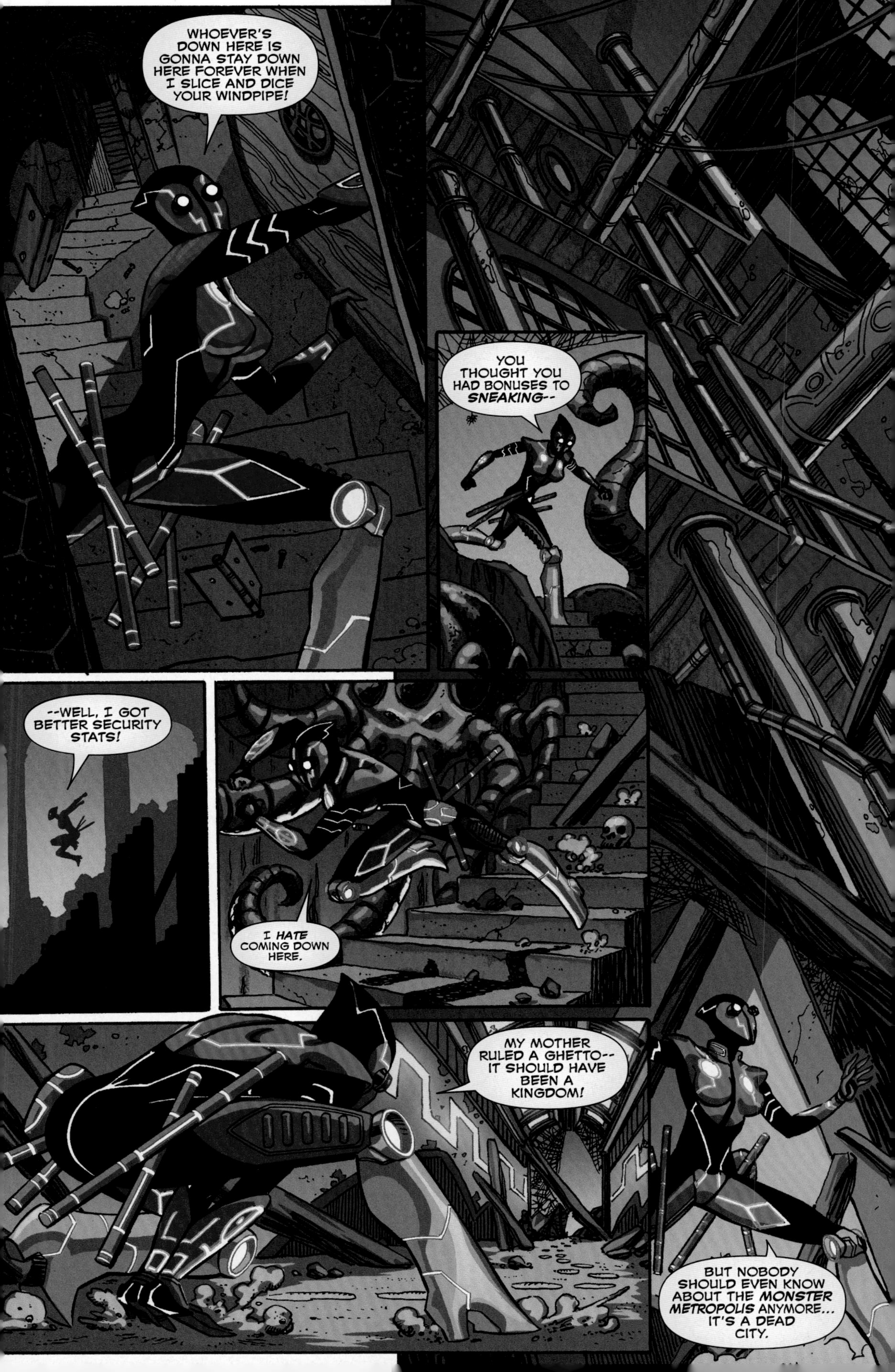
WHOEVER'S DOWN HERE IS GONNA STAY DOWN HERE FOREVER WHEN I SLICE AND DICE YOUR WINDPIPE!
YOU THOUGHT YOU HAD BONUSES TO SNEAKING--
--WELL, I GOT BETTER SECURITY STATS!
I HATE COMING DOWN HERE.
MY MOTHER RULED A GHETTO-- IT SHOULD HAVE BEEN A KINGDOM!
BUT NOBODY SHOULD EVEN KNOW ABOUT THE MONSTER METROPOLIS ANYMORE... IT'S A DEAD CITY.

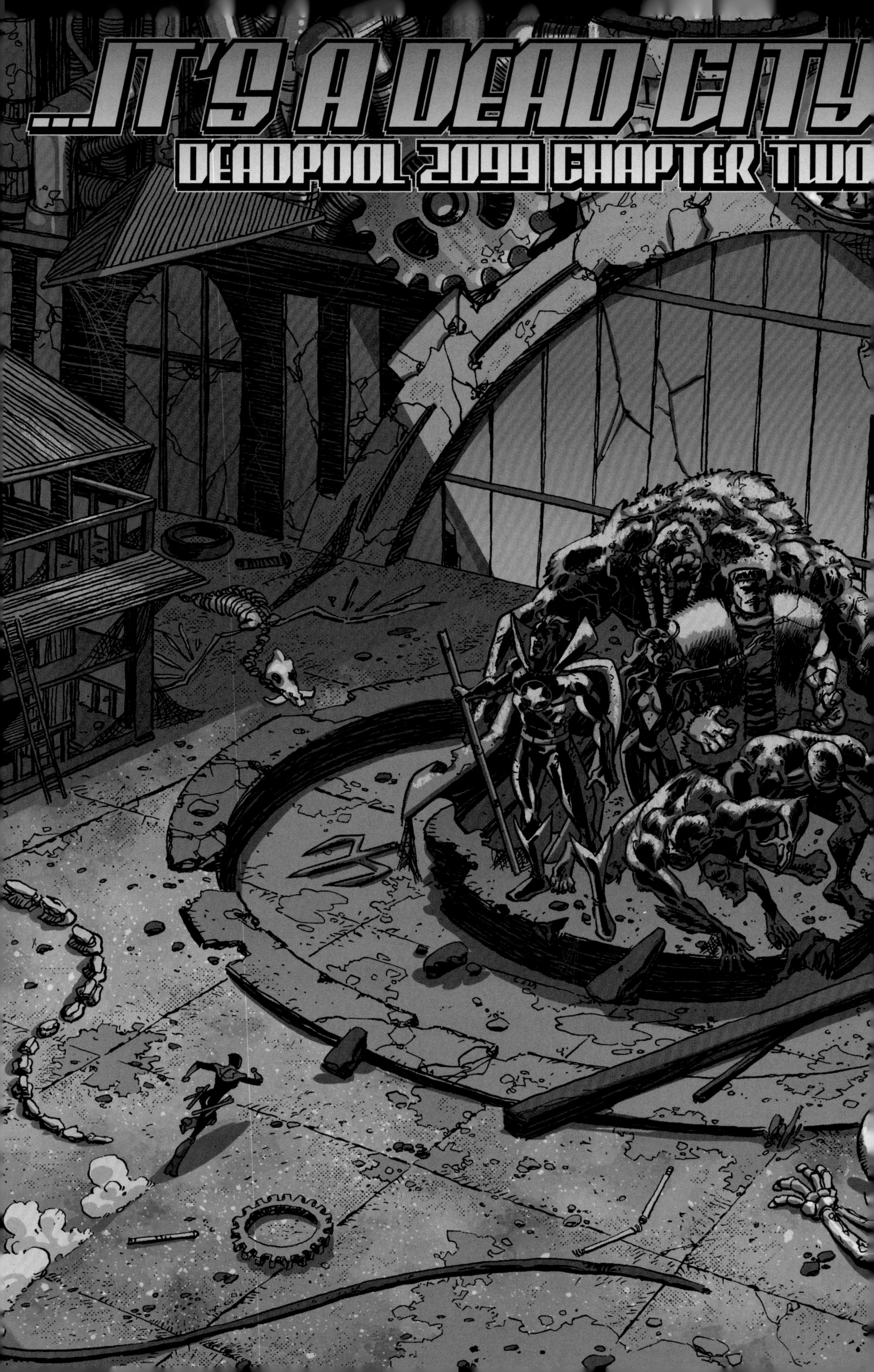

...IT'S A DEAD CITY
DEADPOOL 2099 CHAPTER TWO

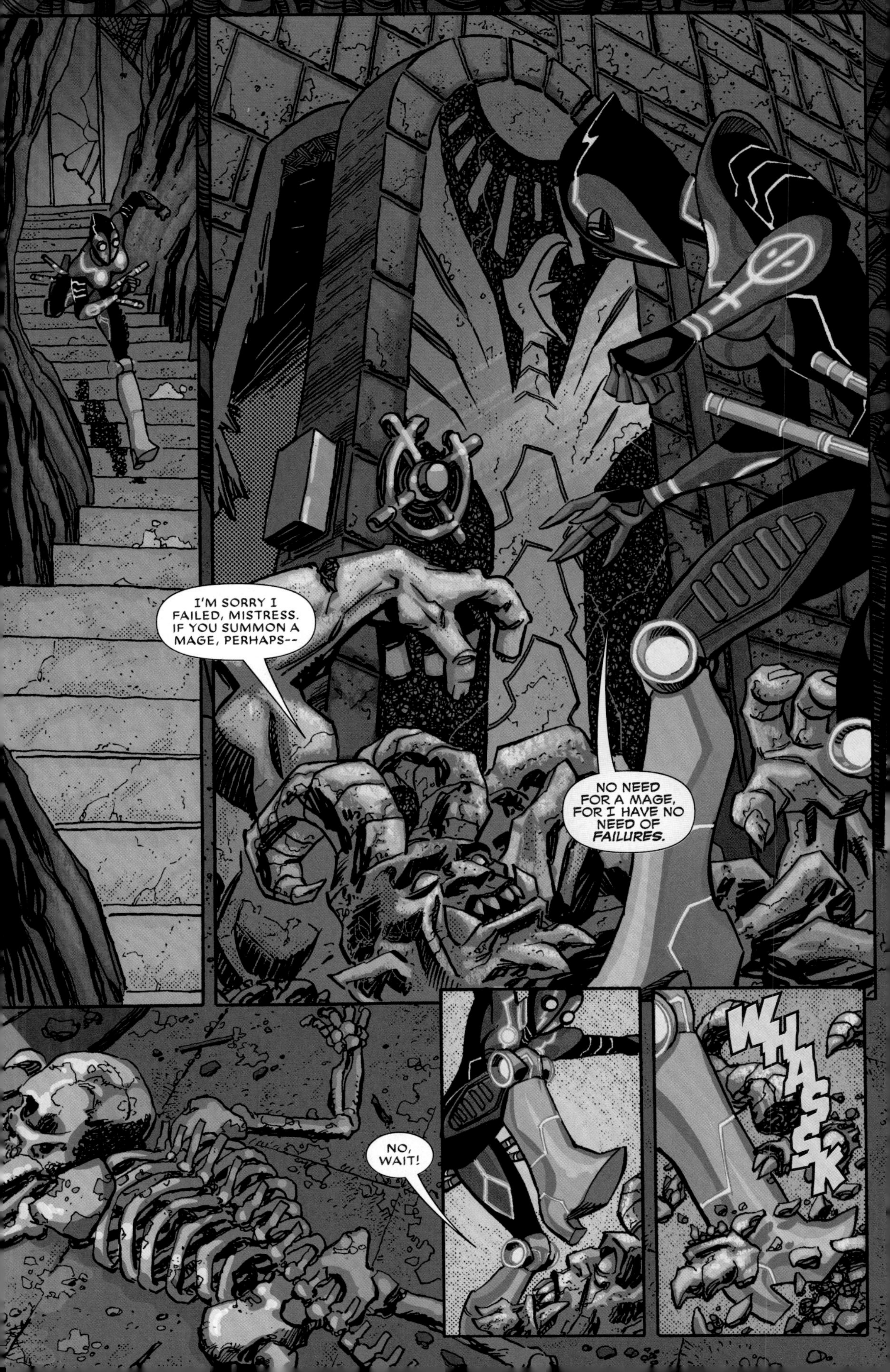
I'M SORRY I FAILED, MISTRESS. IF YOU SUMMON A MAGE, PERHAPS--
NO NEED FOR A MAGE, FOR I HAVE NO NEED OF FAILURES.
NO, WAIT!
WHASSK

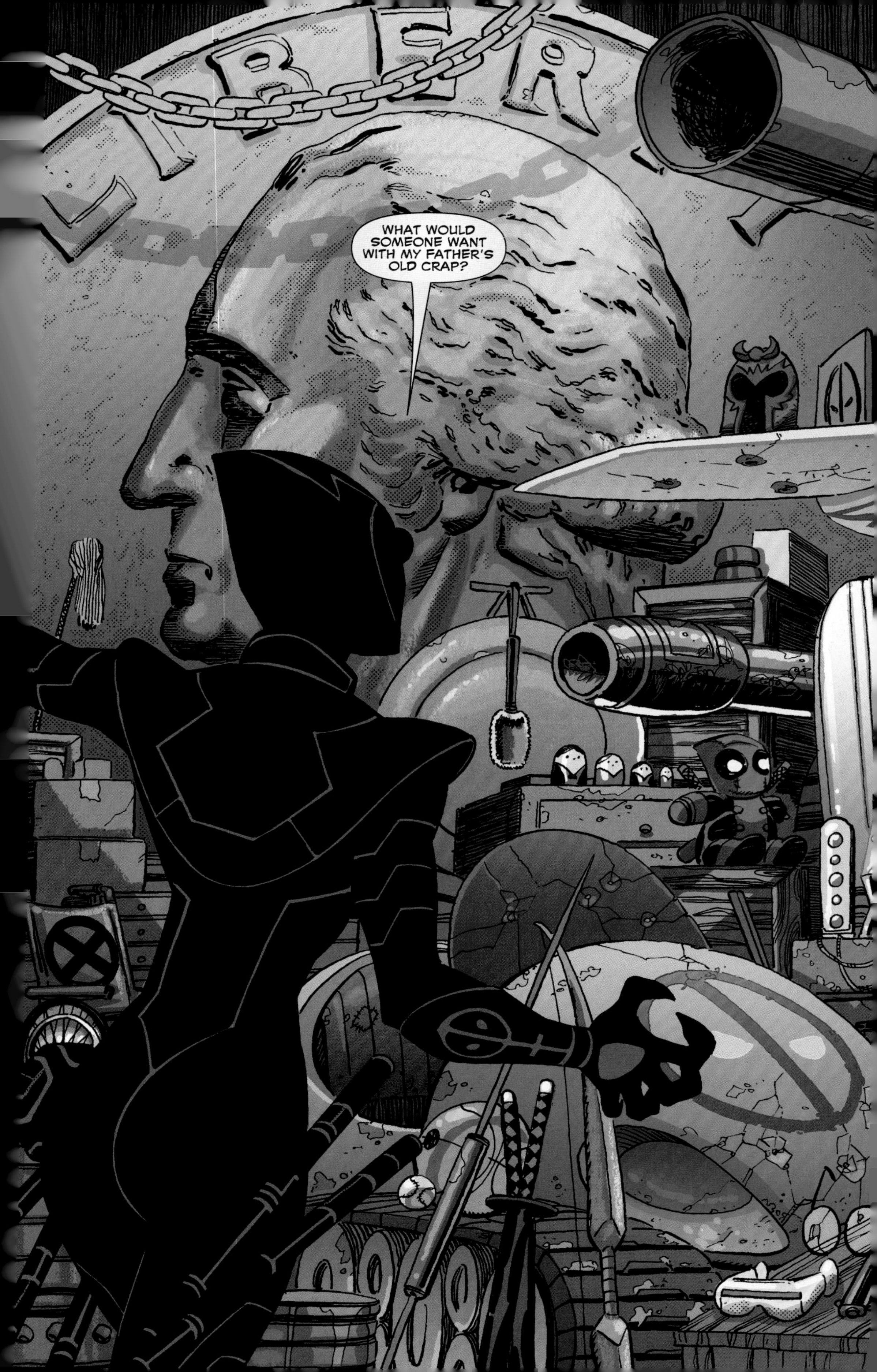
WHAT WOULD SOMEONE WANT WITH MY FATHER'S OLD CRAP?

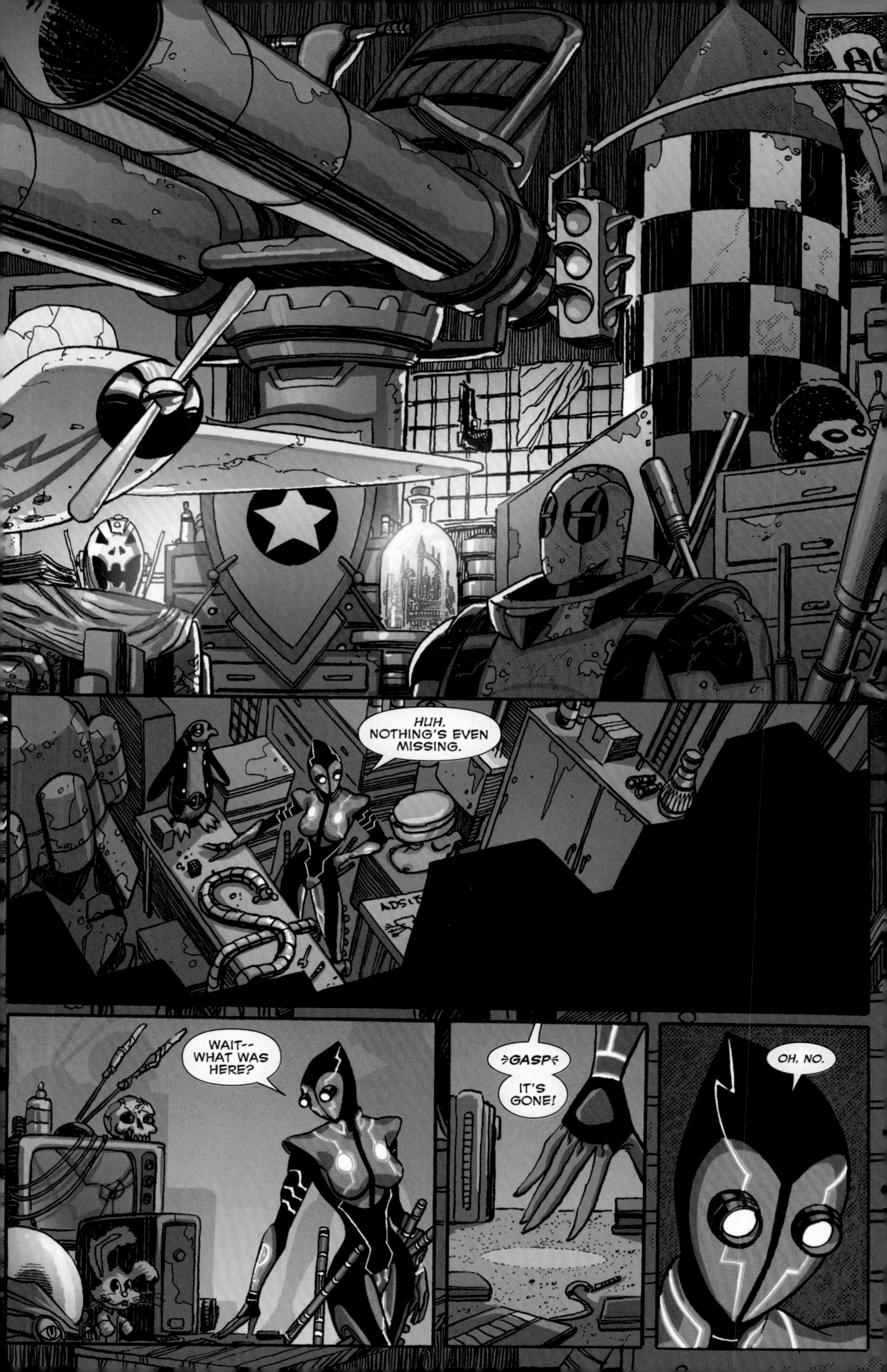
HUH. NOTHING'S EVEN MISSING.
WAIT-- WHAT WAS HERE?
GASP
IT'S GONE!
OH, NO.

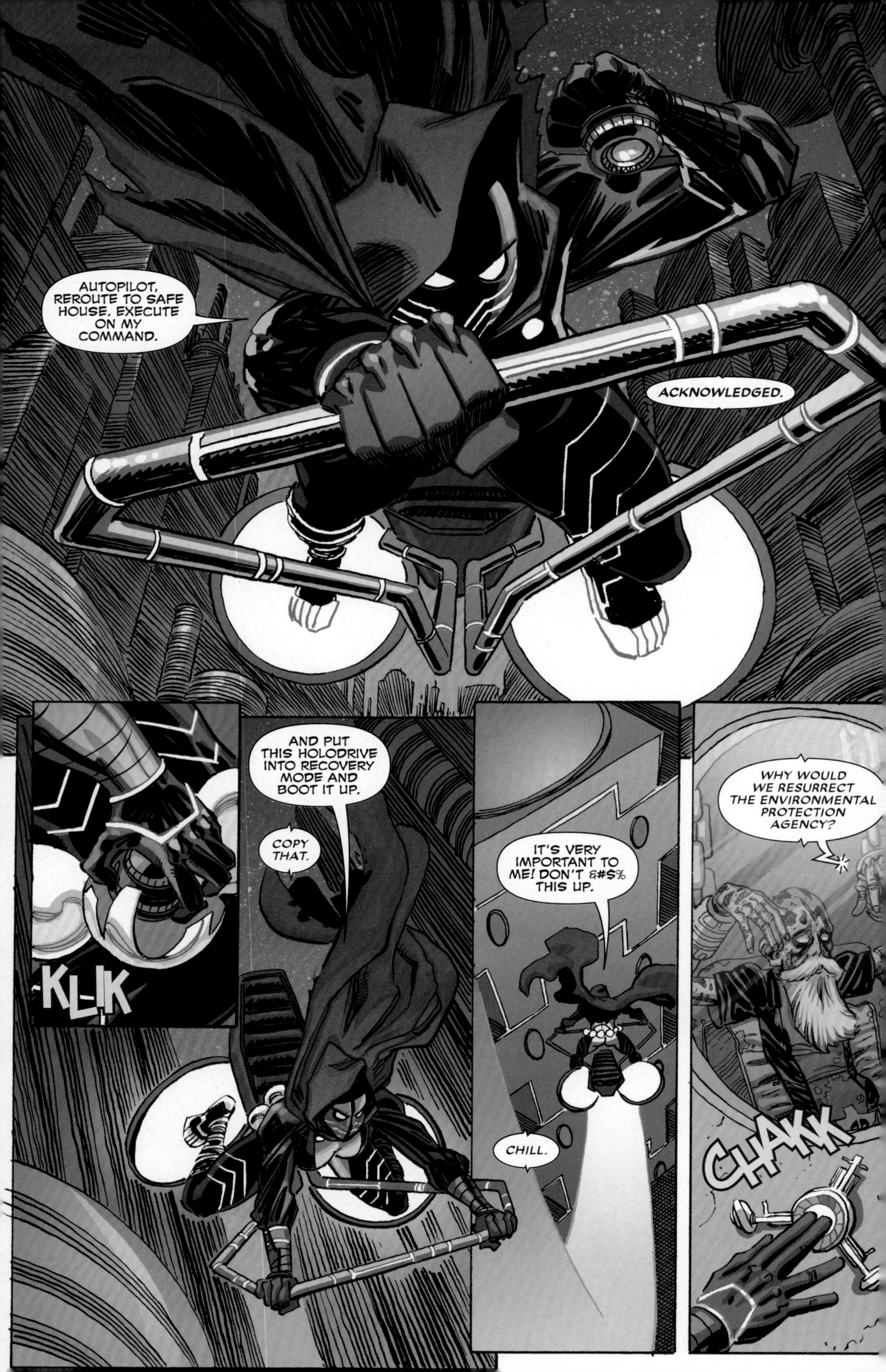
AUTOPILOT, REROUTE TO SAFE HOUSE. EXECUTE ON MY COMMAND.
ACKNOWLEDGED.
KLIK
AND PUT THIS HOLODRIVE INTO RECOVERY MODE AND BOOT IT UP.
COPY THAT.
IT'S VERY IMPORTANT TO ME! DON'T &#$% THIS UP.
CHILL.
WHY WOULD WE RESURRECT THE ENVIRONMENTAL PROTECTION AGENCY?
CHAKK

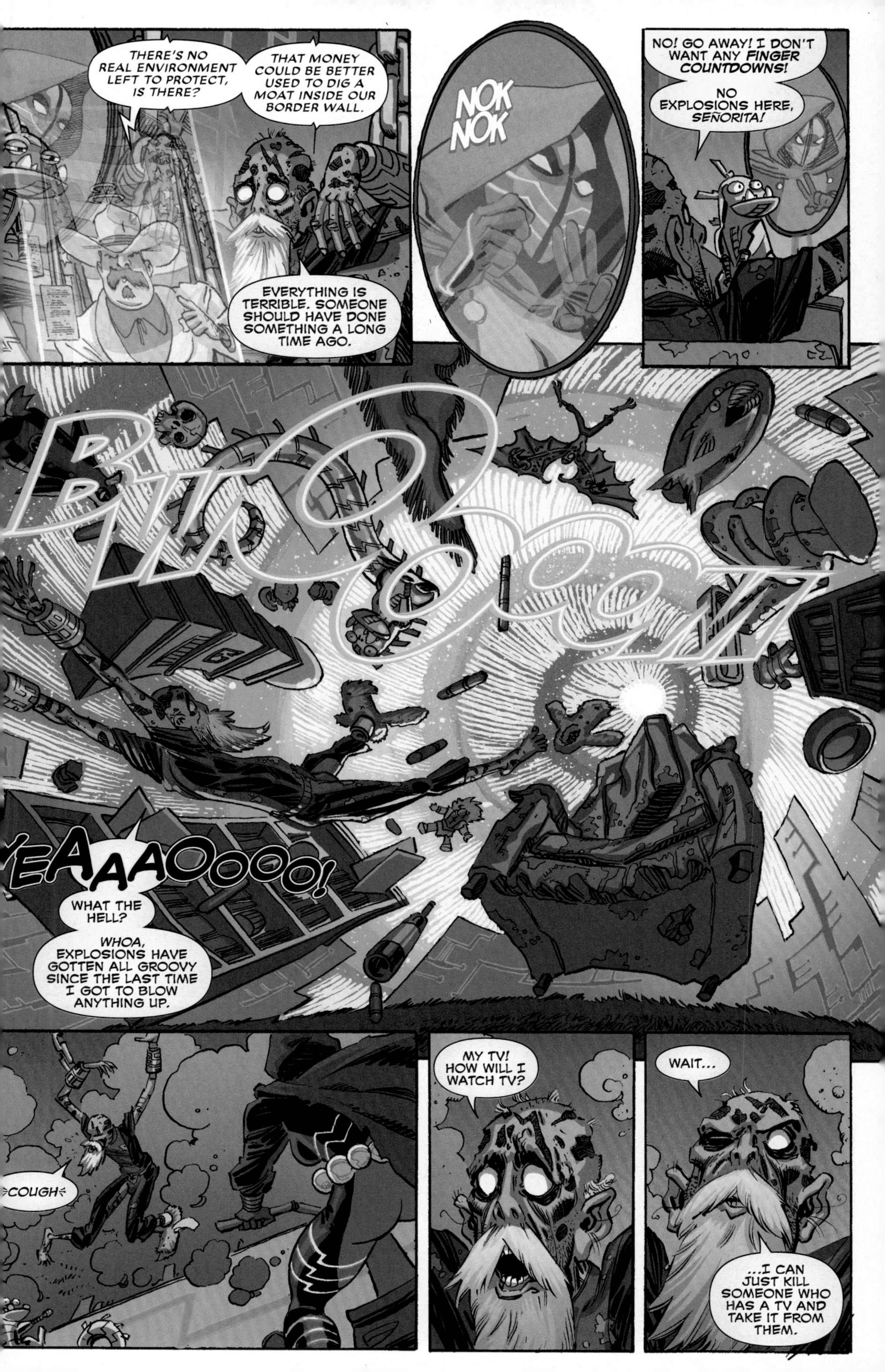
THERE'S NO REAL ENVIRONMENT LEFT TO PROTECT, IS THERE?
THAT MONEY COULD BE BETTER USED TO DIG A MOAT INSIDE OUR BORDER WALL.
EVERYTHING IS TERRIBLE. SOMEONE SHOULD HAVE DONE SOMETHING A LONG TIME AGO.
NOK NOK
NO! GO AWAY! I DON'T WANT ANY *FINGER COUNTDOWNS!*
NO EXPLOSIONS HERE, *SEÑORITA!*
BTHOOOOM
YEAAAOOOOO!
WHAT THE HELL?
WHOA, EXPLOSIONS HAVE GOTTEN ALL GROOVY SINCE THE LAST TIME I GOT TO BLOW ANYTHING UP.
COUGH
MY TV! HOW WILL I WATCH TV?
WAIT...
...I CAN JUST KILL SOMEONE WHO HAS A TV AND TAKE IT FROM THEM.

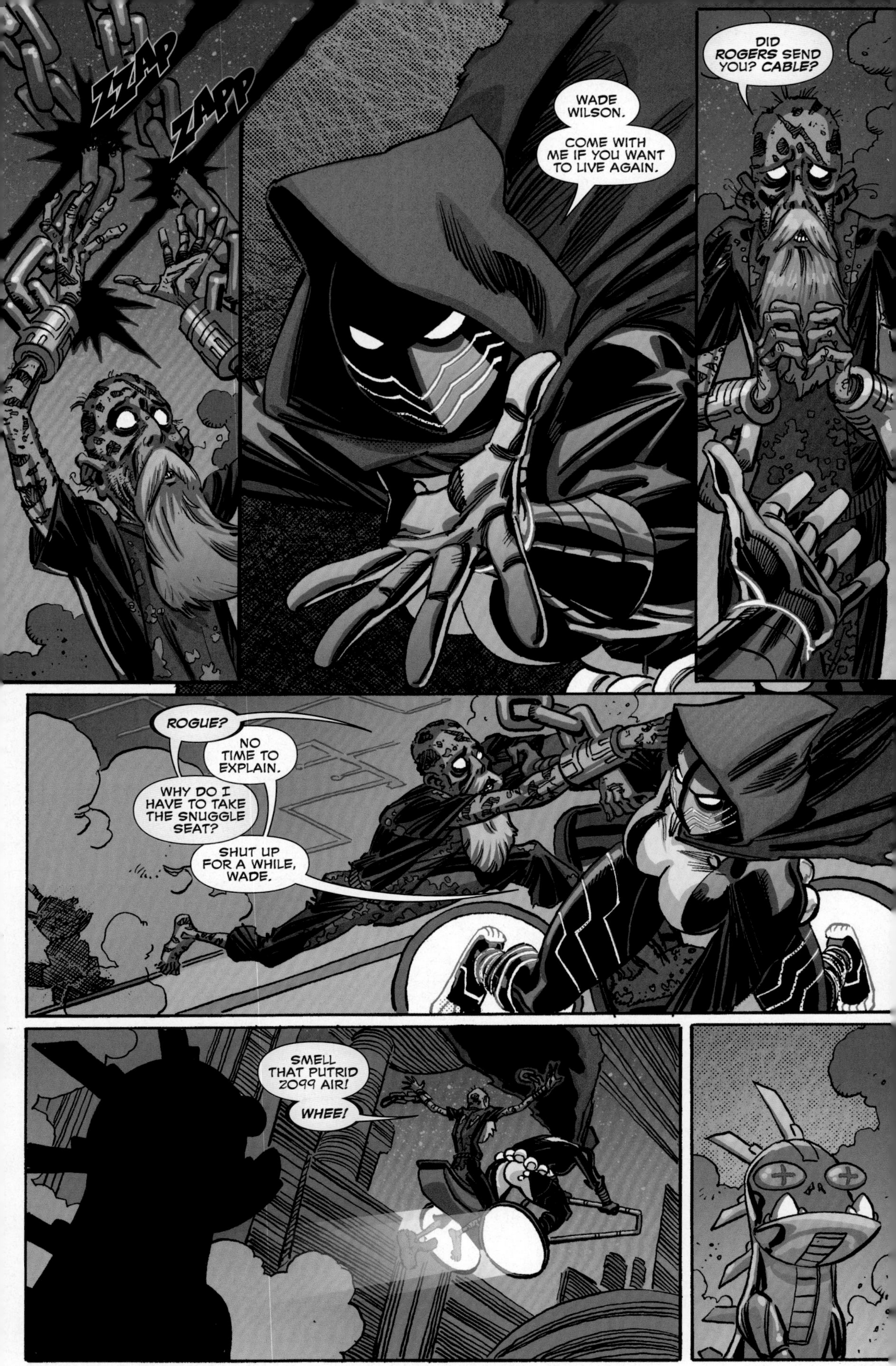
ZZAP
ZAPP
WADE WILSON.
COME WITH ME IF YOU WANT TO LIVE AGAIN.
DID ROGERS SEND YOU? CABLE?
ROGUE?
NO TIME TO EXPLAIN.
WHY DO I HAVE TO TAKE THE SNUGGLE SEAT?
SHUT UP FOR A WHILE, WADE.
SMELL THAT PUTRID 2099 AIR!
WHEE!

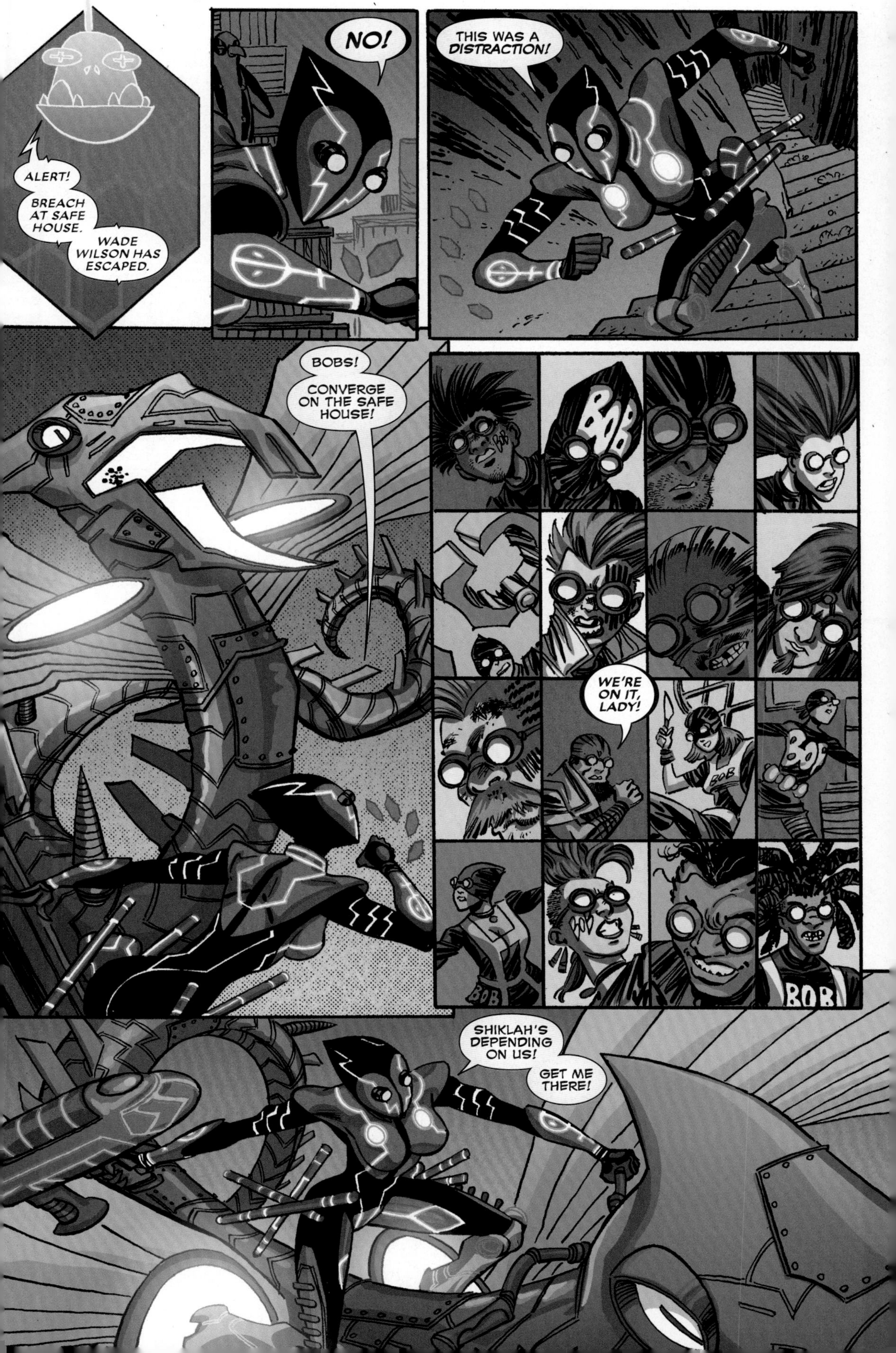
ALERT!
BREACH AT SAFE HOUSE.
WADE WILSON HAS ESCAPED.
NO!
THIS WAS A DISTRACTION!
BOBS!
CONVERGE ON THE SAFE HOUSE!
BOB
WE'RE ON IT, LADY!
BOB
BOB
BOB
SHIKLAH'S DEPENDING ON US!
GET ME THERE!

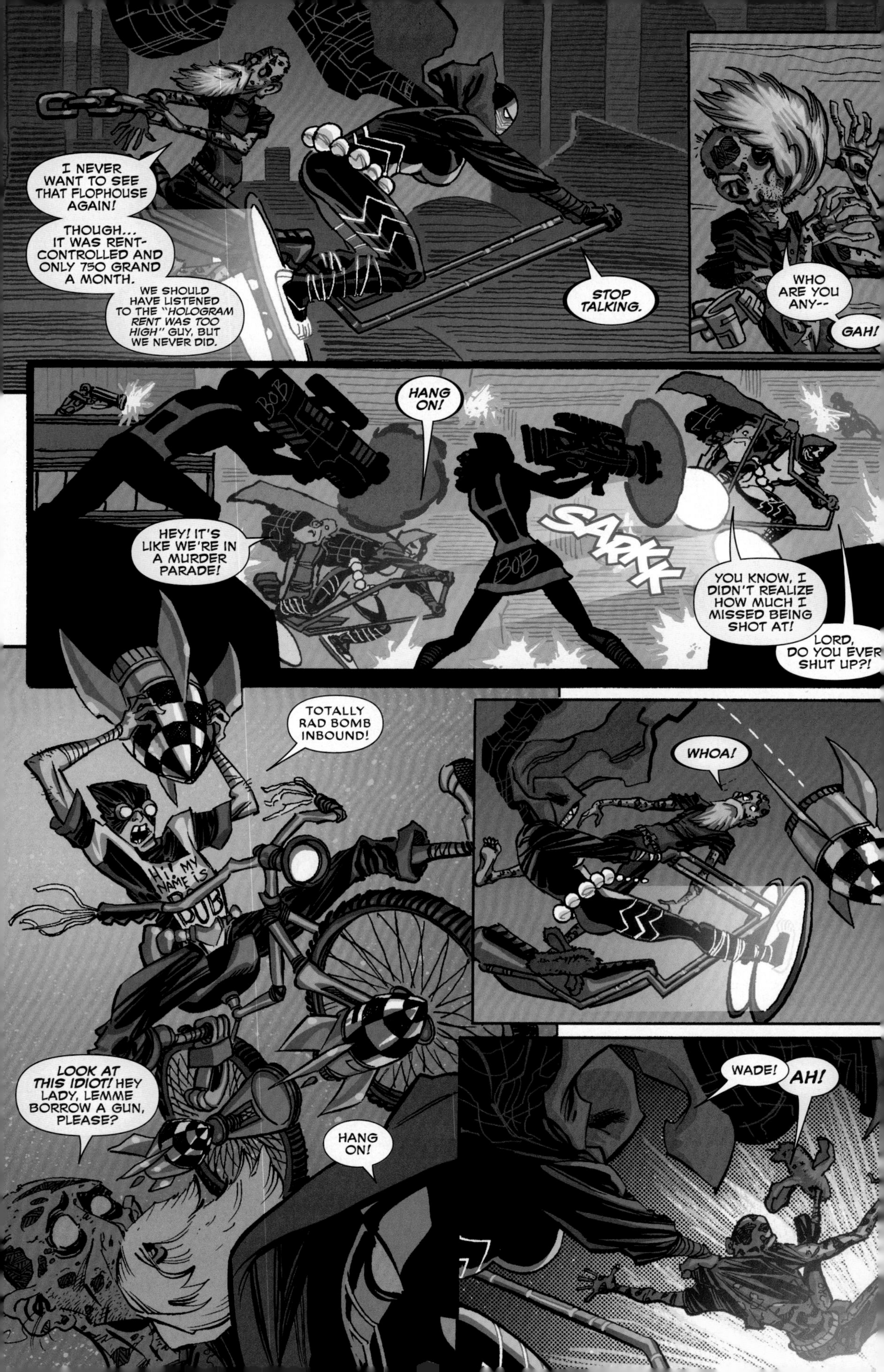
I NEVER WANT TO SEE THAT FLOPHOUSE AGAIN!
THOUGH... IT WAS RENT-CONTROLLED AND ONLY 750 GRAND A MONTH.
WE SHOULD HAVE LISTENED TO THE "HOLOGRAM RENT WAS TOO HIGH" GUY, BUT WE NEVER DID.
STOP TALKING.
WHO ARE YOU ANY--
GAH!
HANG ON!
HEY! IT'S LIKE WE'RE IN A MURDER PARADE!
SARKK
YOU KNOW, I DIDN'T REALIZE HOW MUCH I MISSED BEING SHOT AT!
LORD, DO YOU EVER SHUT UP?!
TOTALLY RAD BOMB INBOUND!
HI! MY NAME IS BOB
WHOA!
LOOK AT THIS IDIOT! HEY LADY, LEMME BORROW A GUN, PLEASE?
HANG ON!
WADE!
AH!

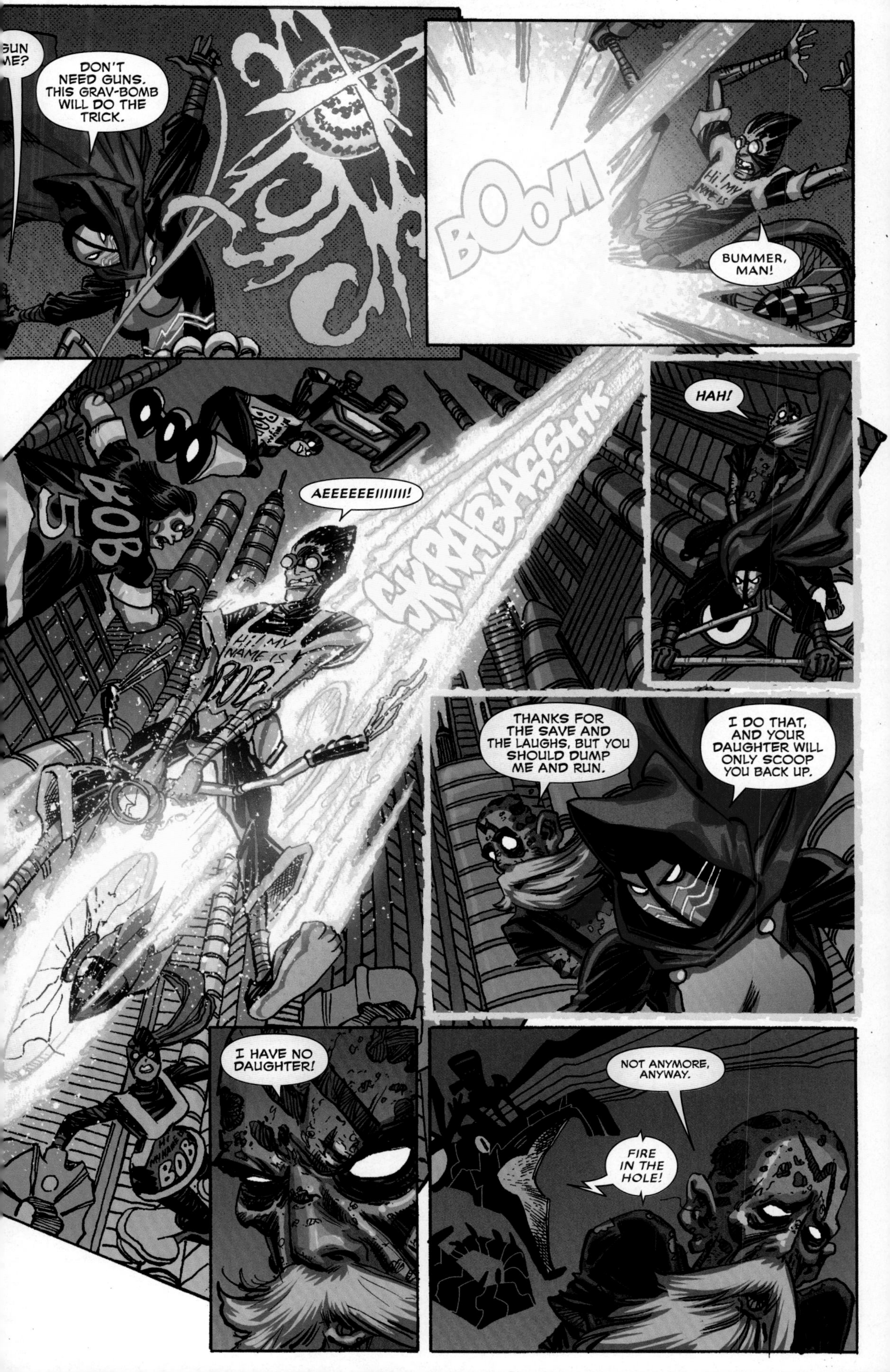
GUN
ME?
DON'T NEED GUNS. THIS GRAV-BOMB WILL DO THE TRICK.
BOOM
BUMMER, MAN!
AEEEEEEIIIIIII!
SKRABASSHK
HAH!
THANKS FOR THE SAVE AND THE LAUGHS, BUT YOU SHOULD DUMP ME AND RUN.
I DO THAT, AND YOUR DAUGHTER WILL ONLY SCOOP YOU BACK UP.
I HAVE NO DAUGHTER!
NOT ANYMORE, ANYWAY.
FIRE IN THE HOLE!

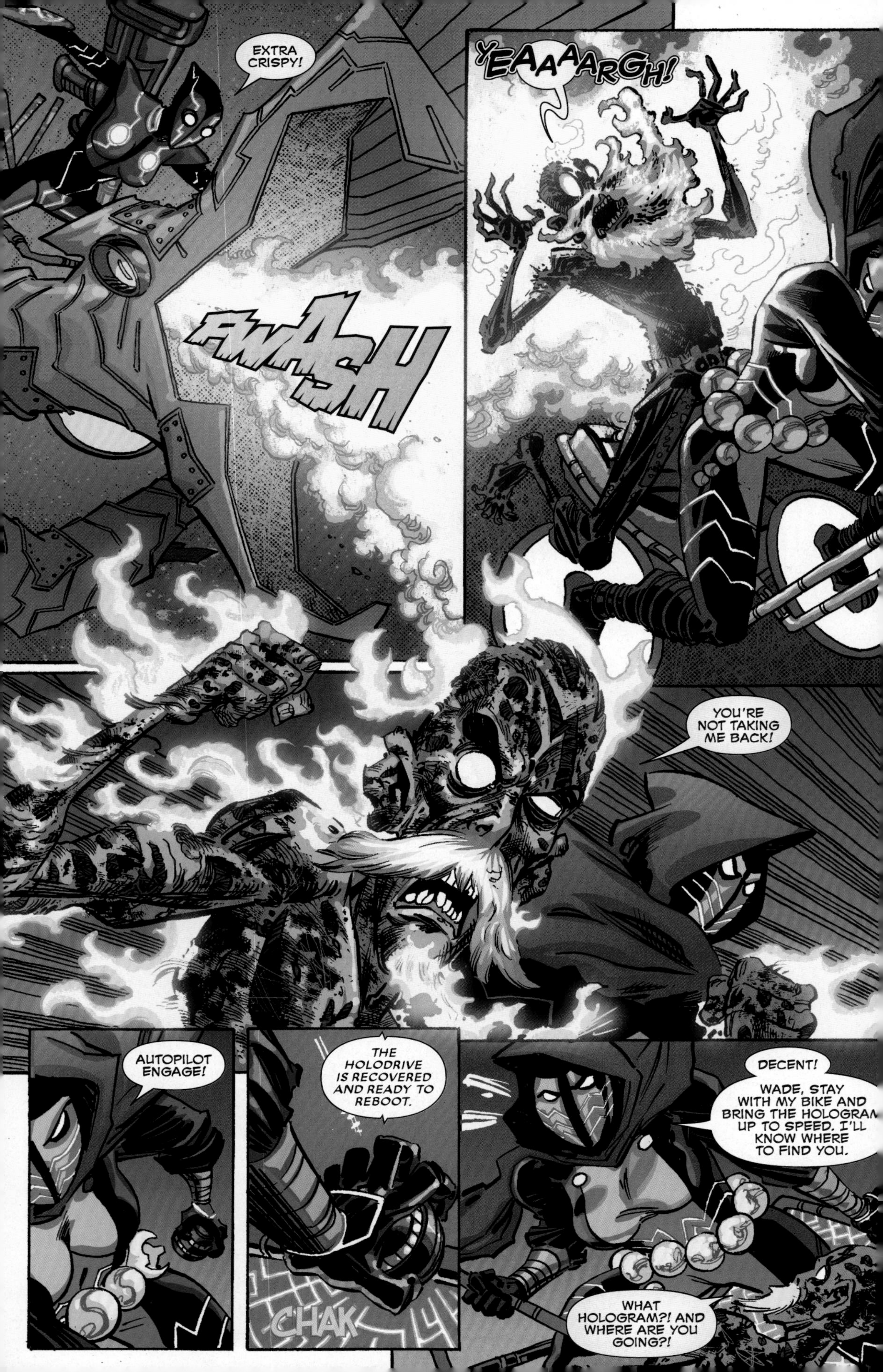
EXTRA CRISPY!
FWAASH
YEAAAARGH!
YOU'RE NOT TAKING ME BACK!
AUTOPILOT ENGAGE!
THE HOLODRIVE IS RECOVERED AND READY TO REBOOT.
CHAK
DECENT!
WADE, STAY WITH MY BIKE AND BRING THE HOLOGRAM UP TO SPEED. I'LL KNOW WHERE TO FIND YOU.
WHAT HOLOGRAM?! AND WHERE ARE YOU GOING?!

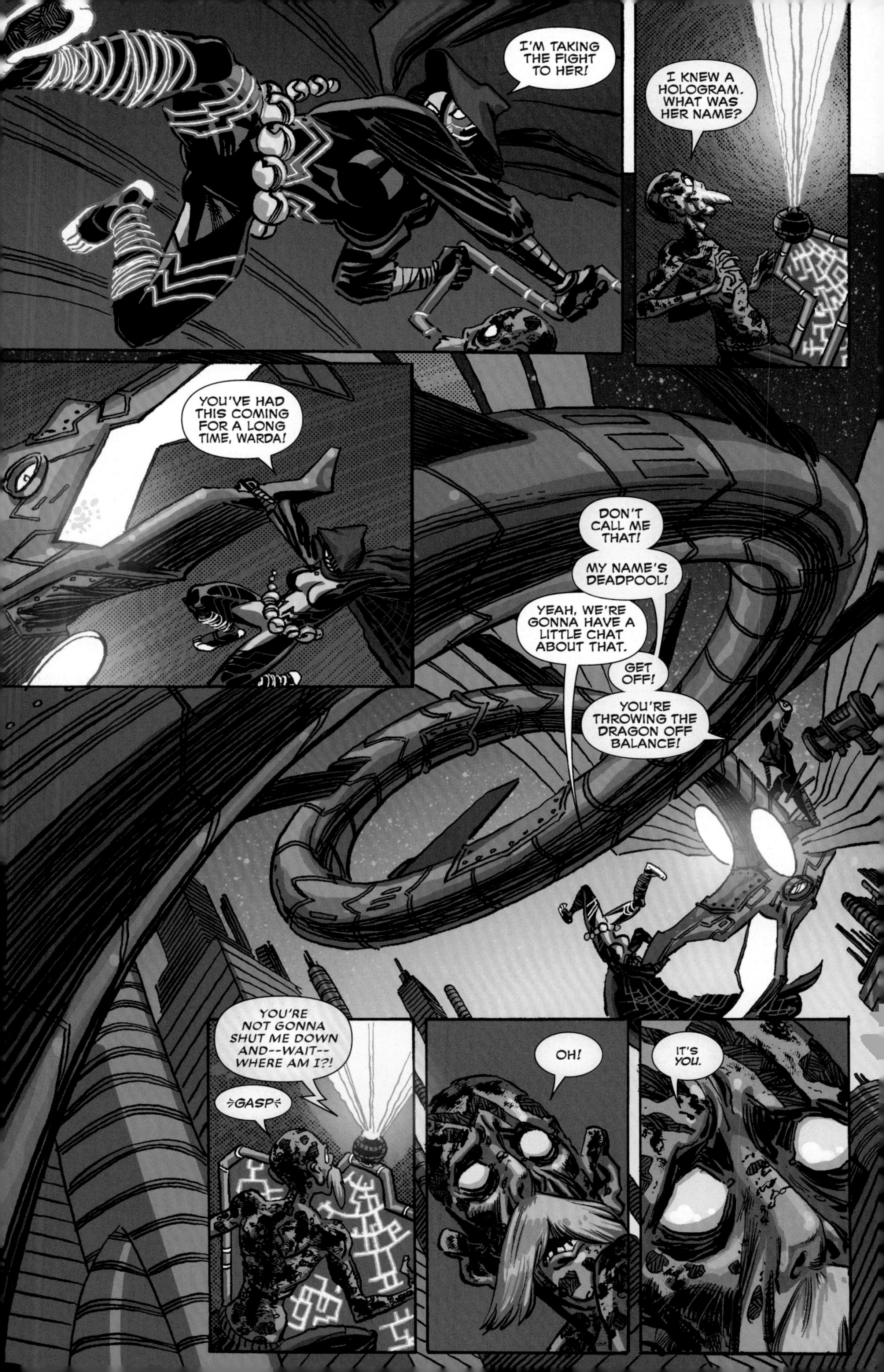
I'M TAKING THE FIGHT TO HER!
I KNEW A HOLOGRAM. WHAT WAS HER NAME?
YOU'VE HAD THIS COMING FOR A LONG TIME, WARDA!
DON'T CALL ME THAT!
MY NAME'S DEADPOOL!
YEAH, WE'RE GONNA HAVE A LITTLE CHAT ABOUT THAT.
GET OFF!
YOU'RE THROWING THE DRAGON OFF BALANCE!
YOU'RE NOT GONNA SHUT ME DOWN AND--WAIT-- WHERE AM I?!
GASP
OH!
IT'S YOU.

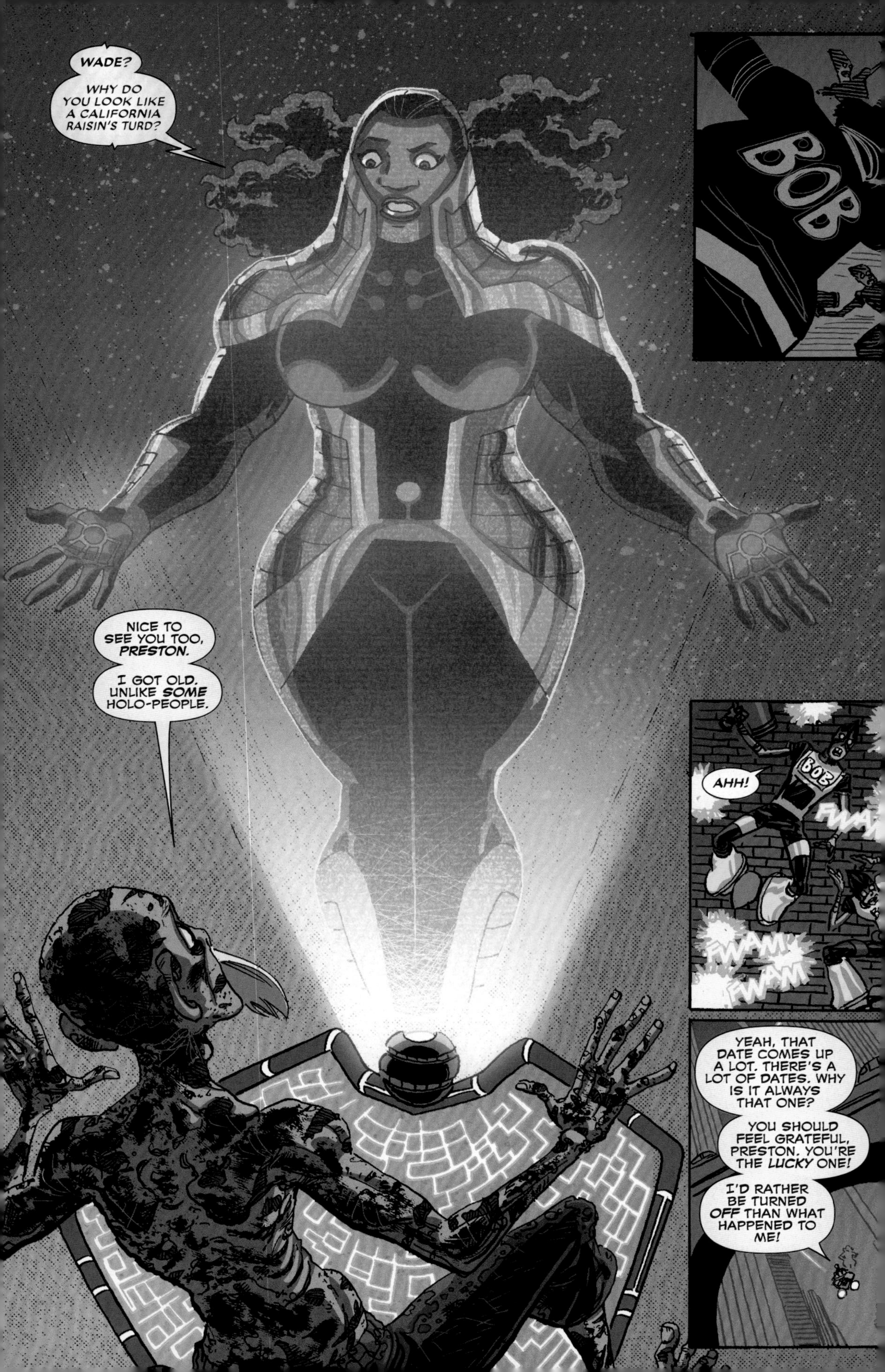
WADE?
WHY DO YOU LOOK LIKE A CALIFORNIA RAISIN'S TURD?
BOB
NICE TO SEE YOU TOO, PRESTON.
I GOT OLD. UNLIKE SOME HOLO-PEOPLE.
BOB
AHH!
FWAM
FWAM!
FWAM
FWAM
YEAH, THAT DATE COMES UP A LOT. THERE'S A LOT OF DATES. WHY IS IT ALWAYS THAT ONE?
YOU SHOULD FEEL GRATEFUL, PRESTON. YOU'RE THE LUCKY ONE!
I'D RATHER BE TURNED OFF THAN WHAT HAPPENED TO ME!

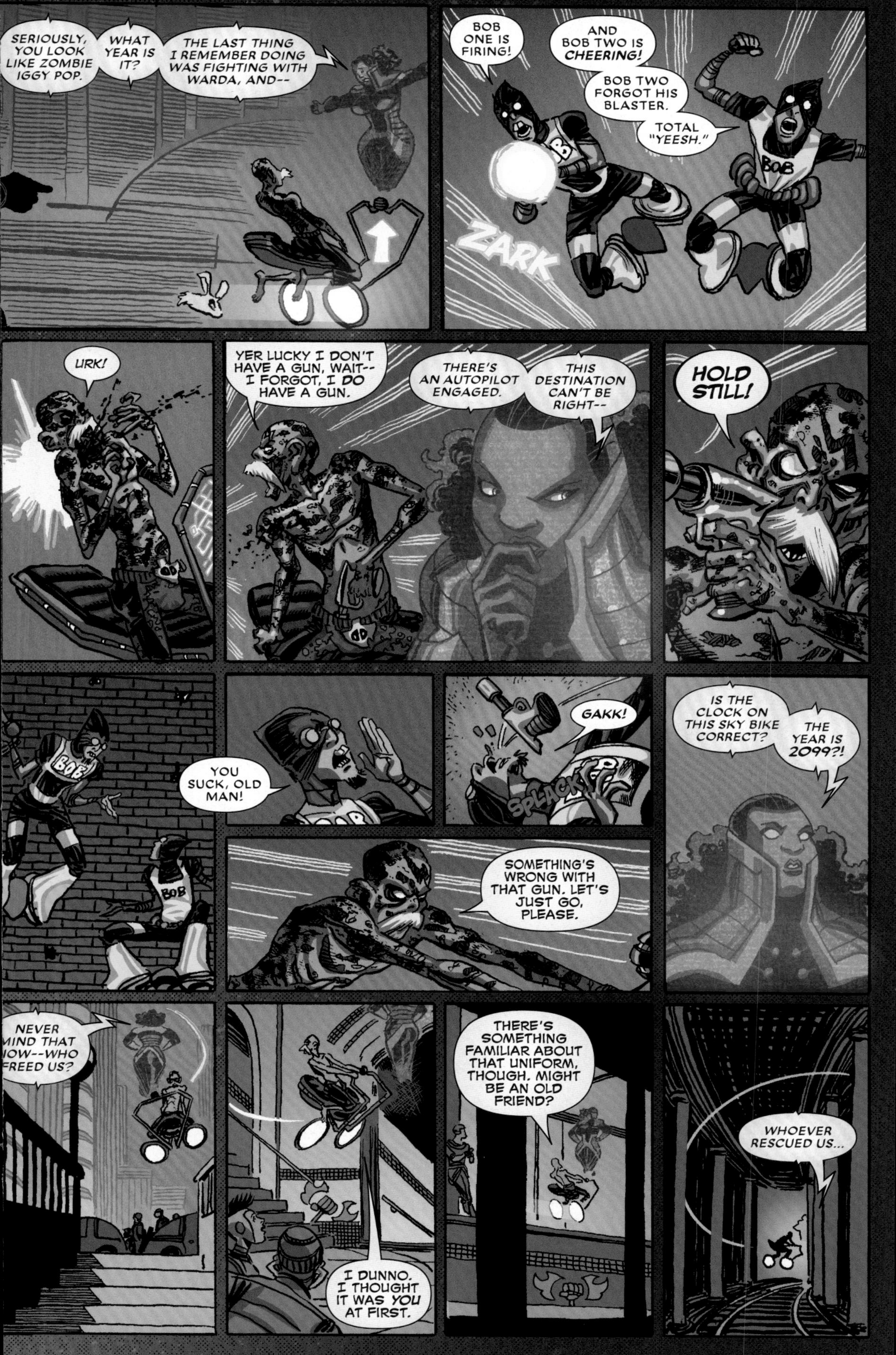
SERIOUSLY, YOU LOOK LIKE ZOMBIE IGGY POP.
WHAT YEAR IS IT?
THE LAST THING I REMEMBER DOING WAS FIGHTING WITH WARDA, AND--
BOB ONE IS FIRING!
AND BOB TWO IS CHEERING!
BOB TWO FORGOT HIS BLASTER.
TOTAL "YEESH."
ZARK
URK!
YER LUCKY I DON'T HAVE A GUN, WAIT-- I FORGOT, I DO HAVE A GUN.
THERE'S AN AUTOPILOT ENGAGED.
THIS DESTINATION CAN'T BE RIGHT--
HOLD STILL!
YOU SUCK, OLD MAN!
GAKK!
SPLACK
IS THE CLOCK ON THIS SKY BIKE CORRECT?
THE YEAR IS 2099?!
SOMETHING'S WRONG WITH THAT GUN. LET'S JUST GO, PLEASE.
NEVER MIND THAT NOW--WHO FREED US?
I DUNNO. I THOUGHT IT WAS YOU AT FIRST.
THERE'S SOMETHING FAMILIAR ABOUT THAT UNIFORM, THOUGH. MIGHT BE AN OLD FRIEND?
WHOEVER RESCUED US...

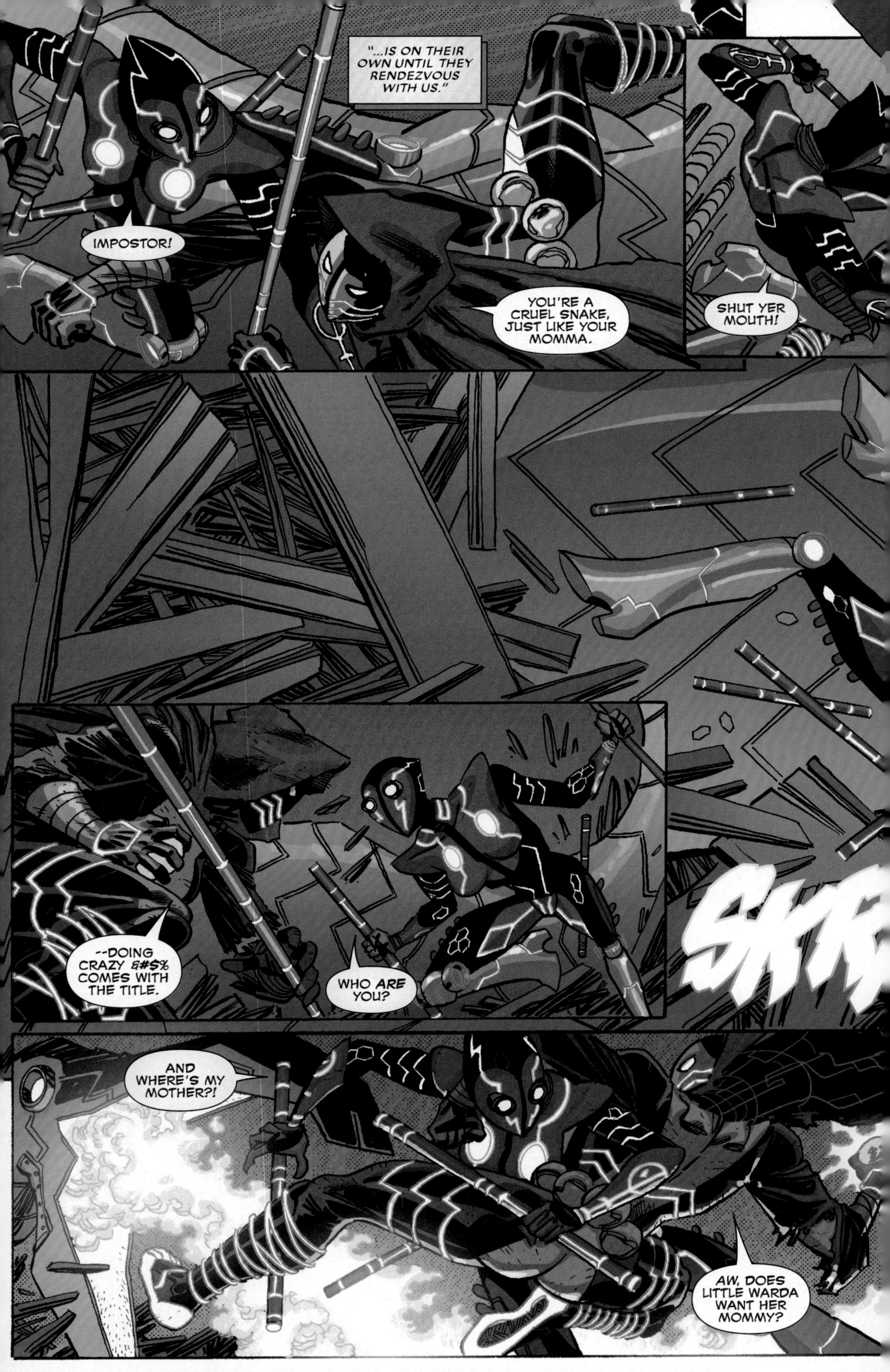
"...IS ON THEIR OWN UNTIL THEY RENDEZVOUS WITH US."
IMPOSTOR!
YOU'RE A CRUEL SNAKE, JUST LIKE YOUR MOMMA.
SHUT YER MOUTH!
--DOING CRAZY &#$% COMES WITH THE TITLE.
WHO ARE YOU?
SKR
AND WHERE'S MY MOTHER?!
AW, DOES LITTLE WARDA WANT HER MOMMY?

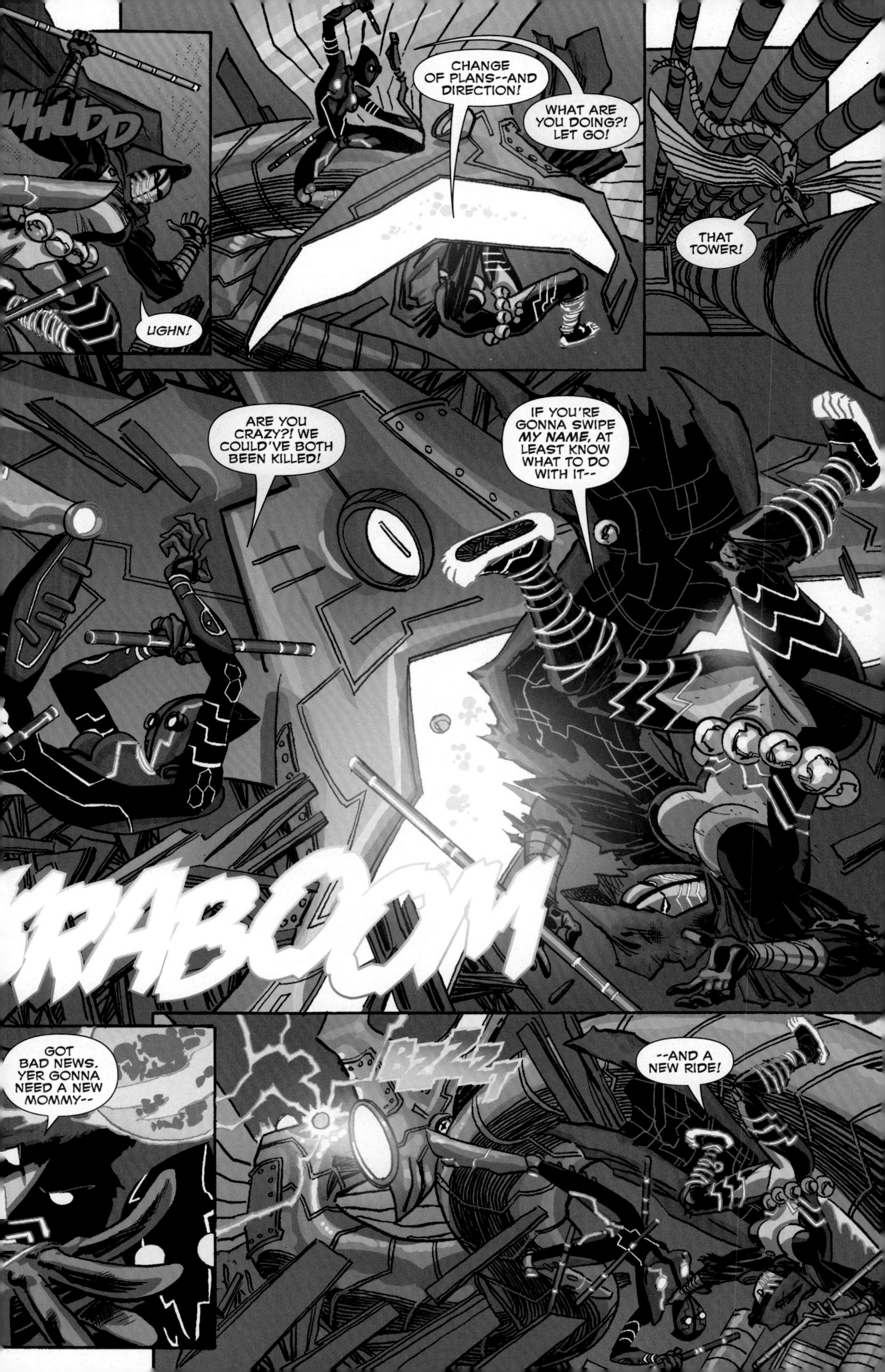
WHUDD
UGHN!
CHANGE OF PLANS--AND DIRECTION!
WHAT ARE YOU DOING?! LET GO!
THAT TOWER!
ARE YOU CRAZY?! WE COULD'VE BOTH BEEN KILLED!
IF YOU'RE GONNA SWIPE *MY NAME*, AT LEAST KNOW WHAT TO DO WITH IT--
KRABOOM
GOT BAD NEWS. YER GONNA NEED A NEW MOMMY--
BZZZT
--AND A NEW RIDE!

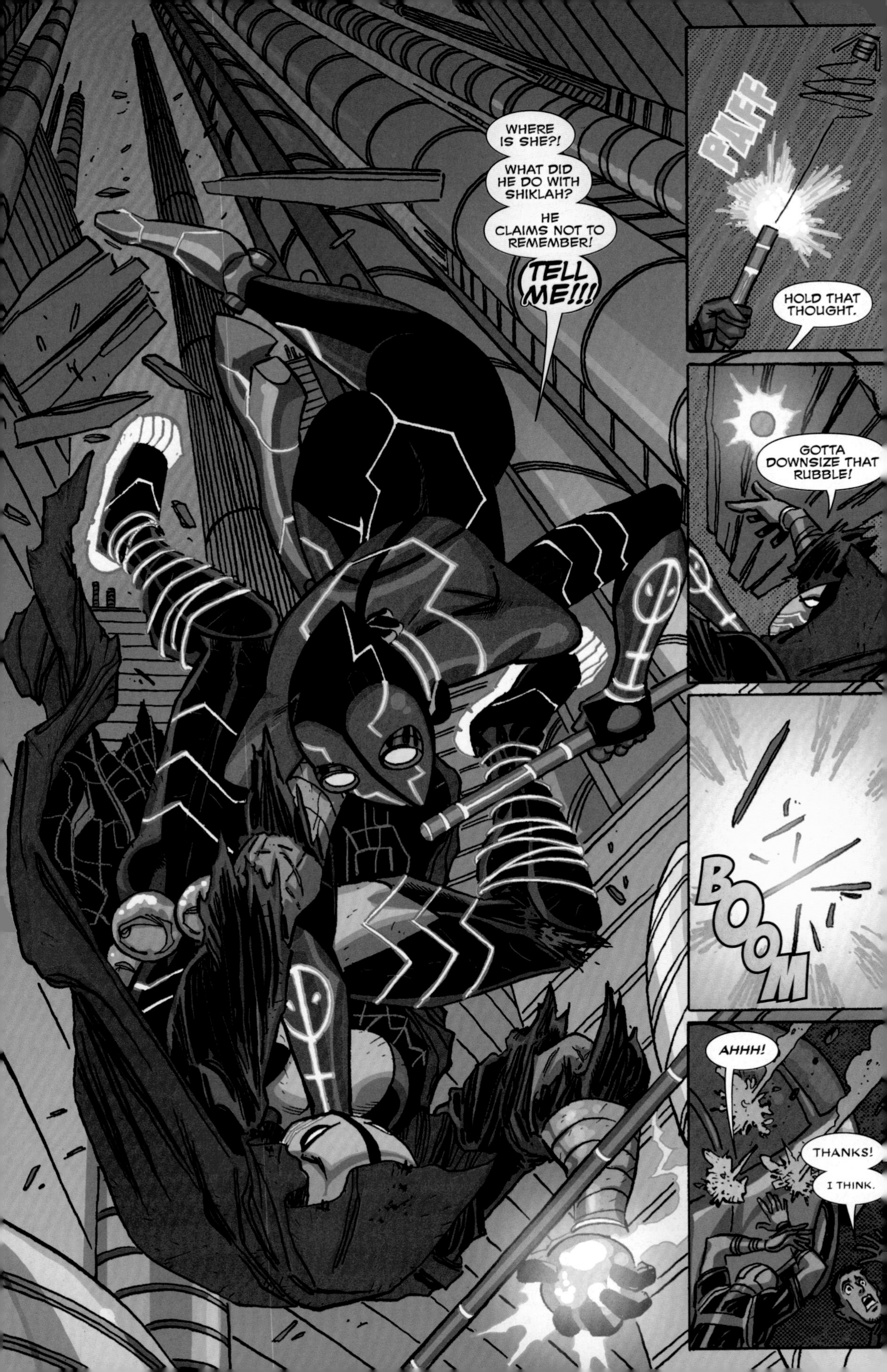
WHERE IS SHE?!
WHAT DID HE DO WITH SHIKLAH?
HE CLAIMS NOT TO REMEMBER!
TELL ME!!!
PAFF
HOLD THAT THOUGHT.
GOTTA DOWNSIZE THAT RUBBLE!
BOOM
AHHH!
THANKS!
I THINK.

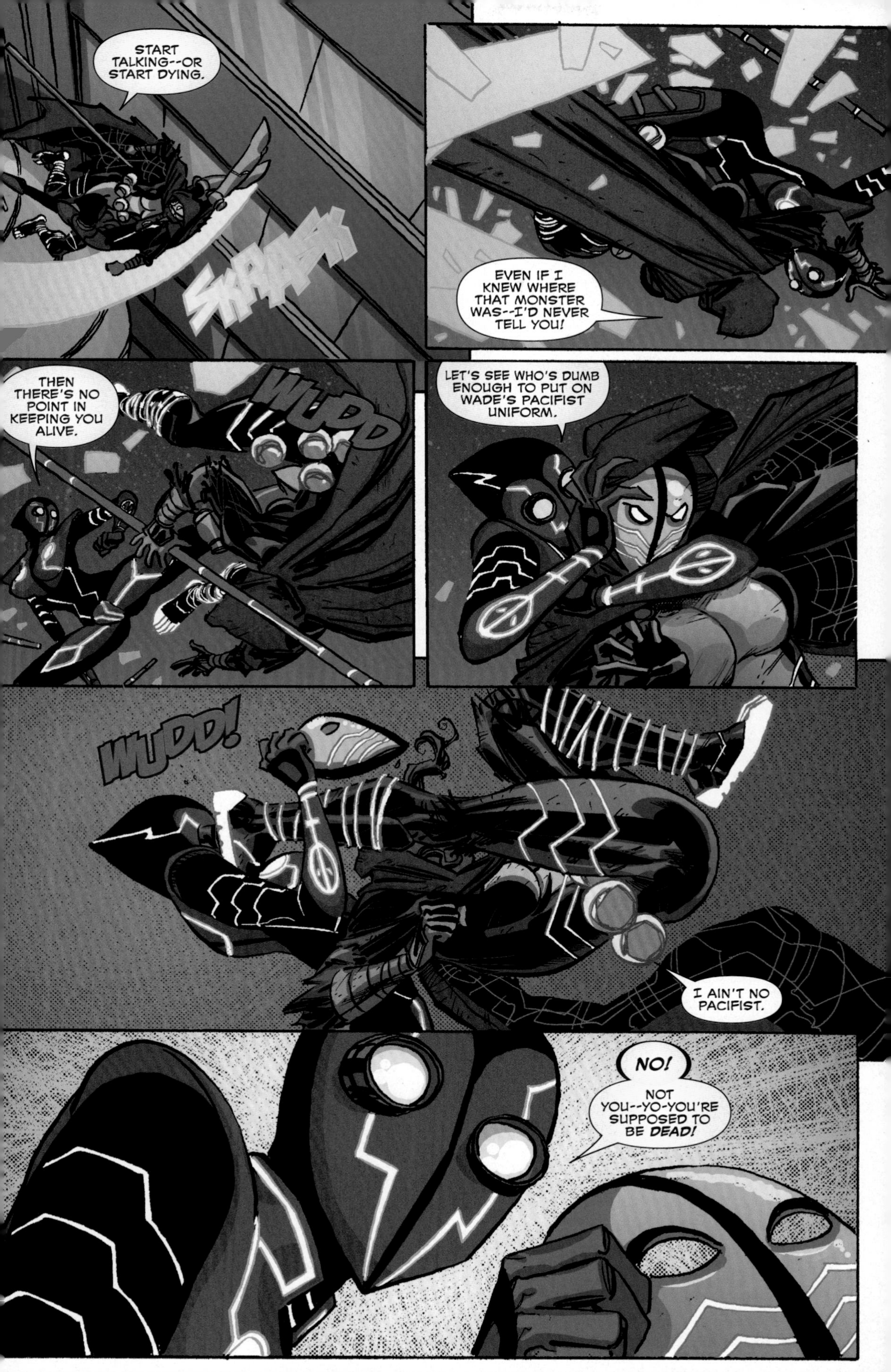

START TALKING--OR START DYING.
SKRASK
EVEN IF I KNEW WHERE THAT MONSTER WAS--I'D NEVER TELL YOU!
THEN THERE'S NO POINT IN KEEPING YOU ALIVE.
WUDD
LET'S SEE WHO'S DUMB ENOUGH TO PUT ON WADE'S PACIFIST UNIFORM.
WUDD!
I AIN'T NO PACIFIST.
NO!
NOT YOU--YO-YOU'RE SUPPOSED TO BE DEAD!

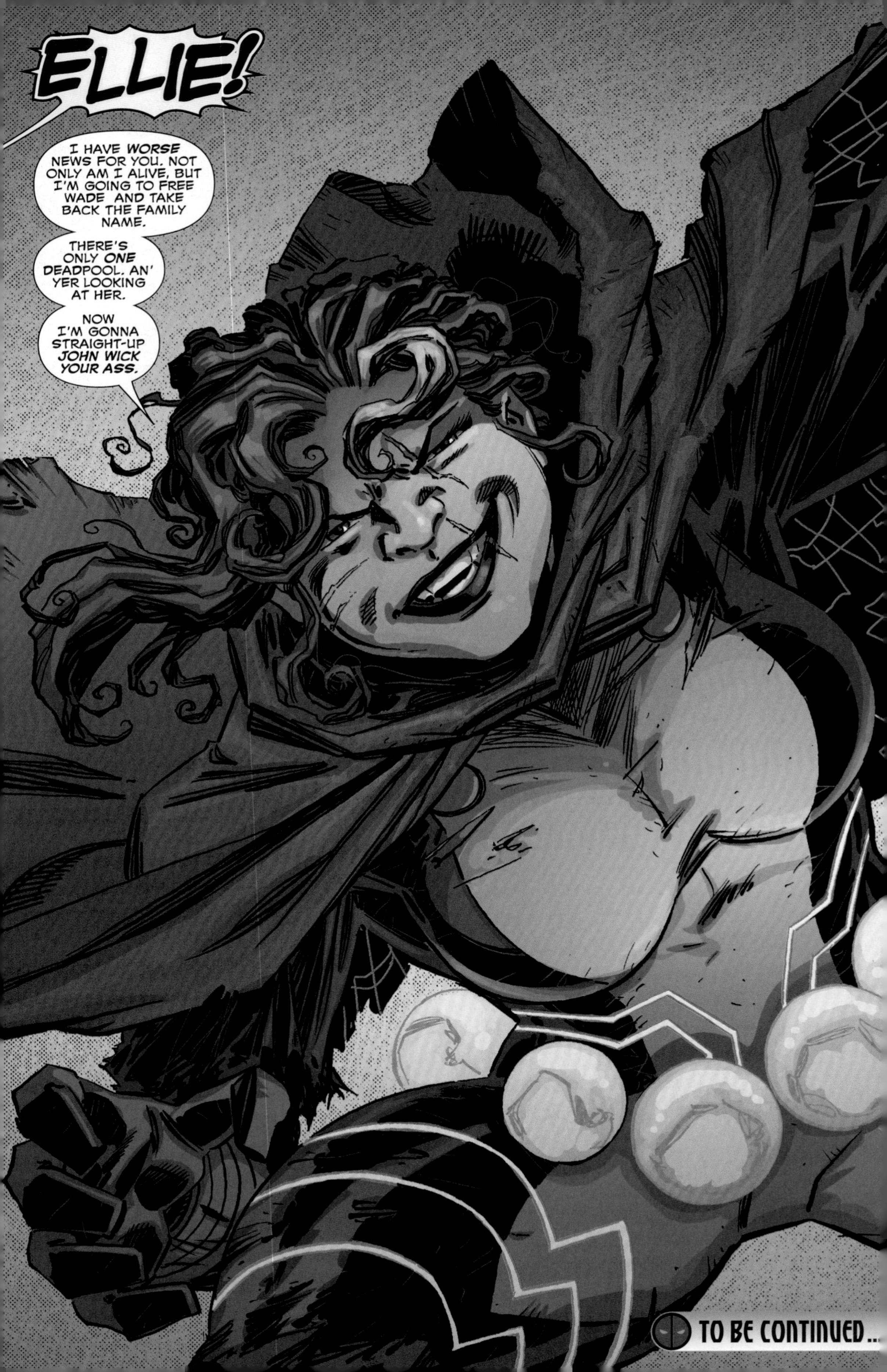
ELLIE!
I HAVE WORSE NEWS FOR YOU. NOT ONLY AM I ALIVE, BUT I'M GOING TO FREE WADE AND TAKE BACK THE FAMILY NAME.
THERE'S ONLY ONE DEADPOOL. AN' YER LOOKING AT HER.
NOW I'M GONNA STRAIGHT-UP JOHN WICK YOUR ASS.
TO BE CONTINUED...

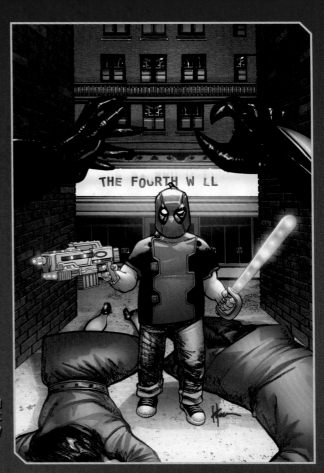

#8 classic variant by
HOWARD CHAYKIN &
JESUS ABURTOV

#8 women of power variant by
ANNIE WU

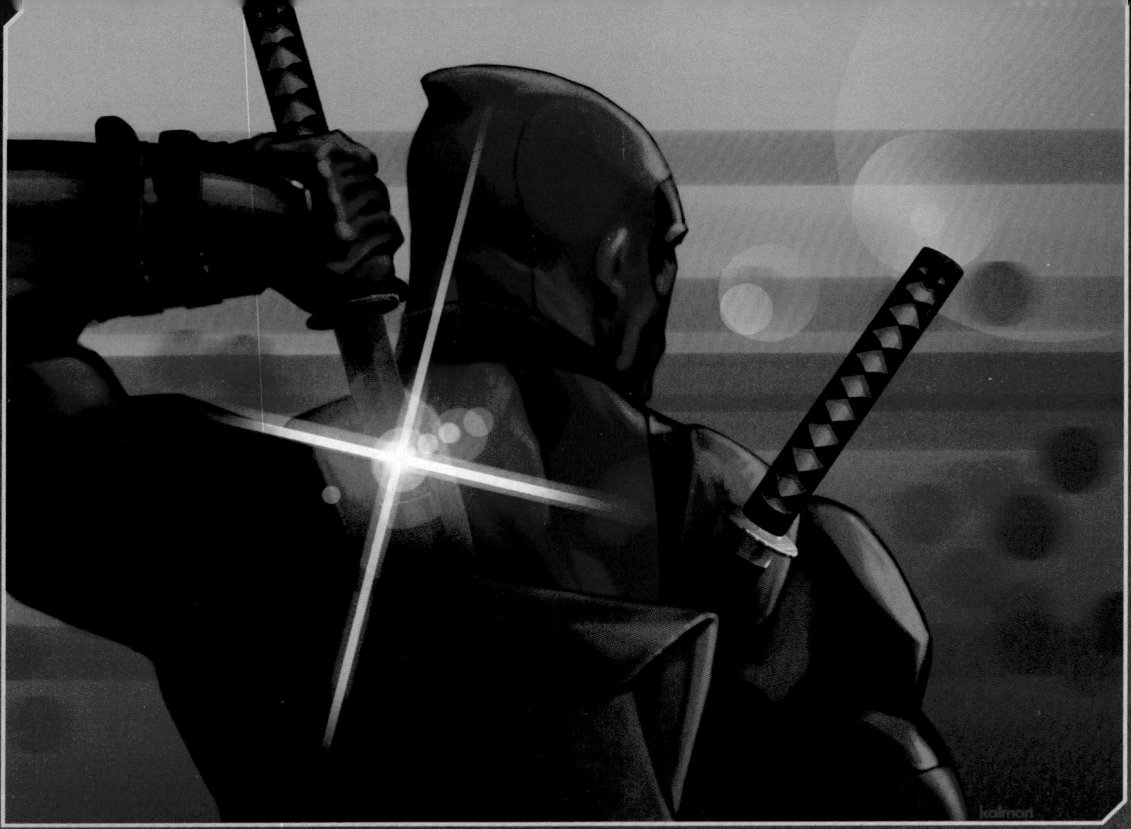
kalman

#10 civil war variant by KALMAN ANDRASOFSZKY

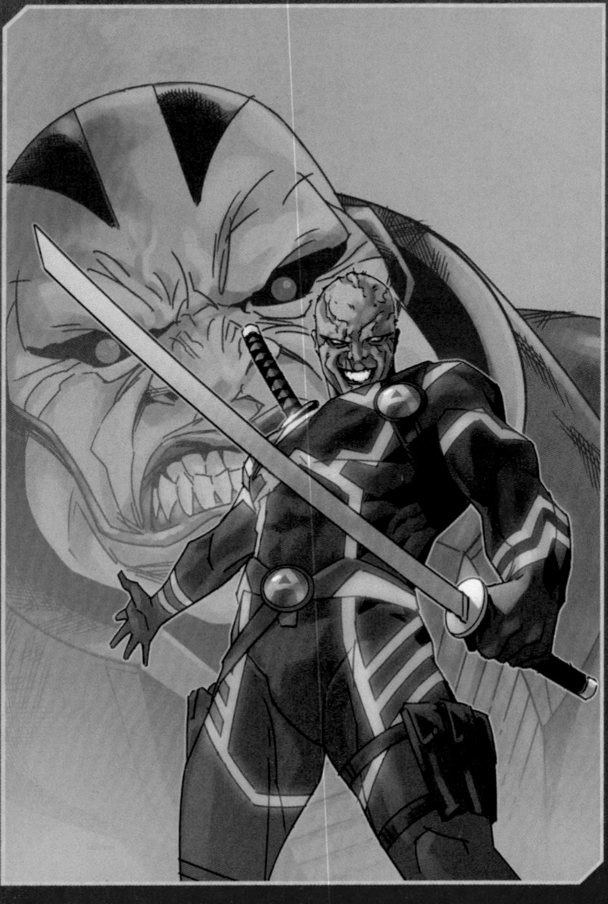

#11 age of apocalypse
variant by
KALMAN ANDRASOFSZKY